Harmony 9

Essential Music Theory

Mark Sarnecki

San Marco Publications

Essential Music Theory © 2023 by Mark Sarnecki. All rights reserved.

All right reserved. No part of this book may be reproduced in any form or by electronic or mechanical means including Information storage and retrieval systems without permission in writing from the author.

ISNB: 9798852530011

Contents

Chapter 1: **The Basics** — 3

Chapter 2: **Diatonic Chords** — 11

Chapter 3: **Seventh Chords** — 17

Chapter 4: **Notating Chords** — 24

Chapter 5: **Tonic and Dominant Harmony** — 31

Chapter 6: **The Subdominant** — 44

Chapter 7: **First Inversion Chords** — 57

Chapter 8: **Harmonizing a Melody** — 66

Chapter 9: **V^7 and Its Inversions** — 71

Chapter 10: **The Supertonic** — 84

Chapter 11: **Cadential Six Four** — 91

Chapter 12: **The Leading Tone Chord** — 105

Chapter 13: **More Six Four Chords** — 111

Chapter 14: **The Submediant and Mediant Chords** — 117

Chapter 15: **The Subtonic Chord** — 126

Chapter 16: **Harmonic Rhythm** — 134

Chapter 17: **The Supertonic Seventh** — 138

Chapter 18: **Secondary Dominants** — 147

Chapter 19: **Modulation** — 155

Chapter 20: **Chorale Harmonization** — 169

Chapter 21: **Form** — 181

Chapter 22: **Melody Writing** — 204

Chapter 23: **Counterpoint** — 220

1
Harmony: The Basics

What is Harmony?

What exactly is harmony? There are probably many definitions of harmony that have nothing to do with the study of music. However, this is a music book so we will focus our discussion in that direction. Harmony could be defined as:

- The combination of two or more musical sounds heard at the same time.
- The study of how chords are constructed and how they relate to each other.

Music theory looks to the past. All music theory examines music that has already been composed. It analyzes it, and tries to explain what it's all about. It does not decide what music could be, it decides what it is.

Almost all great composers looked to the past and studied the work of their predecessors to learn and to hone their craft.

Vocal Music

Some of the earlist music was vocal. This music consisted of a single vocal melody known as monophony (mono meaning one, phony meaning sound or voice).

Eventually more melodies were layered together to create a style of music called polyphony (poly meaning many).

These melodies worked together, complimented each other, and created harmony. When three or four different vocal lines intersected on three or four different notes they created a chord.

Figure 1.1 is an example of a chorale by Johann Sebastian Bach, one of the greatest composers of four part harmony. Here, it is written in open score and each voice gets its own staff. Each line is sung by a different person. If you examine the first notes vertically (from the bottom up), they form a chord. In this case it is the G major chord. Even though there are four different melodies being performed, when they work and meet together they create chords.

Figure 1.1

Key and Tonality

Music written between the the years 1600 and 1900, a time known as the common practice period, and much of the music composed today, is based on major and minor scales. This type of music is called *tonal music*. In tonal music one note is the most important of all, and is considered the tonal center. All other notes are centered around this note, the tonic. This system on which western music is based is called tonality. The tonic is the most important and central note of a key. All other pitches are subordinate to the tonic. We will study the functions of these pitches and their relationships in this system. This is the foundation of harmony based on major and minor scales, commonly known as *tonal harmony*,

The melody in Figure 1.2 is in the key of F major. F occurs on the first strong beat and it is also the last note. Notice the following:

- E occurs 1 time
- F occurs 5 times
- G occurs 3 times
- A occurs 3 times
- B♭ occurs 1 time
- C occurs 3 times

F is the most repeated note in this melody. When a note is repeated a number of times it gives it emphasis and importance. Generally, the note that is repeated the most in tonal music is the tonic. Repeating the tonic emphasises the tonality or key of a composition. This melody is based on the F major scale, F is the tonal center, and it is in the key or tonality of F major.

Figure 1.2

English Air

F major

The Triad

The prefix *tri* implies three. A triangle is a three sided figure. A tricycle is a three wheeled vehicle. A *triad* is a three note *chord*. What is a chord? A chord is three or more notes heard at the same time. A triad is not just any three note chord though. It is a chord constructed by stacking thirds on top of one another.

Figure 1.3 shows a triad created by stacking thirds on the note F. The note the triad is built upon, in this case F, is called the *root*. The three notes of the triad are called the *root*, the *third*, and the *fifth*. The note A which is three notes above the root is the third. The note C which is five notes above the root is the fifth.

Figure 1.3

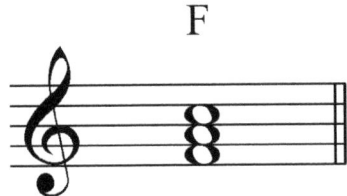

Triads come in different *qualities*. Chord quality, like interval quality can be major, minor, augmented or diminished. Figure 1.3 is the simplest way of looking at a triad. Triads don't always occur in such a clear fashion and are often voiced differently and appear in different forms. A *chord voicing* is the arrangement or rearrangement of the notes of a chord without changing the actual elements of the chord.

Major Triads

A *major triad* consists of the intervals of a major third and a perfect fifth above the root of the chord. Figure 1.4. is a C major triad. The root of the triad is C. The interval from C to E is a major third. The interval from C to G is a perfect fifth. All major triads are built in this way.

Note the symbol above the chord. This is called a *root/quality* chord symbol. An uppercase C is all that is needed to indicate a C major chord. If it was an D major chord, the root/quality symbol would be D. The letter name identifies the root of the chord. If there is no other indication beside the letter, it means the quality of the chord is major. Root/quality chord symbols are common in popular music and jazz lead sheets.

Figure 1.4

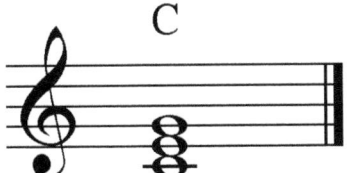

1. Using whole notes and accidentals write the following major triads according to the given root/quality chord symbols.

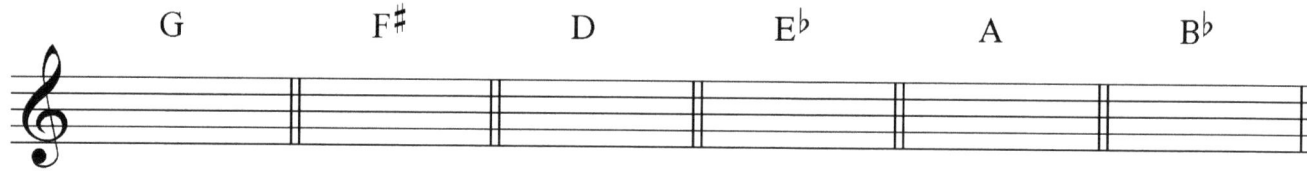

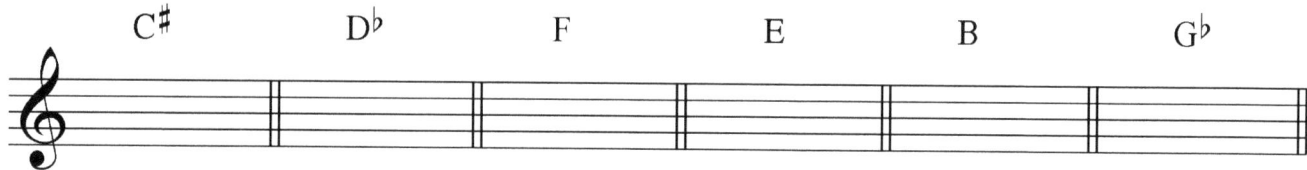

Minor Triads

A *minor triad* consists of the intervals of a minor third and a perfect fifth above the root of the chord. Figure 1.5. is a C minor triad. The root of the triad is C. The interval from C to E♭ is a minor third. The interval from C to G is a perfect fifth. All minor triads are constructed with a minor third and perfect fifth above the root.

Major triads have a major third and perfect fifth. Minor triads have a minor third and perfect fifth. You can relate these triads to their major or minor scales. The C major triad takes its notes from the first, third and fifth notes of the C major scale. The C minor triad takes its notes from the first, third and fifth notes of the C minor scale.
The root/quality symbol for the C minor chord is Cm or Cmin. "C" indicates that the root is C, and "m" indicates that the quality is minor.

Figure 1.5

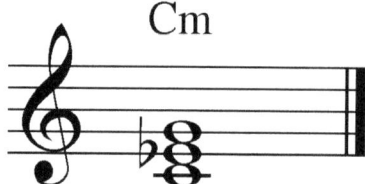

2. Using whole notes and accidentals write the following minor triads according to the given root/quality chord symbols.

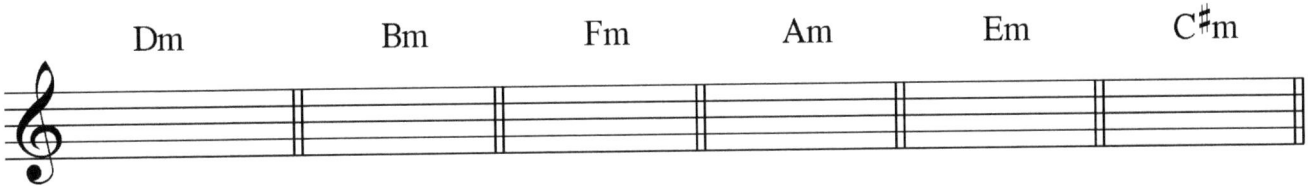

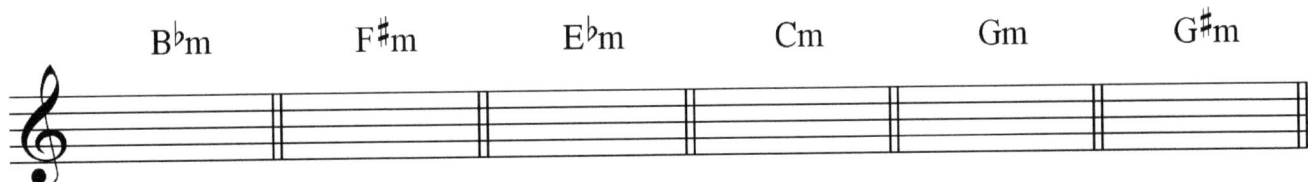

Diminished Triads

A *diminished triad* consists of the intervals of a minor third and a diminished fifth above the root of the chord. Figure 1.6. is a C diminished triad. The root of the triad is C. The interval from C to E♭ is a minor third. The interval from C to G♭ is a diminished fifth. All diminished triads are built in this way. Another way to look at this triad is two minor thirds: C to E♭ is a minor third and E♭ to G♭ is a minor third.

The root/quality symbol for the C diminished chord is Cdim or C°. "C" indicates that the root is C, and "dim" indicates that the quality is diminished. Occasionally, the diminished chord is symbolized with a small degree sign next to the letter.

Figure 1.6

3. Using whole notes and accidentals, write the following diminished triads according to the root/quality chord symbols.

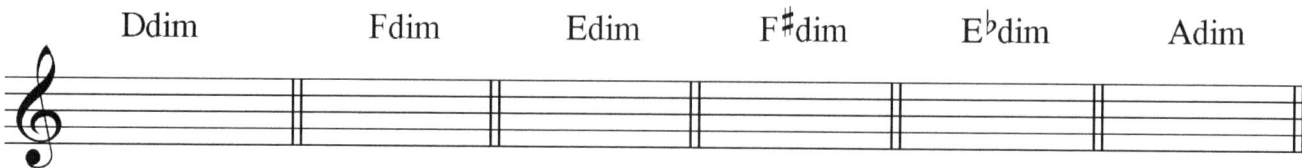

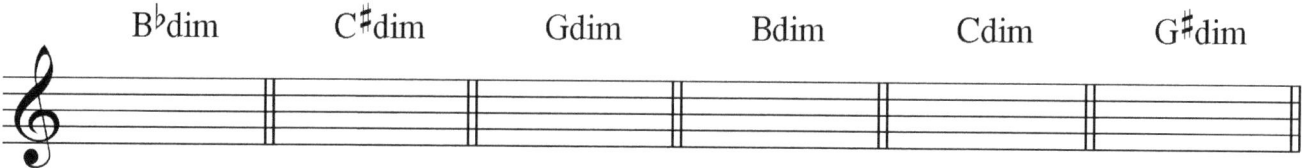

Augmented Triads

An *augmented triad* consists of the intervals of a major third and an augmented fifth above the root of the chord. Figure 1.7. is a C augmented triad. The root of the triad is C. The interval from C to E is a major third. The interval from C to G♯ is and augmented fifth. All augmented triads consist of these intervals. Another way to look at this triad is two major thirds: C to E is a major third and E to G♯ is a major third.

Some augmented chords require double sharps for the augmented fifth interval.

For example, C♯aug is C♯-E♯-G^{x}.

The root/quality symbol for the C augmented chord is Caug or C⁺. "C" indicates that the root is C, and "aug" indicates that the quality is augmented. Sometimes the augmented chord is symbolized with a small plus sign next to the letter.

Figure 1.7

4. Using whole notes and accidentals, write the following augmented triads according to the root/quality chord symbols.

Triad Review

Lets look at the relationship between the four qualities of triads. Here we will use 1, 3, and 5 to represent the root, third, and fifth of the triad. Figure 1.8 outlines the relationship between the four triad qualities.

Figure 1.8

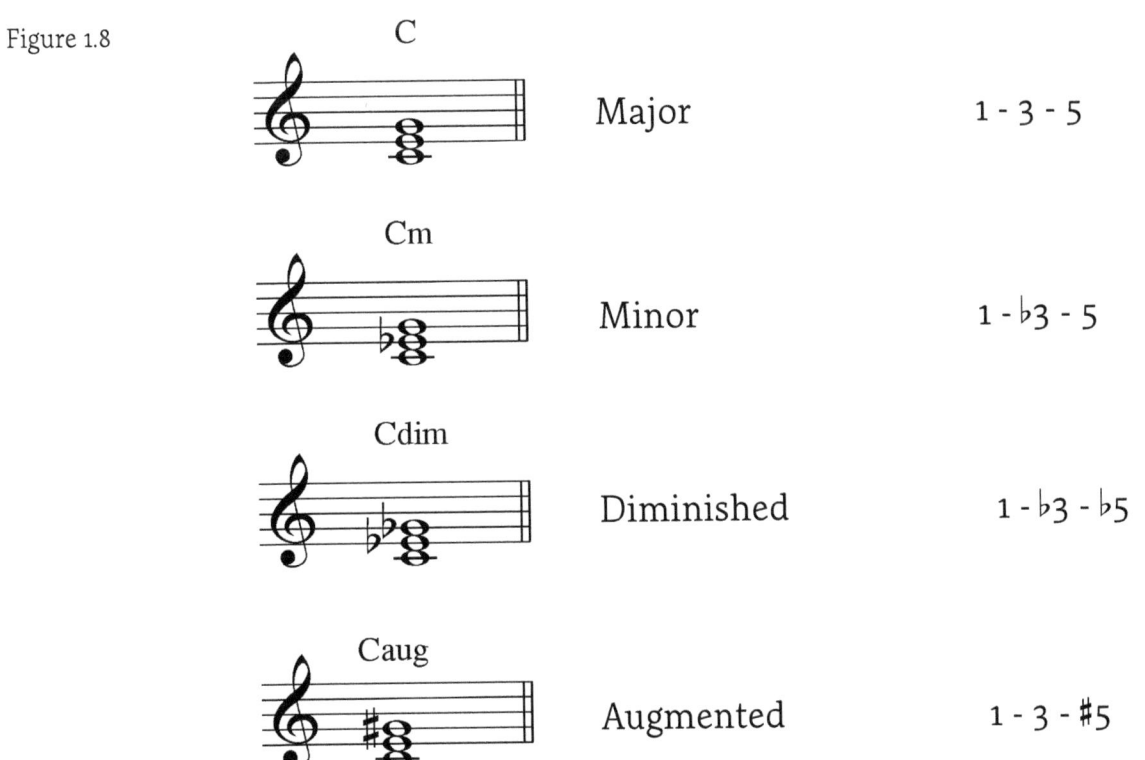

2
Diatonic Chords

Triads in Major Keys

A triad can be built on any note of the scale. All you have to do is stack thirds on each note of the scale and you get seven different chords, one on each scale degree. Figure 2.1 contains the triads that are built on the notes of the C major scale.

The numbers above each triad indicate the *scale degree* each triad is built upon. Scale degrees are indicated by a number with a caret (^) above it. For example, the first note of the scale, the tonic, is scale degree one ($\hat{1}$). The dominant is scale degree five ($\hat{5}$). When naming the key of a piece, the key is indicated by an abbreviation of its name followed by a colon (:). Capital letters are used for major keys and lower case letters for minor keys. C major = C: c minor = c: Different texts use different methods to identify keys. You may also write out the words *C major* or *C minor* to indicate the key if desired.

Figure 2.1

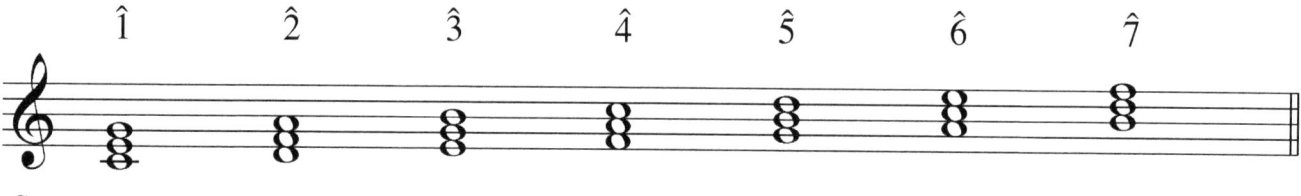

Triad Quality

Triads that are written using the notes of a particular scale are considered *diatonic triads*. This means that they use only the notes of the scale upon which they are built. For example, if you build triads on the F major scale, which contains a B♭, you must use a B♭ for each triad that contains that note.

When you build triads on a major scale you always get the same order and quality of triads. The triads built on $\hat{1}$, $\hat{4}$, and $\hat{5}$ are always major. The triads built on $\hat{2}$, $\hat{3}$, and $\hat{6}$ are always minor. The triad built on $\hat{7}$ is always diminished.

Figure 2.2 uses root/quality chord symbols to illustrate the chord types that occur on each degree of the major scale.

Figure 2.2

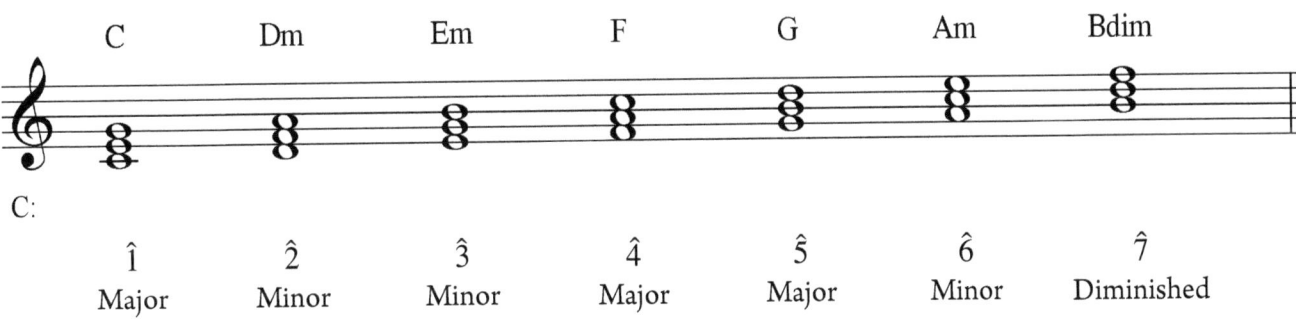

1. Using accidentals instead of a key signature, construct a diatonic triad on each note of the following major scales. Add root/quality chord symbols above each chord.

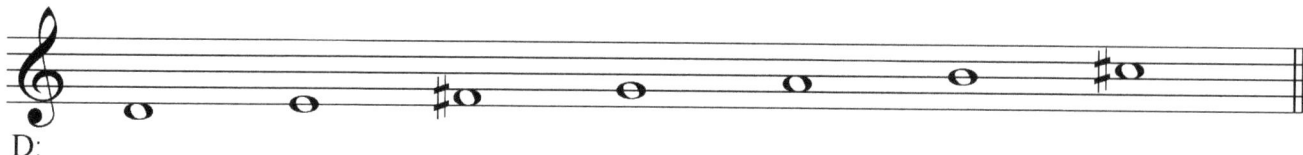
D:

E♭:

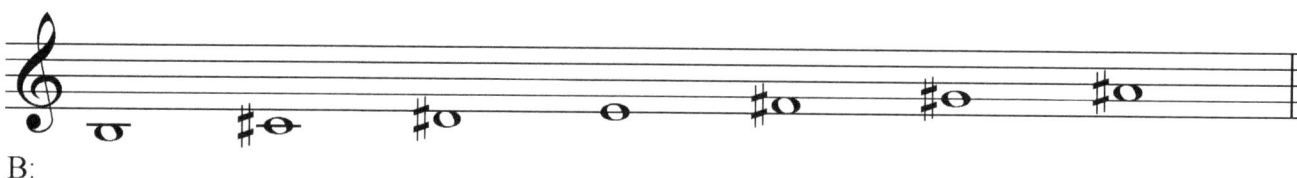
B:

A♭:

F:

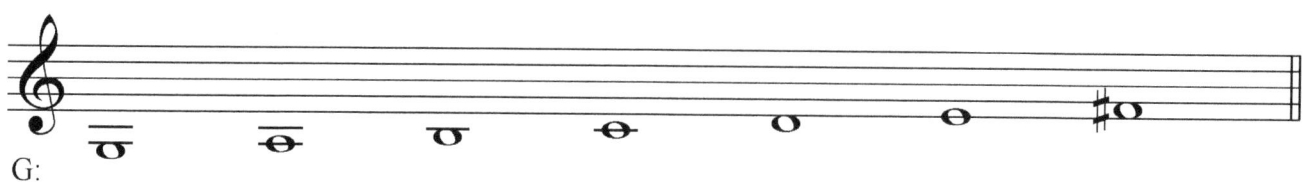
G:

Chapter 2: Diatonic Chords

Roman Numerals

So far, we have studied root/quality chord symbols. Another system is more common in traditional harmony. This is a system of chord symbols using Roman numerals called *functional chord symbols*. Functional chord symbols identify the chord by the scale degree on which it is built.

Figure 2.3 shows functional chord symbols. Notice that they are placed under the chords. The chord built on $\hat{1}$ of a key, gets the Roman numeral I. The chord built on $\hat{2}$ gets the Roman numeral ii, etc. Uppercase Roman numerals are used for major chords and lowercase for minor chords. The diminished chord is indicated with a lowercase Roman numeral and a degree sign (°) to show that the chord is diminished.

Figure 2.3

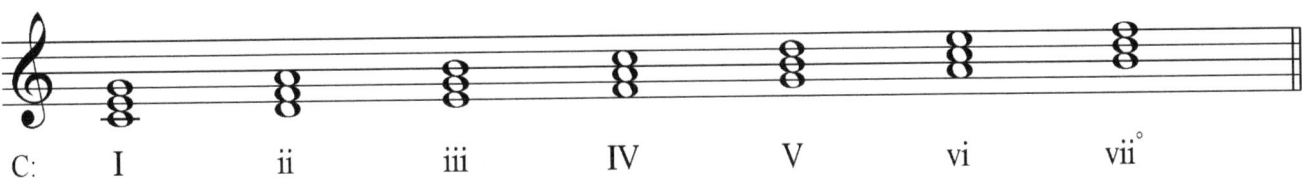

Triads in Minor Keys

The natural minor scale has the same notes as it relative major, but in a different order. In tonal music, this scale is not harmonized, and therefore not used. This is because it does not contain a dominant chord with the raised leading tone. In coming chapters we will discuss the role of the leading tone and dominant harmony.

Figure 2.4 contains triads built on A natural minor. These are the same chords that occur on the C major scale, its relative major. However, they appear in a different order in the natural minor.

Figure 2.4

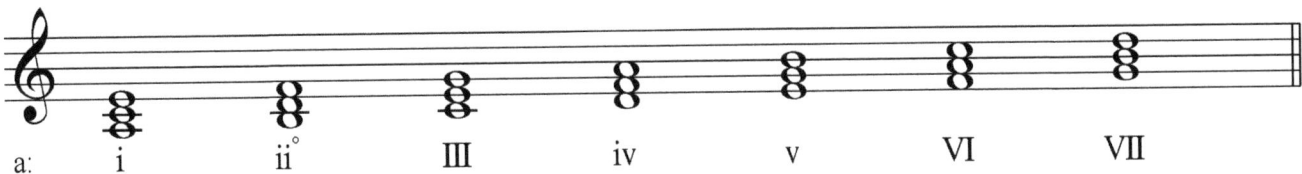

Unlike the natural minor, we do use the harmonic minor scale in harmonization. If you build a triad on each note of the harmonic minor scale you must raise $\hat{7}$ (the leading tone). Raised $\hat{7}$ is part of the harmonic minor scale and is required to create diatonic triads on this scale.

Study Figure 2.5 which contains the diatonic triads built on the A harmonic minor scale. Chord III is an augmented chord. The functional chord symbol for an augmented chord is an uppercase Roman numeral and a small plus sign (+). e.g. III⁺

Figure 2.5

![Figure 2.5: Diatonic triads on A harmonic minor scale labeled a: i, ii°, III⁺, iv, V, VI, vii°]

2. Construct a diatonic triad on each note of the following harmonic minor scales. Add functional chord symbols below each chord.

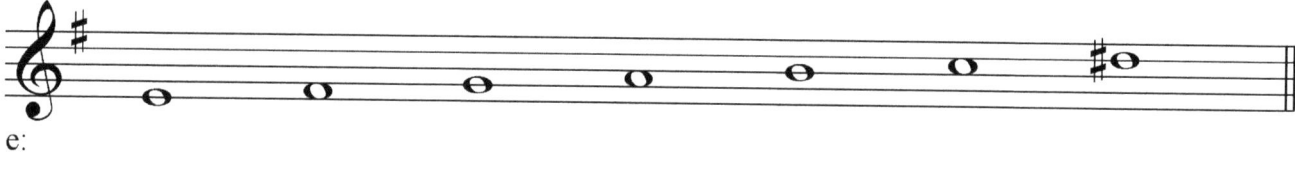

e:

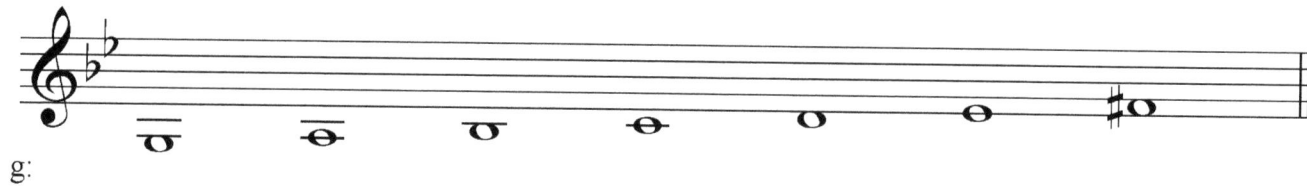

g:

b:

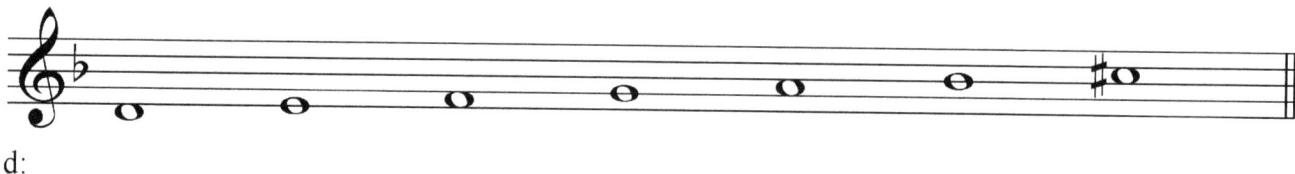

d:

Chapter 2: Diatonic Chords

3. Identify the following chords by writing the functional chord symbols.

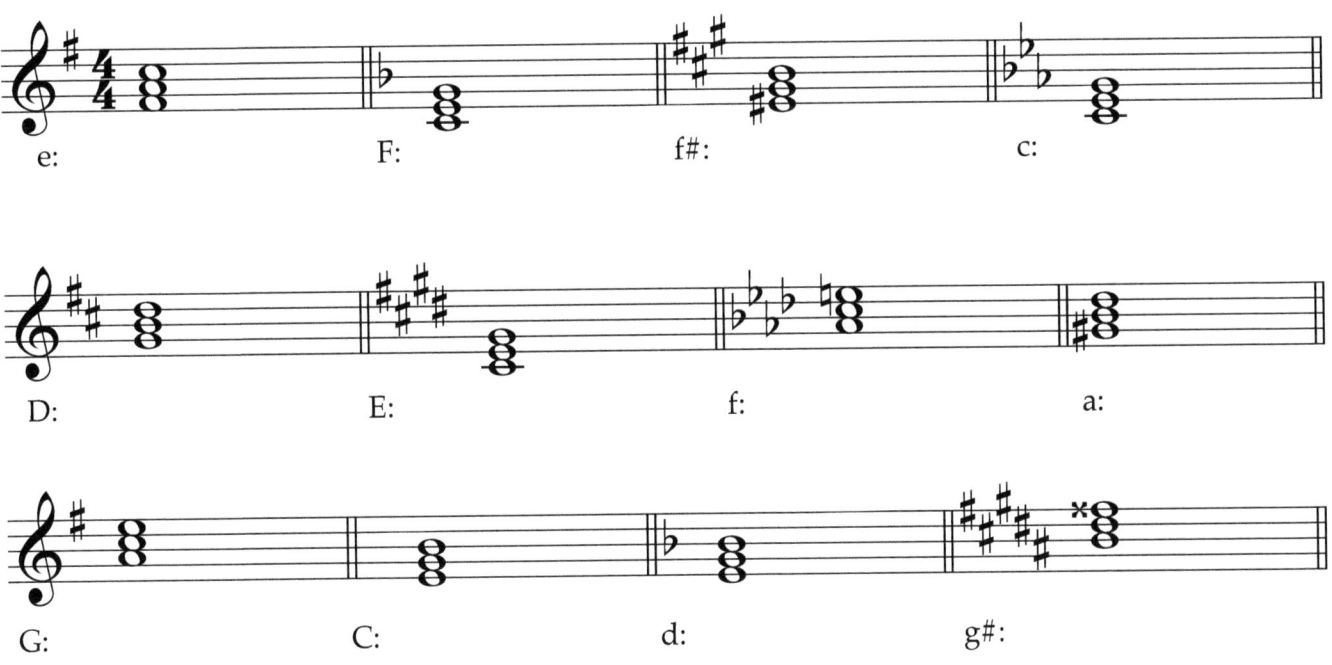

4. Write the following diatonic triads according to the given keys and functional chord symbols. Use accidentals instead of a key signature.

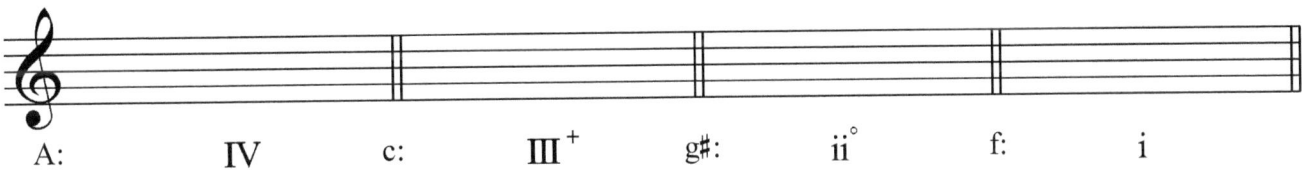

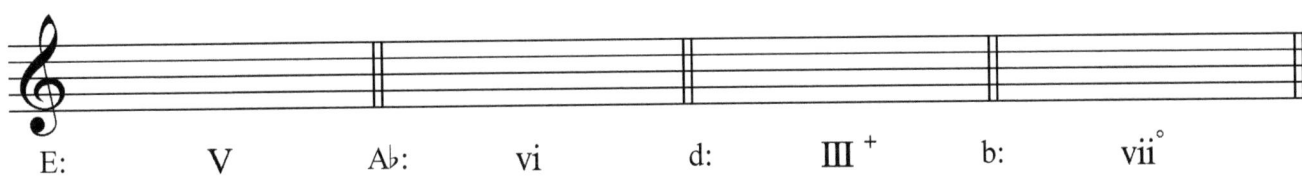

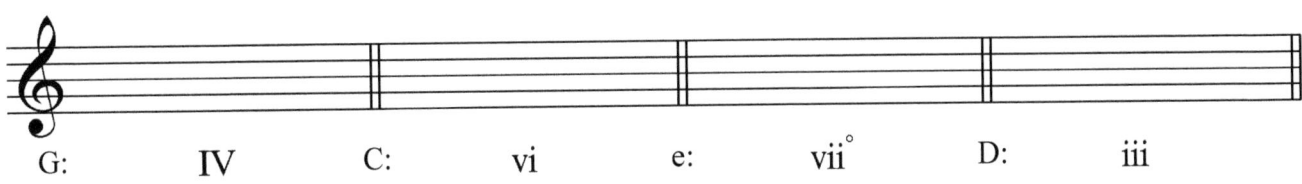

3
Seventh Chords

Seventh chords have been used in music for centuries. After the triad, seventh chords are the next step to a complete understanding of the language of tonal harmony. As a general overview to diatonic 7th chords, this chapter will touch on most of them. This book, however, will focus on three main 7th chords in later chapters.

Diatonic 7th Chords in Major Keys

The triad is the basic building block of harmony. Stacking thirds on the notes of a scale creates various qualities of triads. This harmony, based on third relationships, is called *tertian harmony* and is the basis for the tonal harmony that we are studying here.

If we add another third to a triad we form a *7th chord*. This chord gets its name from the fact that the top note is the interval of a 7th from the root of the chord (Figure 3.1).

Figure 3.1

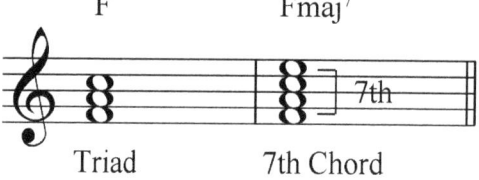

Figure 3.2 shows the *diatonic 7th chords* in C major. We build 7th chords by stacking three thirds on each scale degree. This creates a four note chord with the interval of a 7th between the root and the top note. In order to keep these chords diatonic, we can only use the notes of the scale with which we are working. Here, we are building 7ths in C major. We can only use the notes that make up the C major scale (C D E F G A B C).

Figure 3.2

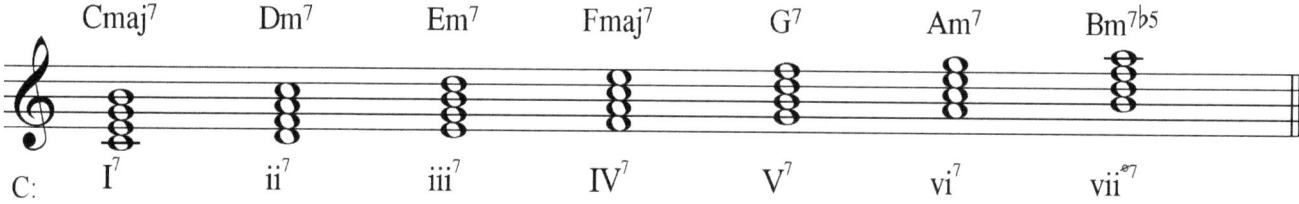

Chapter 3: 7th Chords

The exercise in Figure 3.2 results in four different types of 7th chords. In these examples, the root/quality chord symbols tell us more about the 7th chords than the functional chord symbols. We will discuss each type of 7th in detail.

Major 7th Chords

A major triad with a major 7th is considered a *major 7th chord*. Figure 3.3 is a major 7th chord. Its main features are: It is a major triad (C-E-G), and is contains the interval of a major 7th between the root (C) and the 7th (B). Technically, this chord is a major/major 7th. The first major refers to the major triad and the second major refers to the major 7th interval. However, we abbreviate this and simply call it a major 7th chord. The verbal expression of the chord in Figure 3.3 is: "C major 7th." Major 7th chords occur when you build 7th chords on $\hat{1}$ and $\hat{4}$ of the major scale. A 7th chord built on $\hat{1}$ is considered a *tonic 7th*, and on $\hat{4}$ a *subdominant 7th*. In this level of harmony we will not be dealing extensively with the major 7th chord, but it is important to know what it is.

Figure 3.3

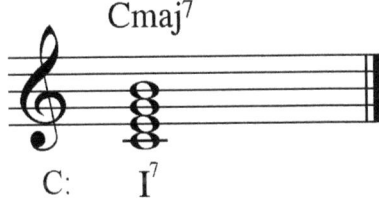

Major/Minor 7th Chords

The chord in Figure 3.4 is a major/minor 7th chord. It is a major triad (G-B-D) with the interval of a minor 7th between the root (G) and the 7th (F). Although this is a major/minor 7th chord it is know as a *dominant 7th*. This is the chord that occurs when you build a 7th chord on $\hat{5}$ (the dominant). The verbal expression for the chord in Figure 3.4 is: "G7" or "G dominant 7th." This chord occurs diatonically only on $\hat{5}$ of the major and harmonic and melodic minor scales. This is a very common chord and we will cover it extensively in this book.

Figure 3.4

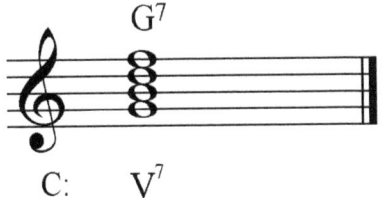

Minor 7th Chords

A *minor 7th chord* is really a minor triad with the interval of a minor 7th above the root. The chord in Figure 3.5 is a minor triad (D-F-A) with a minor 7th between the root (D) and the 7th (C). This could be considered a minor/minor 7th because both the triad and the 7th are minor, but we simply call it a minor 7th chord. The verbal expression of the chord in Figure 3.5 is: "D minor 7th." Minor 7th chords occur on $\hat{2}$, $\hat{3}$, and $\hat{6}$ of the major scale. We will discuss this chord more completely in our study of the *supertonic 7th* (ii^7).

Figure 3.5

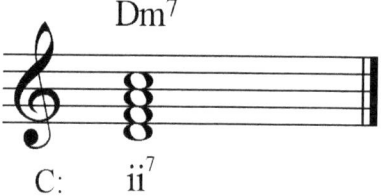

Diminished/Minor 7th Chords

If we build a 7th chord on $\hat{7}$ in a major key we get a chord with a diminished triad and a minor 7th. This diminished/minor 7th chord is commonly known as an *half diminished 7th chord*. The chord in Figure 3.6 contains a diminished triad (B-D-F) with the interval of a minor 7th between the root (B) and the 7th (A). It occurs diatonically on $\hat{7}$ of the major scale. The symbol for this chord contains a degree sign with a slash through it (ø). This sign is used in both the root/quality and functional chord symbols. The verbal expression for the chord in Figure 3.6 is: "B half diminished 7th."

Figure 3.6

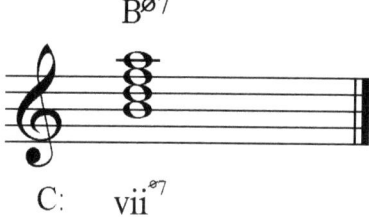

1. Identify the following 7th chords as *major 7th, minor 7th, dominant 7th or half diminished 7th*. Write the root/quality chord symbols above each.

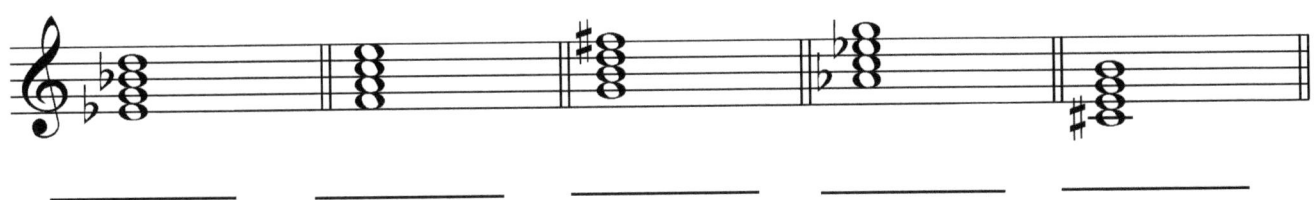

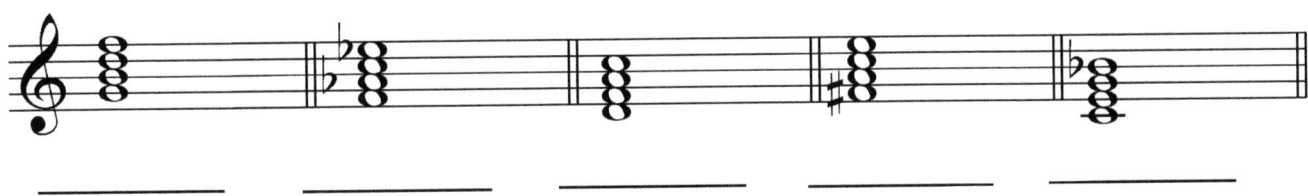

2. Write the following 7th chords according to the root/quality chord symbols.

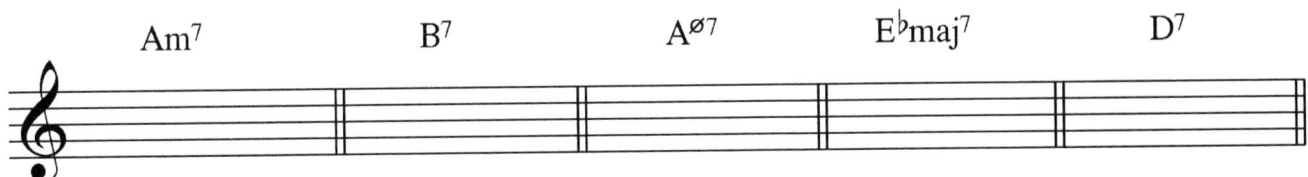

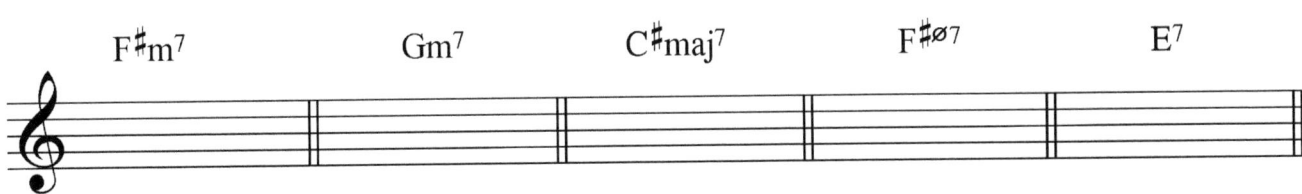

Diatonic 7th Chords in Minor Keys

Figure 3.7 illustrates the 7th chords that occur on the notes of the harmonic minor scale. There are three 7th chords here that we do not see in a major key. They are the *minor/major 7th* (i^7), the *augmented/major 7th* (III^{+7}) and the *diminished/diminished 7th* (vii^{o7}). We will discuss each one in detail.

Figure 3.7

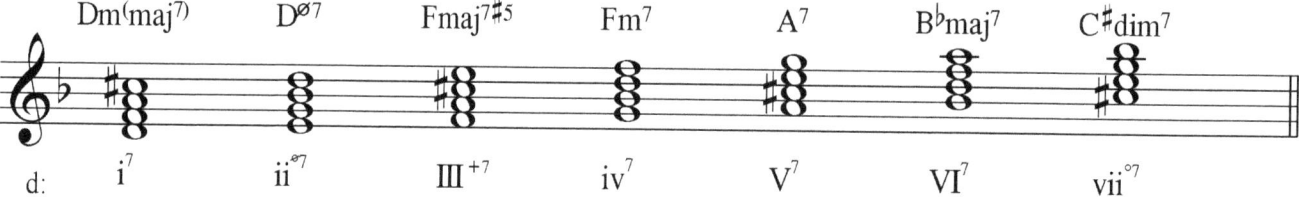

Minor/Major 7th Chords

The minor/major 7th chord has an unusual sound. Figure 3.8 illustrates this chord. It is a minor triad (D-F-A) with a major 7th from the root (D) to the 7th (C♯). There is no shortening of its name. Here, it is called D minor/major 7th. In root/quality chord symbols it may be shown as Dm(maj7), Dmin(maj7), or D-(maj7). This chord only occurs tonally in the harmonic or melodic minor scale. It is sometimes used in pop and jazz music most notably by Pink Floyd.

Figure 3.8

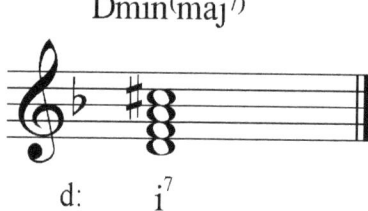

Chapter 3: 7th Chords

Augmented/Major 7th Chords

The *augmented 7th chord/major 7th* is not used frequently. It can be heard in modern music. It is common in jazz, and also the music of the late 19th and the 20th centuries. This chord occurs on III in the minor key with raised $\hat{7}$. Figure 3.9 illustrates this chord in d minor. In d minor, III is an augmented triad (F-A-C♯) and there is a major 7th between the root(F) and the 7th (G). The root/quality symbol may appear as Fmaj7♯5, F+7, or Faug7. The functional chord symbol is an uppercase III with the + sign and a 7.

Figure 3.9

Diminished 7th Chords

The *diminished 7th* chord occurs diatonically on raised $\hat{7}$ in the harmonic and melodic minor scale. It consists of a diminished triad and the interval of a diminished 7th above the root. We know that the half diminished is a diminished triad with a minor 7th. However, in the diminished 7th chord, both the triad and the 7th are diminished, and it is considered a *fully* diminished 7th chord. It's really a diminshed/diminished 7th, but we simply call it a "diminished 7th." Figure 3.10 is a diminished 7th in d minor. It is built on raised $\hat{7}$ (C♯). The diminshed triad is (C♯-E-G) and the diminished 7th occurs between the root (C♯) and the 7th (B♭). The functional chord symbol is a lower case vii with a degree sign (°) and a 7. The verbal expression for the this is: "seven diminished 7th." The root/quality chord symbol is C♯dim7 or C♯°7. This is expressed as: "C♯ diminished 7th."

Figure 3.10

3. Supply the correct functional chord symbol for each chord.

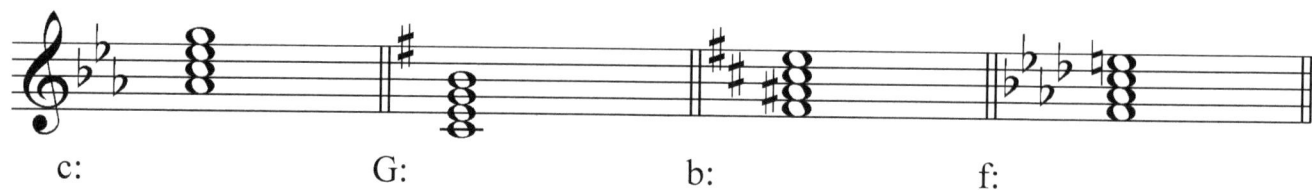

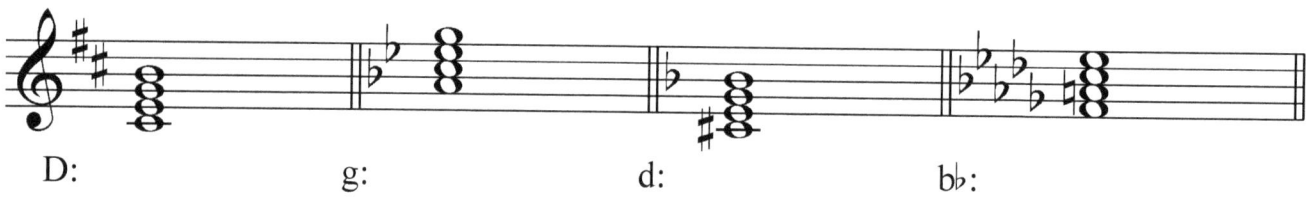

4. Write the following chords according to the given chord symbols.

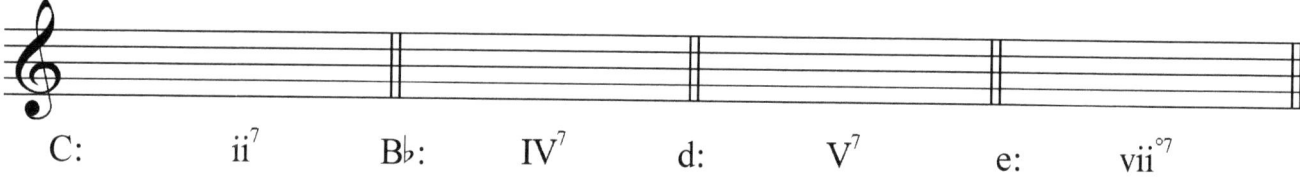

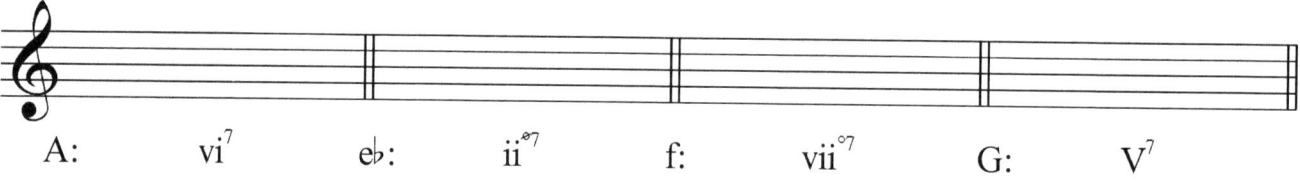

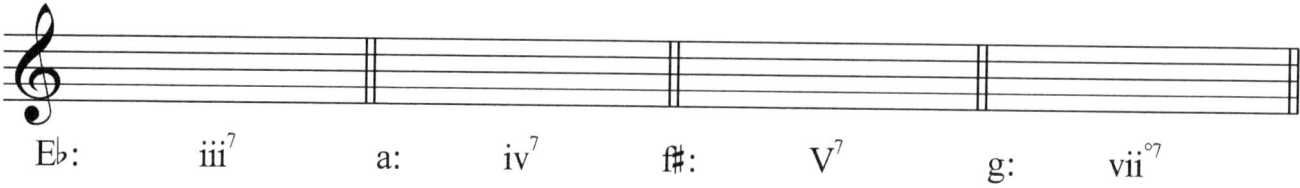

4
Notating Chords

In this book we are going to study four part harmony also known as *four part style*. Much of the music composed since the 18th century is written for four voices or parts. This writing was common in the baroque, classical and romantic eras. We are going to write for the four voices of a choir. These four voices from the top to the bottom are the *soprano, alto, tenor* and *bass*. SATB is the abbreviation for the four voices and this writing is sometimes called *SATB style*. The soprano and alto are womens voices written on the upper staff in the treble clef. The tenor and bass are mens voices written on the lower staff in the bass clef. When we write for these (human) voices we must consider that there are ranges in which each person can sing. These ranges are shown in Figure 4.1. There are not really absolute limits to voice range. Every singer is different, but you should try to keep within the ranges outlined here.

Figure 4.1

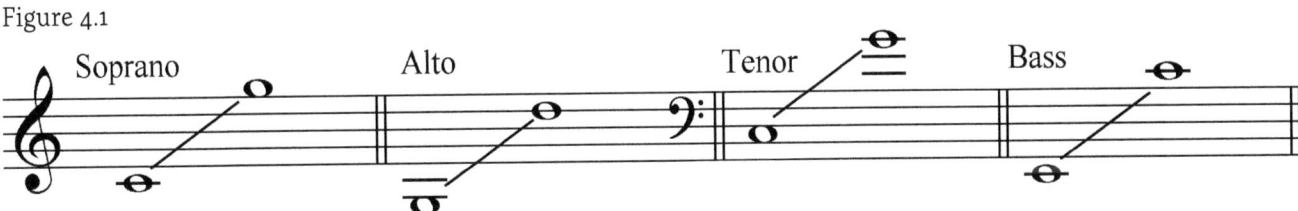

Notation and Voicing

The voice configuration for the four part choir is shown in Figure 4.2. It should be noted that:

- The soprano is the highest voice and is written in the treble clef with the stems going up.
- The alto is the next highest voice and is written in the treble staff with the stems going down.
- The tenor is written in the bass staff with the stems going up.
- The bass is written in the bass staff with the stems going down.

Figure 4.2

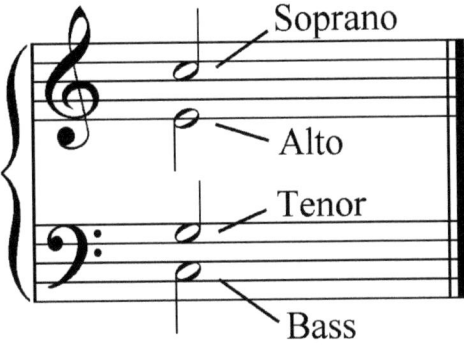

1. 1. Place stems in the correct direction on each note according to four part style.

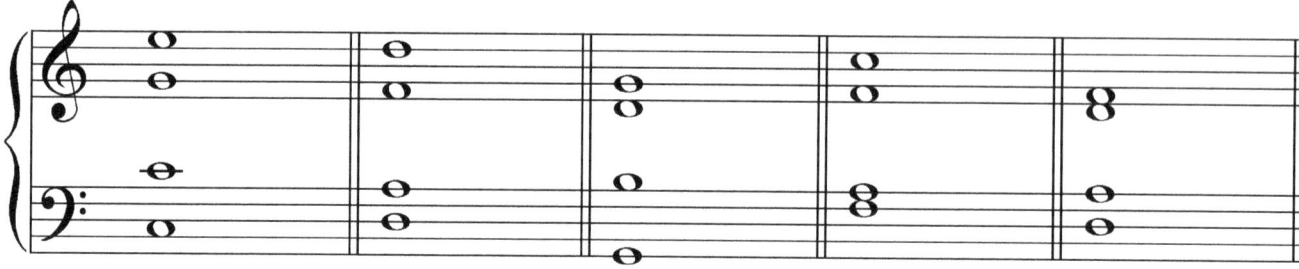

Doubling

The term *voicing* refers to how the notes are distributed among the four voices. Since triads have three pitches, and we are writing for four voices, one of the pitches must be *doubled*. When we learn to connect several different chords the doubling may be determined by the voice leading between the chords. For now, if possible, double the root of the chord. The second best choice to double is the fifth, followed by the third. This refers to major and minor triads only.

When two voices sing the same note on different staves Figure 4.3 (a) one note is written on each staff. When two voices sing the same note on the same staff (b), two stems are attached to one notehead. When two voices sing whole notes on the same staff (c), two notes are used.

Figure 4.3

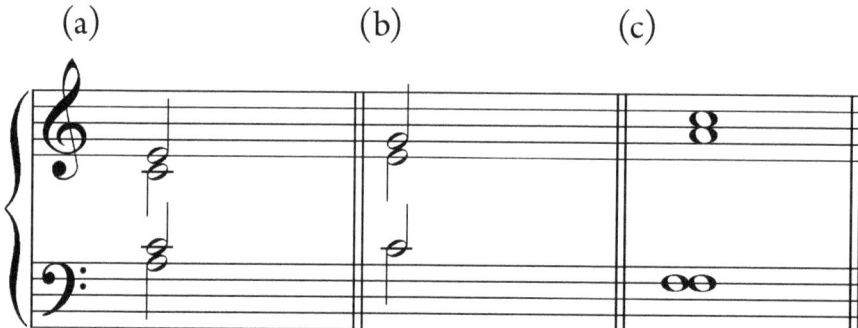

Note Spacing

The spacing between the top three voices of a chord (soprano, alto, tenor) should not exceed the interval of an octave. The chords in Figure 4.4 (a), (b) and (c) are all correct. The tenth between the bass and tenor in (b) is fine. In fact there is not really a limit between the space between these two voices as long as you stay within their vocal ranges. However, the chord in (d) is incorrect. There is a tenth between the tenor and alto (E and G). The distance here should not exceed one octave. This sort of writing creates a hollow, sparse sound and should be avoided.

Figure 4.4

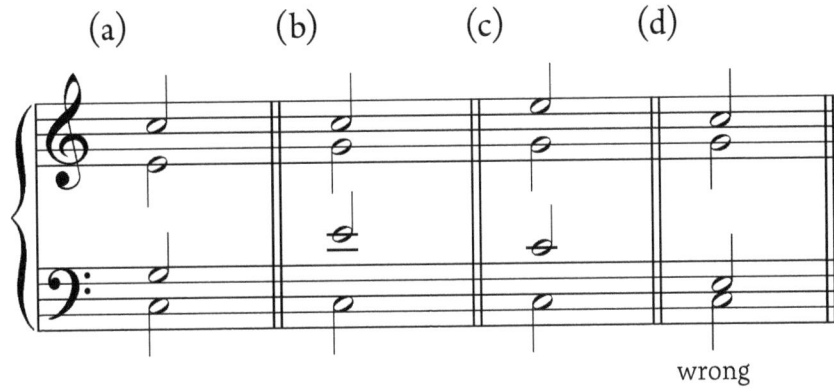

2. Find and mark the chords containing incorrect spacing in the following examples.

Crossed Parts

In four part writing, the soprano is the highest voice followed in downward order by the alto, tenor and bass. When this order is not followed, a fault called *crossed parts* occurs. In Figure 4.5, the error of crossed parts occurs between the tenor and alto in (a) and between the alto and soprano in (b). (c) and (d) show the corrected versions.

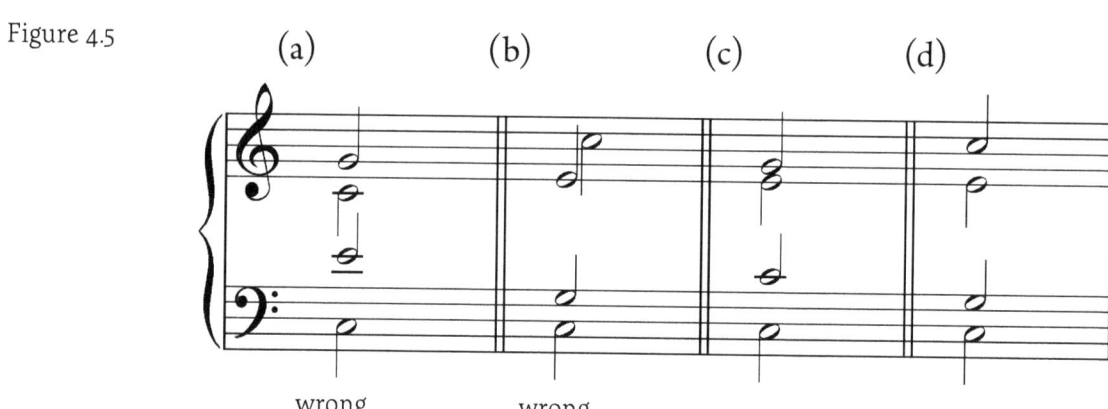

Figure 4.5

3. Some of the following chords contain errors. Find and mark any errors involving crossed parts or incorrect spacing.

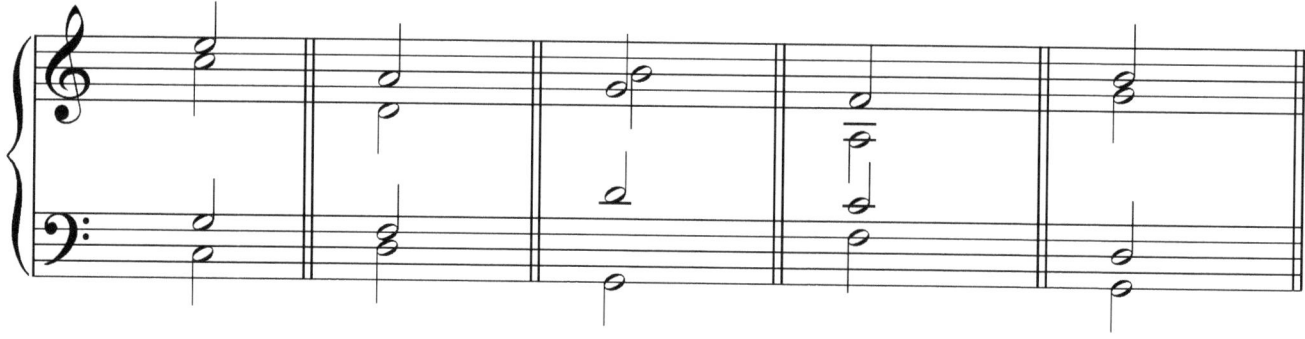

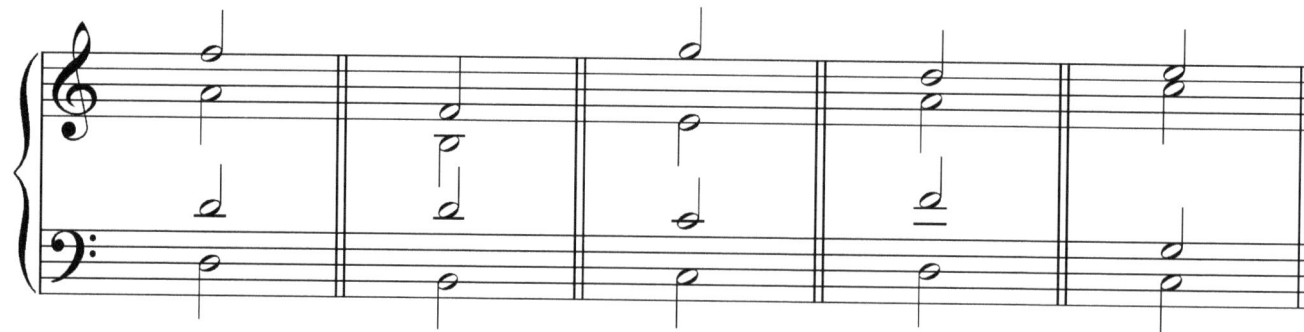

Chapter 4: Notating Chords

Voice Overlap

Figure 4.6 (a) and (b) are examples of an error called *voice overlap*. In (a) the alto moves to a pitch (A) higher than the soprano just sang (G). In (b) the tenor moves to a pitch (E) lower than the bass just sang (F). These are incorrect. (c) is acceptable because the overlap is approached by step. Overlaps should be avoided in four part writing.

Figure 4.6
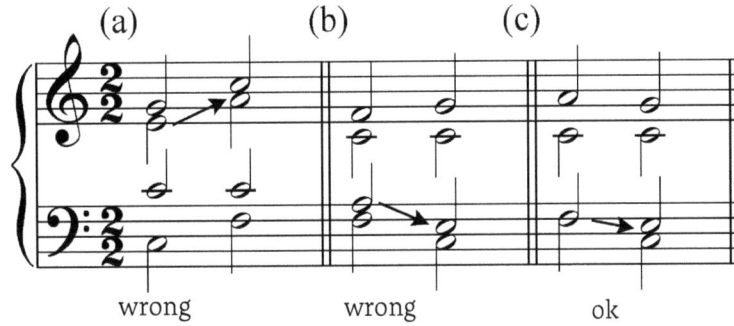

Open and Closed Spacing

Chords may be written in *open spacing* or *closed spacing*. In open spacing there is an octave or more between the soprano and tenor as in Figure 4.7 (a). In open spacing you should be able to fit one or more chord tones between some of the three upper voices. In (a) you could fit a C between the tenor and the alto and a G between the alto and the soprano. In closed spacing there is less than an octave betweeen the soprano and tenor as in Figure 4.7 (b). Here, the three upper voices are as close together as possible, and there is no room to fit another chord tone between them.

Figure 4.7
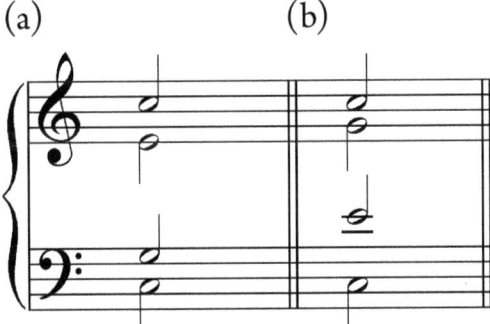

4. Identify the following chords as using open or closed spacing.

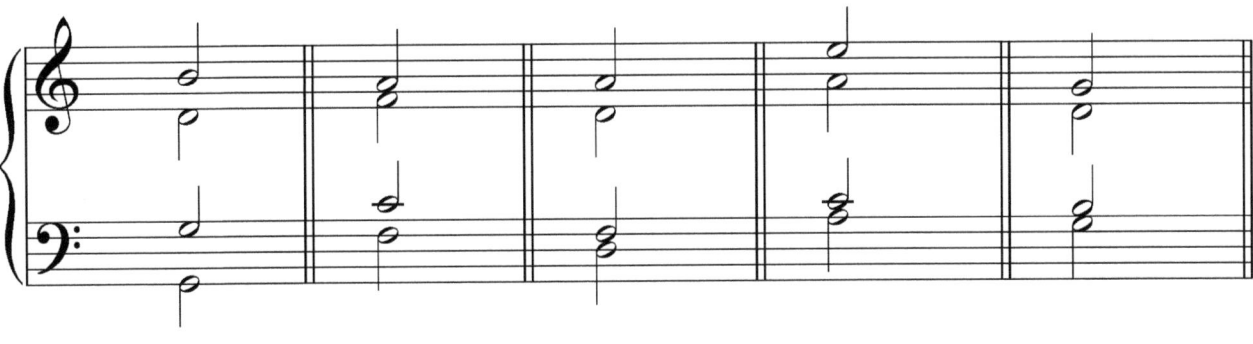

5. Write the alto and tenor for the following chords. Use closed spacing. Double the root in each chord.

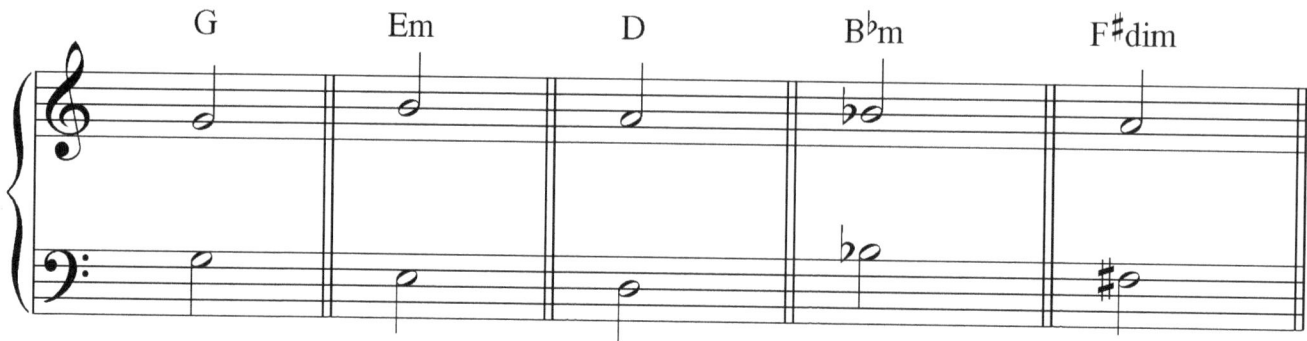

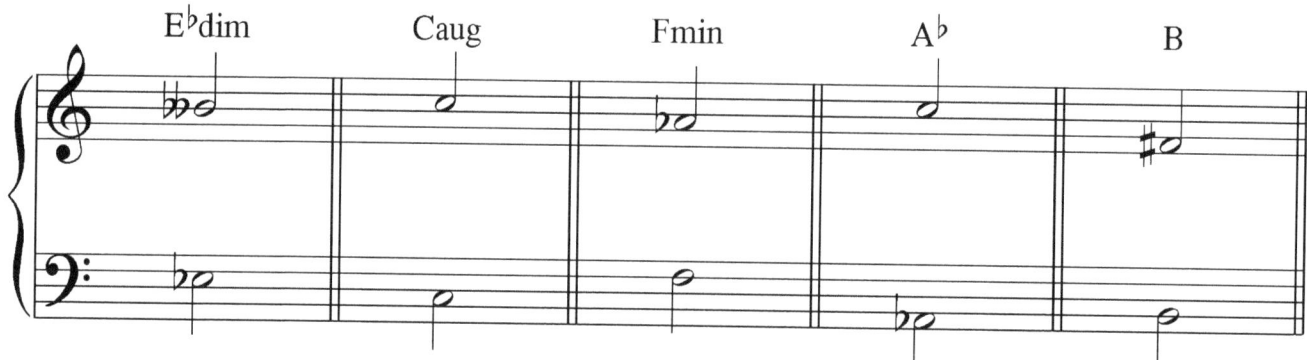

6. Write the alto and tenor for the following chords. Use open spacing. Double the root in each chord.

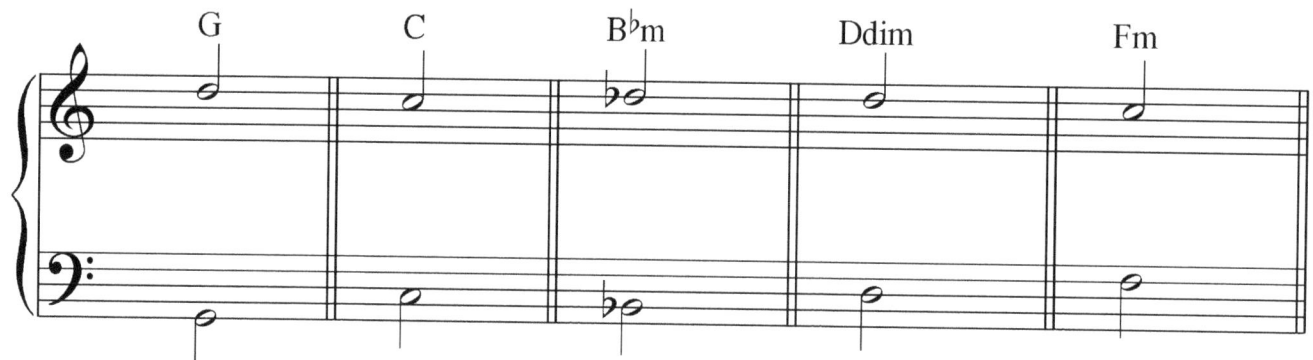

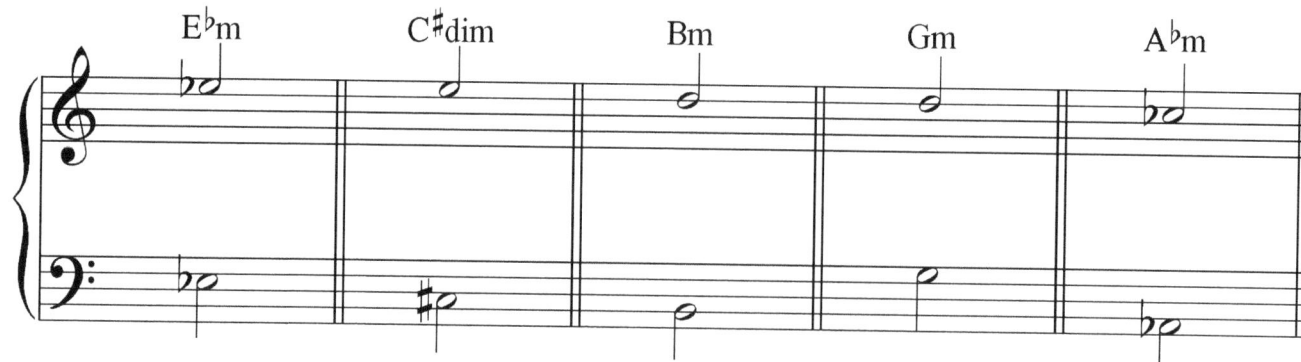

Chapter 4: Notating Chords

We have studied doubling and spacing for a four part choir. Other music based on four parts will often display these charctericstics. Compositions written for instrumental ensembles, orchestra and piano are often based on four part texture. Study Figure 4.8.

7. Is this writing based on open or closed spacing? Mark each chord that contains a doubled root.

Figure 4.8

Frédéric Chopin
Nocturne, Op. 37, No. 1

8. Write the following chords in four part style. Use open or closed spacing and half notes.

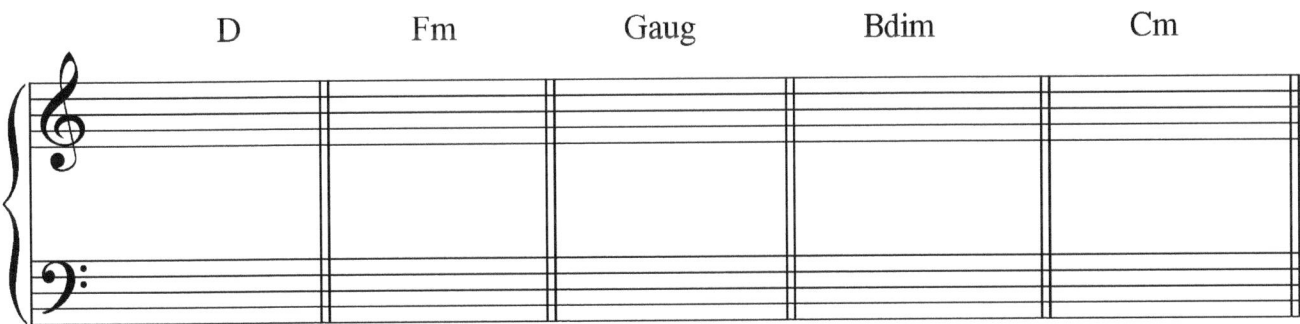

Chapter 4: Notating Chords

5

Tonic & Dominant Harmony

The *tonic* and *dominant* are the two most fundamental chords in tonal music. These chords have a role in the beginning and ending of a composition. The tonic chord is the starting point of a composition, and both the tonic or dominant can function as a point of rest or arrival at the end of a phrase. The tonic chord varies with the key (I in major and i in minor) but the dominant remains a major chord (V) in both major and minor keys.

The two basic harmonic progressions are: I →V - I and I → V. Figure 5.1 illustrates these two types of harmonic motion. The first phrase is a progression ending on I - V (a half cadence). The second phrase ends on V - I (an authentic cadence). We will discuss cadences in greater detail later on.

Figure 5.1

Welsh Air

The Tonic Chord

The word tonic means "tone." The *tonic chord* (I) is built using scale degrees $\hat{1}$, $\hat{3}$, and $\hat{5}$. It is the principle chord and central pitch in a key in tonal music. Phrases, sections and whole compositions often begin and end on the tonic. This chord can serve as a goal in tonal harmony. In Figure 5.2 Beethoven establishes the key of E♭ by using the I chord for the opening six measures of this movement.

Figure 5.2

Ludwig van Beethoven
Symphony III, Op. 55

The Dominant Chord

After the tonic, the *dominant chord* (V) is the next most important chord in tonal harmony. It is built using scale degrees $\hat{5}$, $\hat{7}$, and $\hat{2}$. This chord contains the leading tone. The leading tone gets its name because it has a strong tendency to "lead" to the tonic ($\hat{7}$ - $\hat{1}$). Because of this tendency it is considered a *tendency tone*. Generally, a tendency tone is an unstable tone (like $\hat{7}$) that needs resolution to a stable tone (like $\hat{1}$). The dominant chord also contains scale degree $\hat{2}$, which although is not considered a tendency tone, is an unstable tone that wants to resolve to $\hat{1}$ or $\hat{3}$ (both notes of chord I). For this reason, chord V often resolves to chord I. Figure 5.3 illustrates a basic harmonic progression from I to V and back to I again.

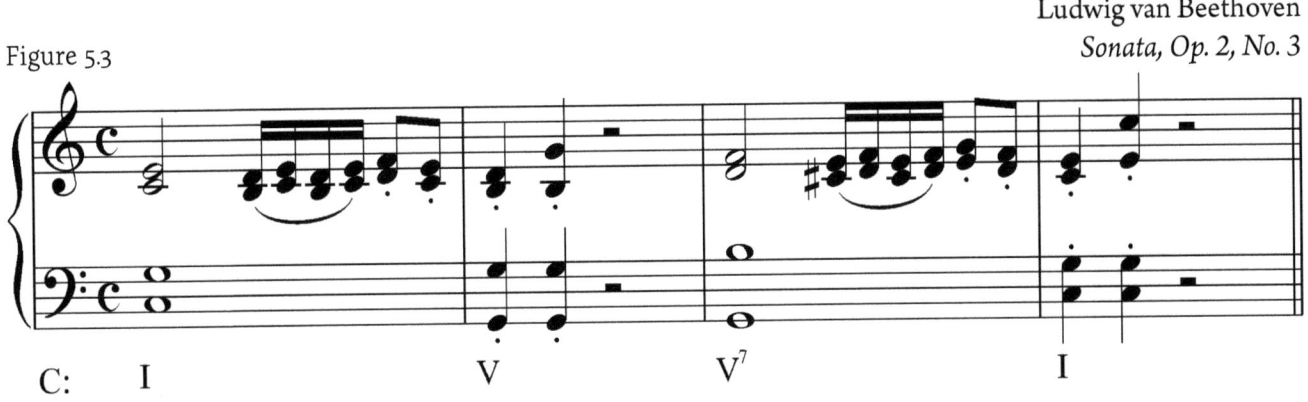

Figure 5.3

Ludwig van Beethoven
Sonata, Op. 2, No. 3

1. Write tonic chords in four part style in the following keys.

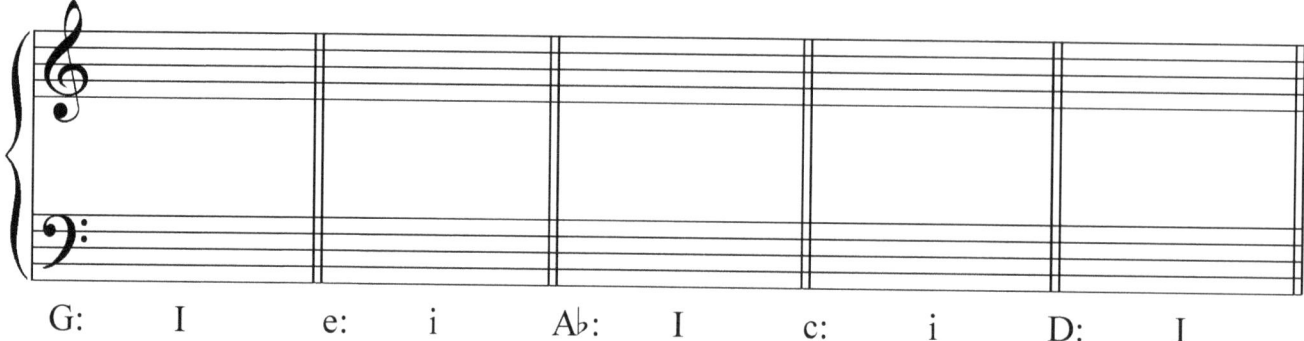

G: I   e: i   A♭:   I   c: i   D: I

2. Write dominant chords in four part style in the following keys.

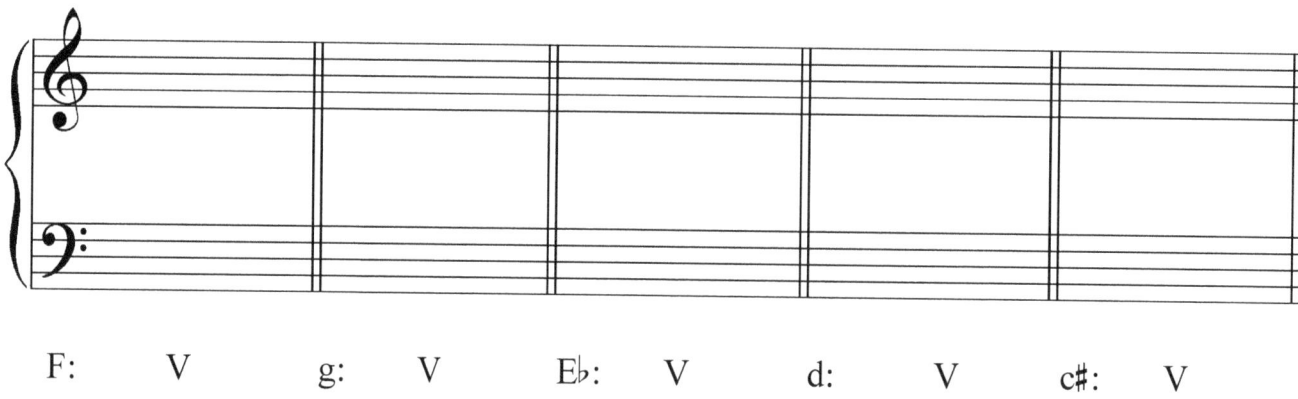

F: V   g: V   E♭:   V   d: V   c♯:   V

The Authentic Cadence

Music is organized into sections or segments called *phrases*. Most phrases in traditional music are four measures long. A *cadence*, which is a two chord ending, occurs at the end of a phrase. The end of a phrase is a point of rest in music. The cadence serves as a goal for the phrase and as a result has structural importance in a harmonic progression.

There are two types of cadences: *final cadences* and *non-final cadences*. Final cadences bring a phrase to a complete close. Non-final cadences are not closed, but continue to look forward and need another phrase to act as completion. The *authentic cadence*, sometimes called a *perfect cadence*, is a final cadence. It can finish an entire composition or a major section within a composition. The authentic cadence consists of the chord progression V - I (or V - i in minor keys). Figure 5.4 shows an authentic cadence in G major at the end of Bach's Chorale: *Allein Gott in der Höh' sei Ehr'*. Bach doubles the root in each chord V (D-F♯-A-D) and I (G-B-D-G).

Figure 5.4

G: V I

An authentic cadence with both chords in root position and $\hat{1}$ in the top voice in the final chord is considered a *perfect authentic cadence*. This cadence has a final or complete sound. The cadence in Figure 5.5 (a) is a perfect authentic cadence. Both chords are in root position. The final chord (I) ends with scale degree $\hat{1}$ in the soprano. Here it is approached from a step above using scale degree $\hat{2}$. Example (b) is also a perfect authentic cadence. The final soprano note is $\hat{1}$ and it is approached from a step below using scale degree $\hat{7}$. These are very strong sounding final cadences. They would be very effective at the end of a composition or at the end of a major section within a piece. Ending on the tonic in the soprano reinforces the tonality and provides a strong affirmation of the key. Make note of the rhythm in these examples. As a rule, the first chord of a cadence should occur on a weaker beat than the second chord.

Figure 5.5

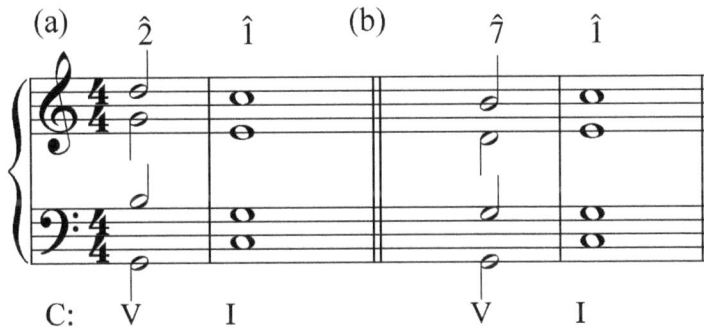

An authentic cadence where at least one of the chords is not in root position or in which $\hat{1}$ is not in the top voice in the final chord is considered an *imperfect authentic cadence*. This cadence has a less final or complete sound. The cadences in Figure 5.6 (a) and (b) are imperfect authentic cadences. They end on $\hat{3}$ and $\hat{5}$ in the soprano respectively. Ending on these notes has a less conclusive sound than ending on $\hat{1}$. Although these are authentic cadences, they would not be the strongest choice for the final cadence of a composition.

Figure 5.6

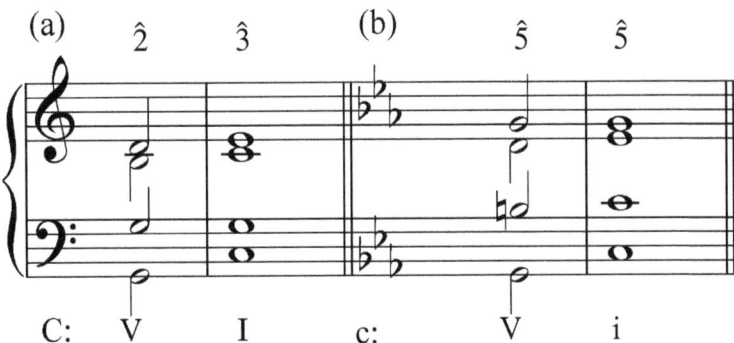

3. For the following authentic cadences: Name the key. Label the scale degree that occurs in the soprano for each cadence. Provide a functional chord analysis using Roman numerals. Identify each cadence as perfect authentic or imperfect authentic.

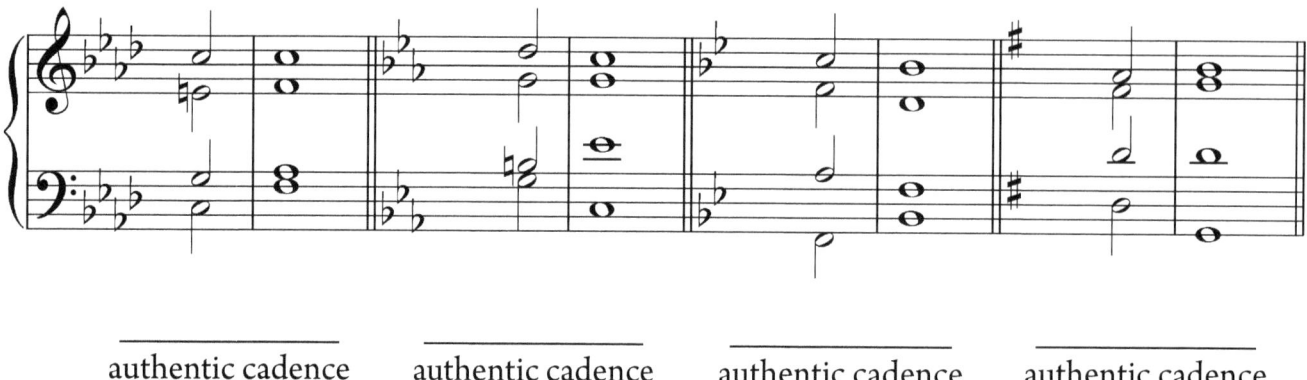

_____   _____   _____   _____
authentic cadence   authentic cadence   authentic cadence   authentic cadence

Writing the Authentic Cadence

We will now examine some part writing techniques to connect V and I and create authentic cadences. For now we will continue to double the root in each chord. There are two ways to connect these chords. V and I have one note in common, in C major that note is G (G-B-D-**G**) (C-E-**G**-C). If possible, try to repeat the common tone in the same voice and move the other voices stepwise. You should retain either open or closed spacing for both chords. In Figure 5.7 (a) the common tone (G) is repeated in the alto, the bass moves from the root of V (G) to the root of I (C), and the soprano and tenor step up. Both chords use closed spacing. Example (b) is in c minor. The common tone is repeated in the tenor here. The soprano and alto step up and the bass moves from the root of V to the root of i. Both chords use open spacing. It should be noted that in the minor key $\hat{7}$ must be raised since it is functioning as the leading tone. In both of these examples the leading tone is in the soprano. **When the leading tone occurs in an outer voice it must rise to the tonic.** In a minor key i is a minor chord and must be notated with a lower case Roman numeral.

Figure 5.7

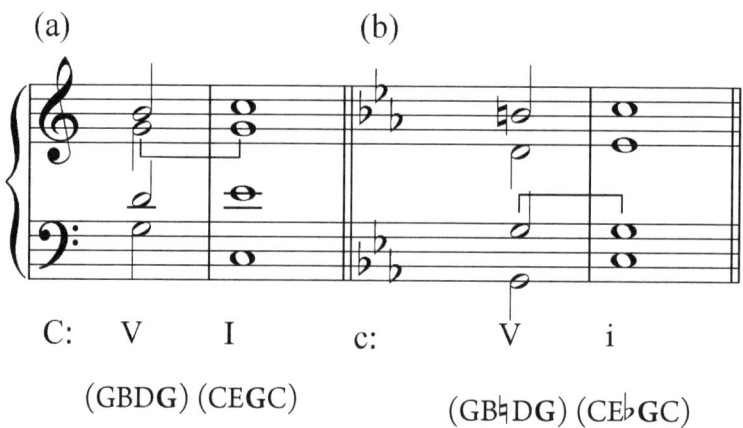

C: V   I   c: V   i

(GBDG) (CEGC)   (GB♮DG) (CE♭GC)

Chapter 5: Tonic and Dominant Harmony

4. Name the keys. Complete the following authentic cadences by adding the alto and tenor. Repeat the common tone in the same voice.

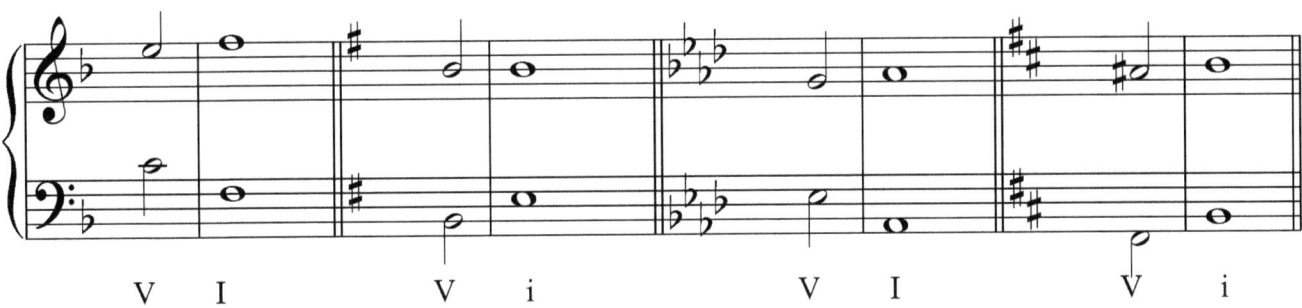

V I   V i   V I   V i

The second option for writing the authentic cadence is shown in Figure 5.8 (a) and (b). Ideally, when there is a common tone, it is good to repeat it in the same voice. However, you may encounter melodies or chord progressions that will not allow you to repeat the common tone. In the following examples the common tone is not repeated in the same voice. All voices move to the nearest chord tones using correct doubling and spacing. Here, all of the upper voices move in the same direction. Two by skip, and one by step. The leading tone is in an inner voice in both examples so it can skip down. Use either closed spacing (a) or open spacing (b) for both chords of this cadence.

Figure 5.8

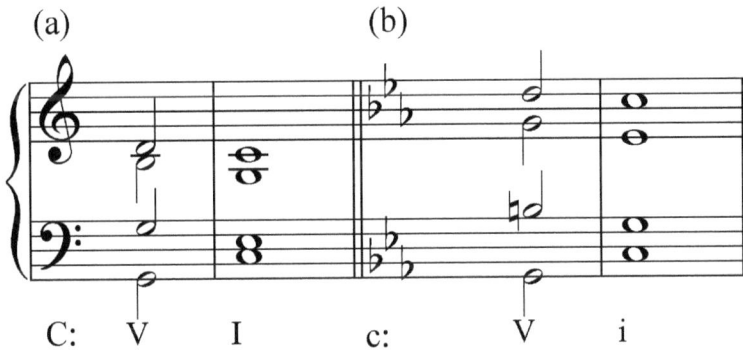

C: V I   c: V i

5. Add the soprano, alto and tenor to complete the following authentic cadences.

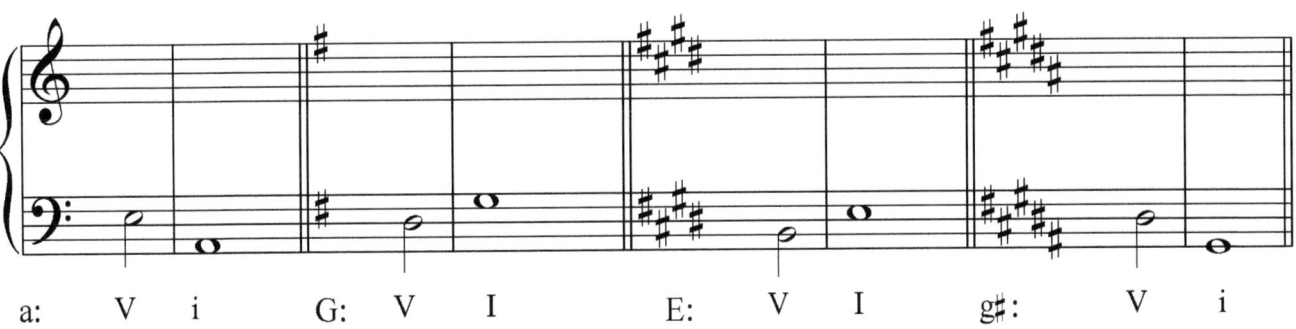

a: V i   G: V I   E: V I   g♯: V i

36   Chapter 5: Tonic and Dominant Harmony

The Half Cadence

The *half cadence* is a non-final cadence ending on V. This cadence lacks finality. It concludes a phrase but it is not the end of a complete musical idea. Because it lacks closure, it is not used to conclude a composition. The half cadence we will study is I - V. Like the authentic cadence, this cadence should be written with both chords in either open or closed spacing. Figure 5.9 shows two versions of the half cadence. (a) repeats the common tone in the tenor, the alto and soprano step down, and the bass moves from the root of I to the root of V. In (b), the tenor and alto skip up and the soprano steps up while the bass moves from the root of I to he root of V. This is essentially the opposite motion of the authentic cadence.

Figure 5.9

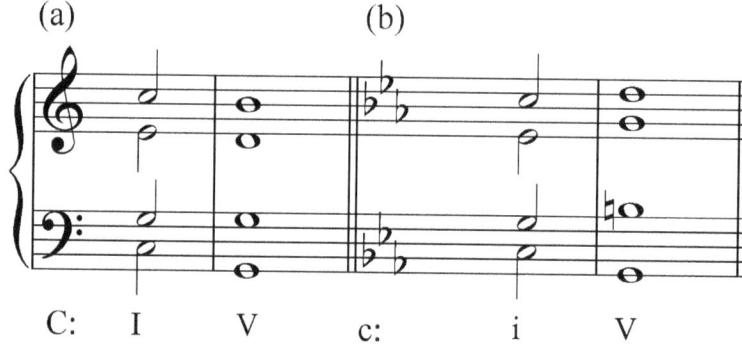

6. Write half cadences in four parts in the following keys.

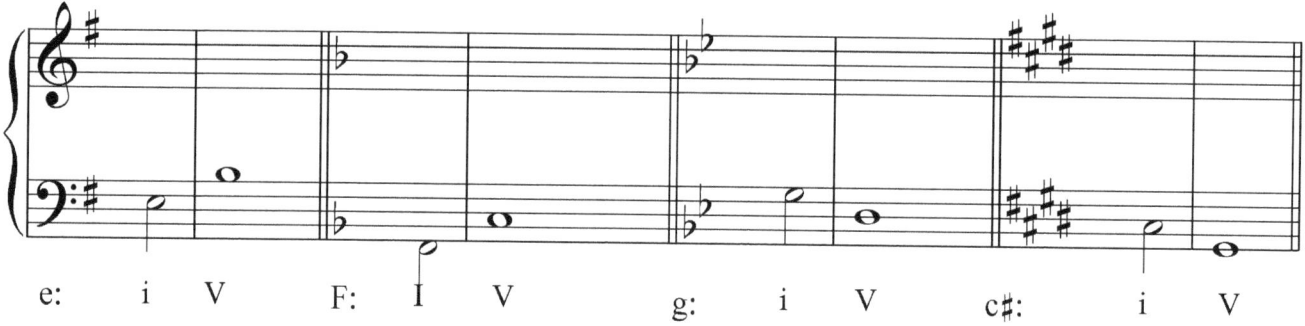

7. Write cadences in four parts the following keys.

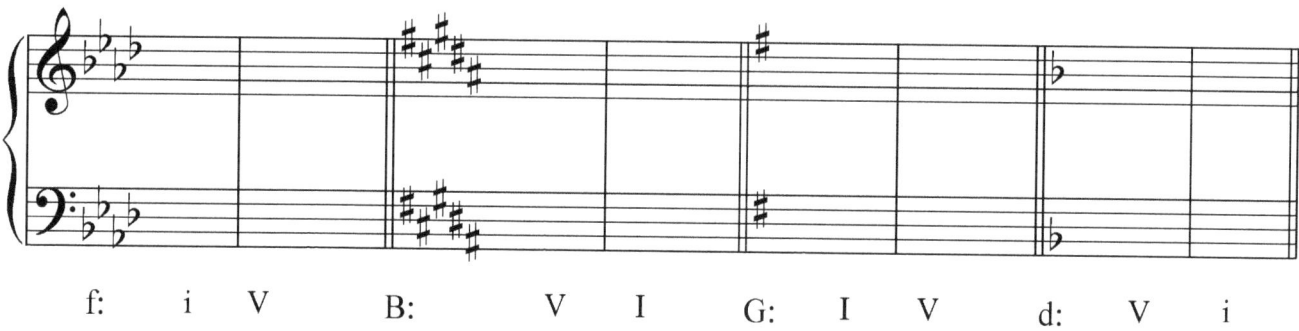

Review of Part Writing Techniques

It is important to grasp the two principles we have studied in this chapter when connecting V to I or I to V. The roots of these two chords are a fifth apart. These principles apply whenever you are connecting two chords whose roots are a fifth apart.

1. *When connecting V and I or I and V whose roots are a fifth apart, repeat the common tone in the same voice and move the remaining voices to the nearest chord tones using correct doubling and spacing. Maintain either open or closed spacing for both chords.*

2. *When connecting these chords and the common tone is not repeated in the same voice, move all voices to the nearest chord tones using correct doubling and spacing. Maintain either open or closed spacing for both chords.*

Remember to be careful when moving to the nearest available chord tones. It is seldom necessary to leap more than a third in the three upper voices. If you have a leap larger than a third you should look at it carefully to see if you have a part writing error.

8. Write the three lower voices for the following cadences. **Repeat** the common tone in the same voice.

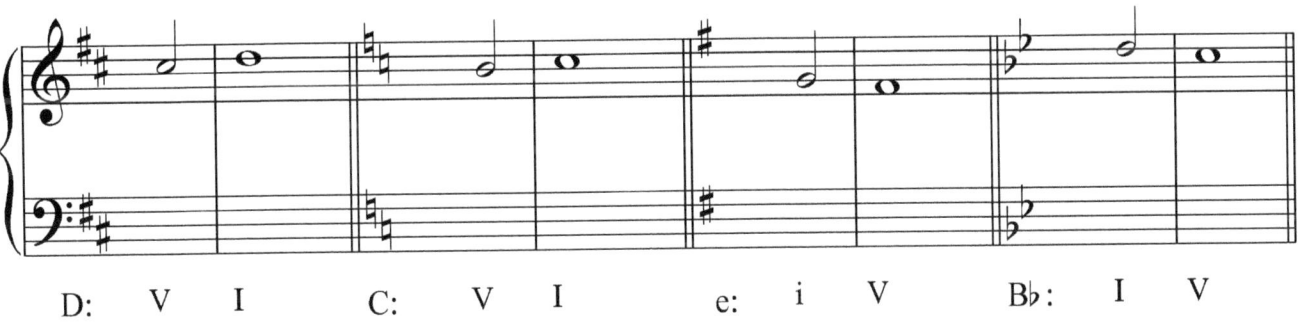

9. Write the three lower voices for the following cadences. **Do not repeat** the common tone in the same voice.

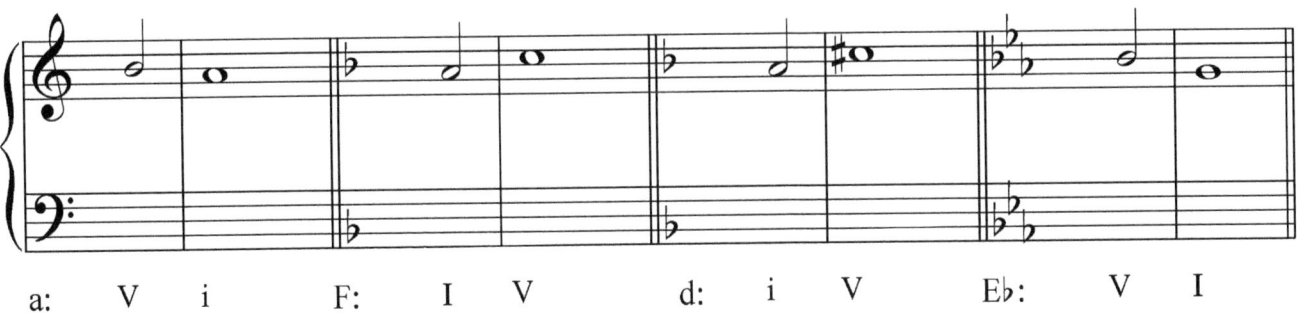

Harmonic Progression

The study of harmony is the study of the way chords relate to one another. A series of chords is a *harmonic progression*. I - V - I is the simplest harmonic progression in tonal music. These three chords create three areas of harmonization. The I chord that opens the progression is considered the *beginning tonic area.* The V in the middle is considered the *dominant area* and creates tension. The I chord that closes the progression is considered the *ending tonic area* and provides resolution to the tension created by the dominant.

I	V	I
Beginning tonic	Dominant	Ending tonic

The smoothest way to write this progression is to repeat the common tone in the same voice throughout and move the other voices by step. In Figure 5.10 the common tone (G) is repeated in the alto. The soprano and tenor move in stepwise motion and the bass moves from the root of I to the root of V and back to I.

Figure 5.10

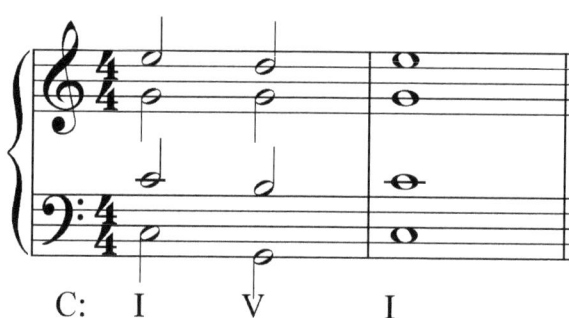

10. Name the keys. Complete the following progressions in four parts for SATB.

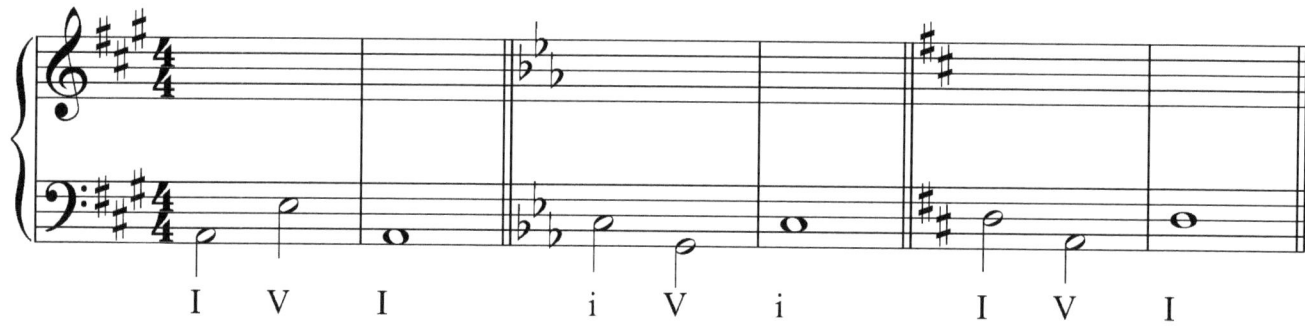

Parallel Perfect Intervals

Harmony is made up of several melodic lines or voices that work together to produce chords. These voices move and relate to one another through four types of motion:

1. *Oblique motion*: One voice moves up or down while the other voice remains on the same pitch. Figure 5.11 (a).

2. *Parallel motion*: Voices move in the same direction keeping the same interval between them Figure 5.11 (b).

3. *Contrary motion*: Voices move in the opposite direction. Figure 5.11 (c).

4. *Similar motion*: Voices move in the same direction but the interval between them does not remain the same. Figure 5.11 (d).

Figure 5.11

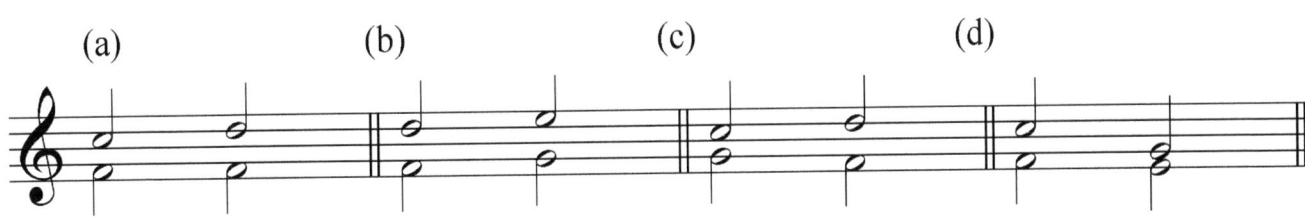

11. Identify the following as oblique, parallel, contrary or similar motion.

_____   _____   _____   _____

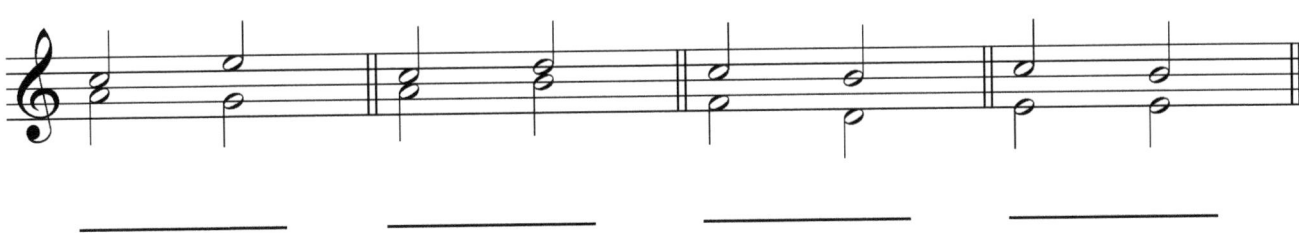

_____   _____   _____   _____

In four part writing certain parallel motion between voices is forbidden. Parallel motion occurs when two voices move in the same direction by the same interval. The following parallel intervals are considered faulty and are forbidden:

- *Parallel unisons* are not allowed between two voices. In Figure 5.11 (a) the alto and tenor move in parallel unison and in (b) the soprano and alto move in parallel unison. When two voices sing the same note, it sounds like one voice has dropped out and there are only three parts remaining.
- *Parallel octaves* are forbidden. 5.11(c) and (d) illustrate parallel perfect octaves. Here, the same pitch and motion is duplicated in a different voice and the individuality and independence of the voices are lost.
- *Parallel perfect fifths* are considered wrong. 5.11(e) and (f) contain faulty parallel perfect fifths. The fifth is a very stable interval. In a texture of individual voices, parallel fifths sound out of character and unstylistic.

Figure 5.11

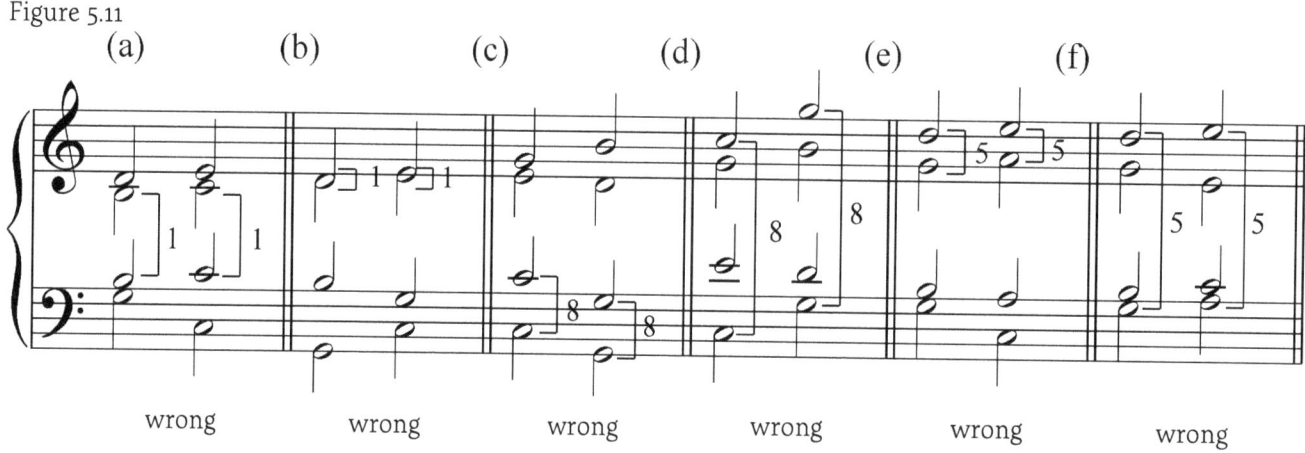

You should always check your writing for faulty parallel motion. To do this examine the progressions you write carefully. Let us examine Figure 5.12 for faulty parallels. Look for an octave between voices in the first chord. An octave occurs between the bass and tenor (C-C). Next, look at the bass and tenor in the next chord. Is there an octave between these two voices? No, so no problem. Look for a perfect fifth in the first chord. There are two perfect fifths. One between the bass and alto (C-G) and one between the tenor and alto (C-G). Look at the next chord. Does a perfect fifth occur in either place in this chord? Yes! The bass and alto have a perfect fifth (D-A). This is a mistake and considered faulty parallel motion. It must be corrected.

Figure 5.12

Faulty parallel intervals require motion in both voices. Figure 5.13 is **not** considered an example of faulty parallel octaves because they are not moving up or down, they are repeating.

Figure 5.13

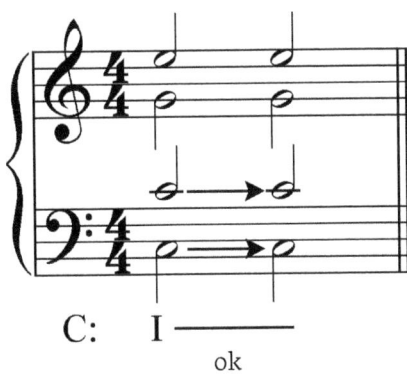

C: I ———
        ok

Hidden or Direct 8ves and 5ths

A fault called *hidden* or *direct 8ves* or *5ths* occurs when an octave or perfect fifth between outer voices is approached by similar motion with a leap in the soprano (Figure 5.14 (a) and (b)). The sound of these is similar to a parallel 8ve or 5th. If the soprano is approached by step the 8ve or 5th is fine (Figure 5.14 (c)).

Figure 5.14

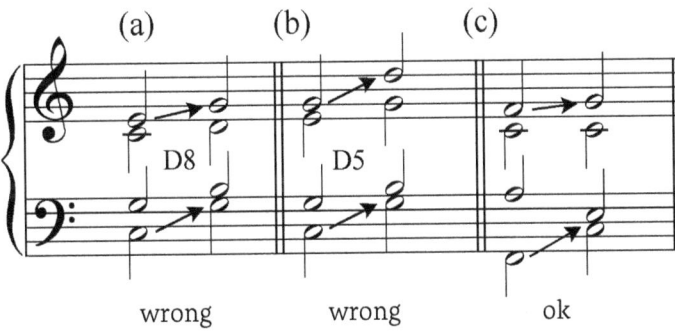

12. Find and mark any faulty parallel, hidden or direct motion, in the following progressions.

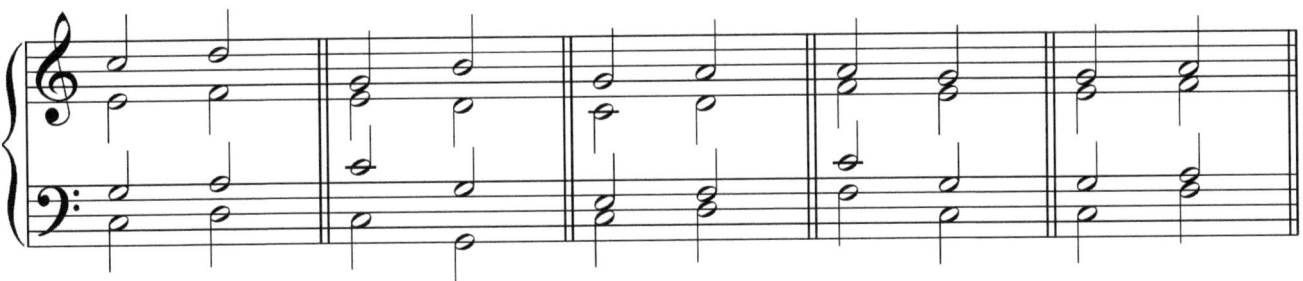

Steps for Harmonizing a Progression with Functional Chord Symbols

1. Complete the bass line according to the given Roman numerals.
2. Write the soprano, alto and tenor of the first chord with correct spacing and doubling.
3. Sketch in the soprano, moving to the nearest available chord tones of each chord.
4. Complete the inner voices (alto and tenor), repeating the common tones in the same voice if possible, and moving the notes to the nearest available chord tones of the next chord.
5. Check your work for faulty parallels, direct 8ves and 5ths, spacing, and crossed voices. Raise the leading tone in minor keys. If the leading tone is in an outer voice be sure it moves to the tonic.

13. Write the following progressions in four parts according to the functional chord symbols.

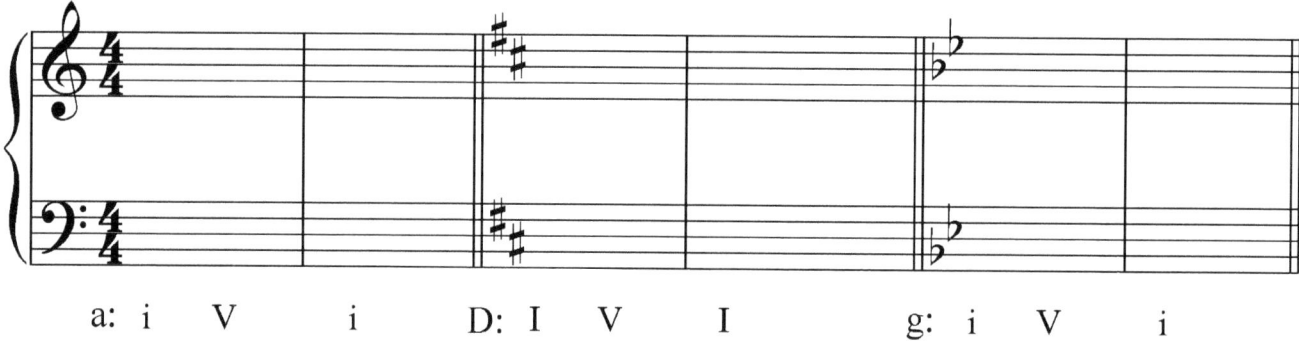

a: i   V   i   D: I   V   I   g: i   V   i

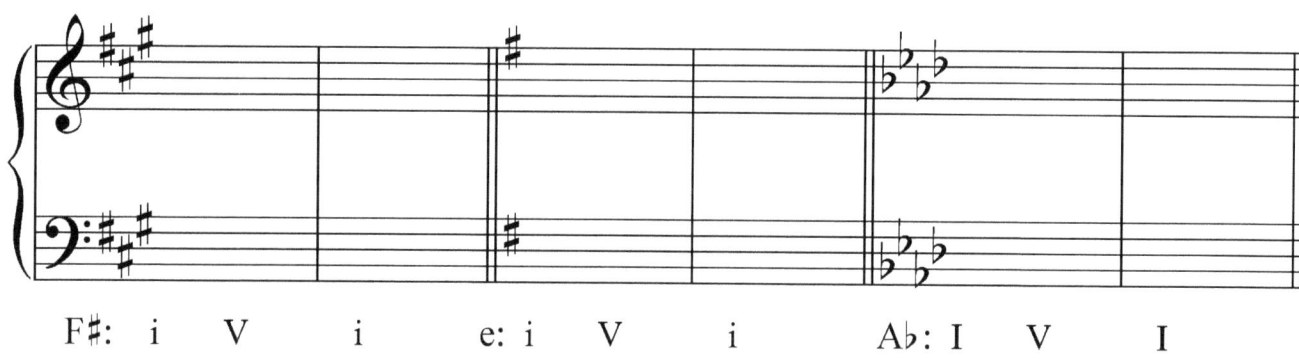

F#: i   V   i   e: i   V   i   Ab: I   V   I

6
The Subdominant

Different chords have different functions in a harmonic progression. A harmonic progression is a series of chords working together, and each chord has a function and a reason for being in the progression. This is called the *harmonic function* of the chord. The I chord has a tonic function and the V chord has a dominant function. These two chords form the main structure of a harmonic progression. The subdominant chord (IV) is a chord built on scale degree $\hat{4}$. It has more than one harmonic function. It can function as a *predominant chord*, that is, a chord that comes before and prepares the dominant chord. It can also function as a *prolongational chord*. In this capacity it extends or prolongs other chords, like the tonic. We will study these two main functions of IV in this chapter.

IV as a Predominant Chord

Chapter 5 introduced the progression I - V - I. Chord IV can be added to this progression before the V chord, giving us the progression I - IV - V - I. Here, IV is functioning as a predominant chord. The prefix "pre" means before, so predominant simply means before the dominant. This adds a new area to our basic harmonic progression:

Beginning Tonic	Predominant	Dominant	Ending Tonic
I	IV	V	I

When IV moves to V, its function is to prepare the dominant. The IV in Figure 6.1 functions as a predominant and prepares the dominant and the authentic cadence that follows it.

Figure 6.1

Muzio Clementi
Sonatina, Op. 36, III

Voice Leading

The roots of I and IV are a fifth (or fourth) apart. The easiest way to connect these two chords is to repeat the common tone in the same voice and move the other voices to the nearest available chord tones. See Figure 6.2. This works equally well in major and minor keys. In minor keys both i and iv are minor chords.

Figure 6.2

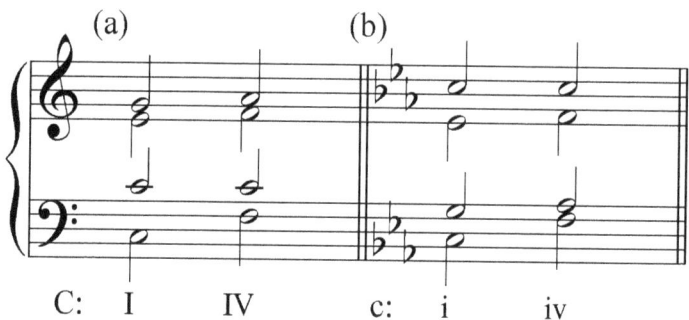

1. Name the keys and complete the following progressions in four parts.

Chapter 6: The Subdominant

IV - V is different than other progressions we have seen. The roots of IV and V are a second apart. There are no common tones between two chords whose roots are a second apart. There is a general rule to follow when writing this progression:

- *When connecting chords whose roots are a second apart, move the three upper voices to the nearest available chord tones in contrary motion to the bass.*

Figure 6.3 illustrates movement from IV to V. The bass steps up in each case and the top three voices move down, two by step, and one by a third. It is very important to follow these rules to avoid faulty parallel motion when writing this progression.

Figure 6.3

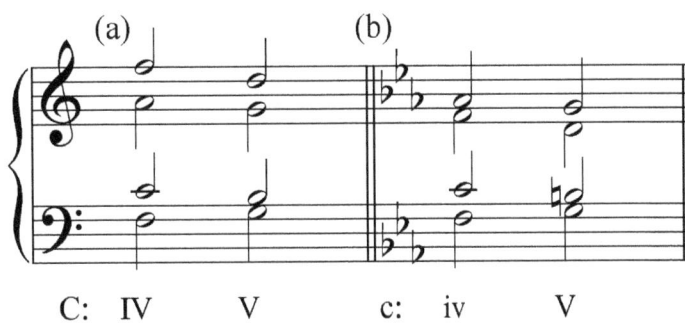

C: IV V   c: iv V

2. Name the keys and complete the following progressions in four parts.

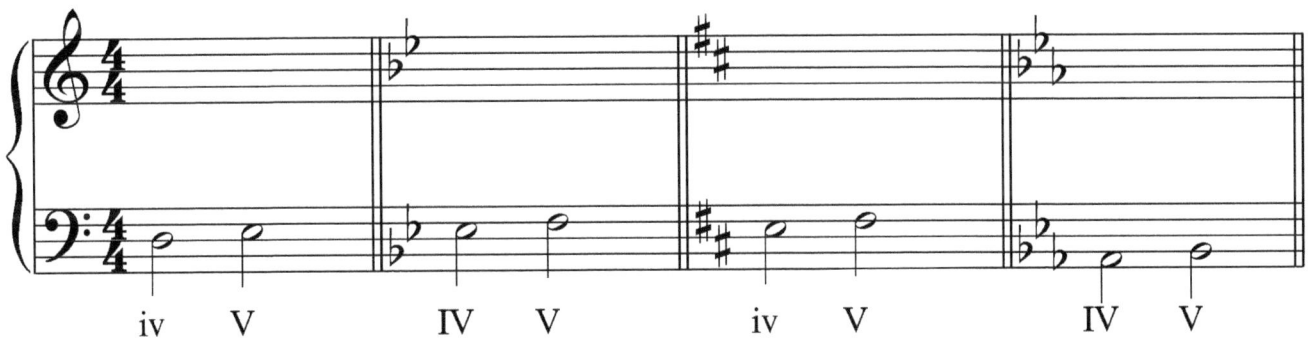

iv V   IV V   iv V   IV V

iv V   IV V   iv V   IV V

Chapter 6: The Subdominant

3. Name the keys and complete the following progressions in four parts.

IV as a Prolongation of the Beginning Tonic

Chord IV may be used between two statements of I to prolong tonic harmony. When we prolong a chord it means we make it last longer or expand it. IV is like the icing between two cookies. It makes the beginning tonic area larger. Instead of just a I chord, we have an expansion of I using I - IV - I. Our harmonic progression now looks like this:

Beginning Tonic	Predominant	Dominant	Ending Tonic
I - IV - I	IV	V	I

IV is functioning in two ways: As a prolongation of I and as a predominant. Figure 6.4 illustrates the voice leading for this progression. It is best to repeat the common tone in the same voice and move the other voices by step. In these examples the bass moves from the root of I to the root of IV and back to I. One voice repeats the common tone and the other voices move by step.

Figure 6.4

47

Chapter 6: The Subdominant

4. Name the keys and complete the following progressions in four parts.

IV as a Prolongation of the Ending Tonic: The Plagal Cadence

The progression IV - I may occur at the end of a phrase after an authentic cadence to prolong the ending tonic area of a harmonic progression. IV - I at the end of a phrase is also known as a *plagal cadence*. This has been called an *Amen cadence* since it was often used to harmonize the word "Amen" at the end of protestant hymns. Our harmonic progression can now be expanded even further:

Beginning Tonic	Predominant	Dominant	Ending Tonic
I - IV - I	IV	V	I - IV - I

Figure 6.5 is an example of this harmonic progression. Since we are only working with three chords, it is not the most exciting sounding progression, but it is a progression none the less. We will continue to learn new chords and our harmonic repertoire will become more interesting as we progress. Take note of the voice leading here. The common tone is repeated in the same voice whenever possible. In the progression IV - V, which involves roots moving by second, the upper voices move in contrary motion to the bass.

Figure 6.5

The previous progression can be written so it sounds more interesting by using different voice leading. The soprano in Figure 6.5 used only two notes, C and B. Figure 6.6 does not repeat the common tone throughout, allowing for a more interesting melody in the soprano. The soprano carries the main melody and if it does not offer variety and interest the whole progression can sound bland. The common tone is not repeated from I to IV at the end of measure one. This allows for a more interesting melody in the soprano and a better sounding progression. Experiment with voice leading, but always be careful to follow the rules and avoid faulty parallel motion, incorrect spacing, crossed voices, etc.

Figure 6.6

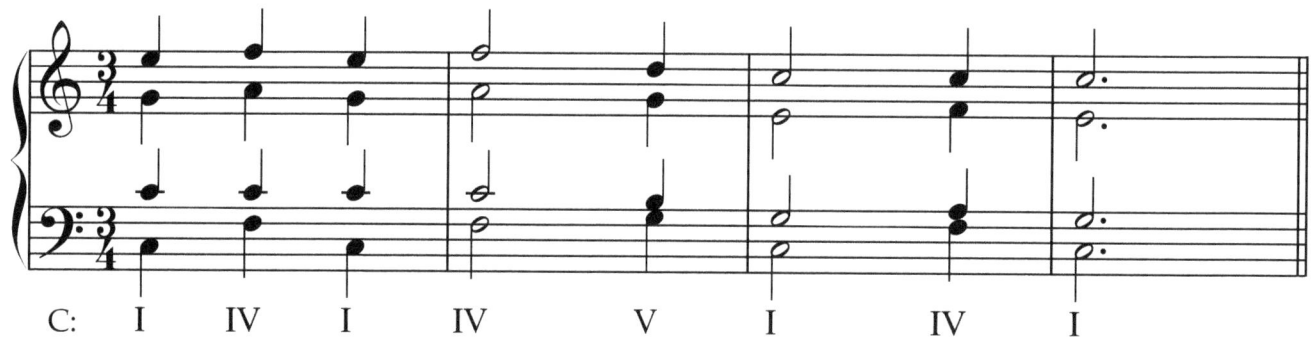

5. Name the keys and complete the following progressions in four parts.

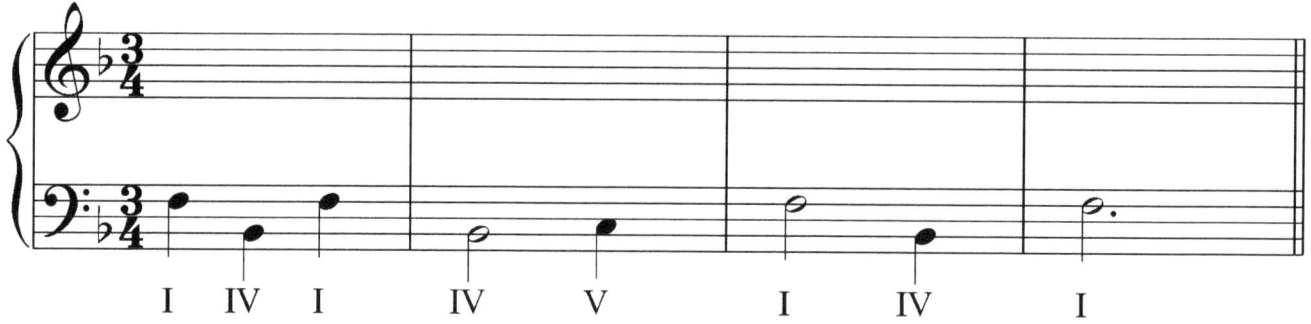

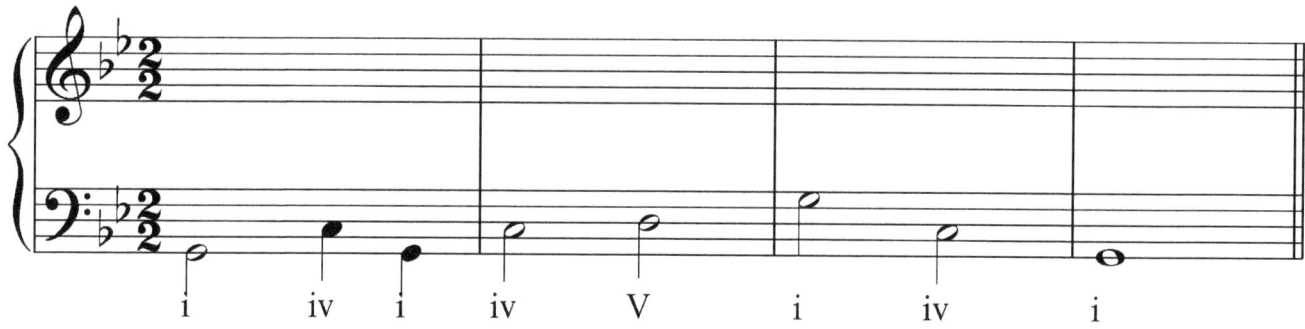

Chapter 6: The Subdominant

Harmonic Analysis

Music theory looks to the past. Composers learned to compose by studying the works of the great masters who came before them. Part of the study of harmony involves examining and analyzing music in order to understand it. This involves analyzing melodies and identifying chords and providing chord symbols.

Music can be written in a number of different textures. In music, *texture* is the way the melody, rhythm, and harmony are combined. The texture of a piece for a four part choir is different than the texture of a piano piece or a symphony for a large orchestra.

To analyze the chords in music in four part texture determine the key of the example and examine the chord. It may be helpful to stack the notes in thirds in order to identify it. Write the chord symbol under each chord using a Roman numeral (Figure 6.7).

Figure 6.7

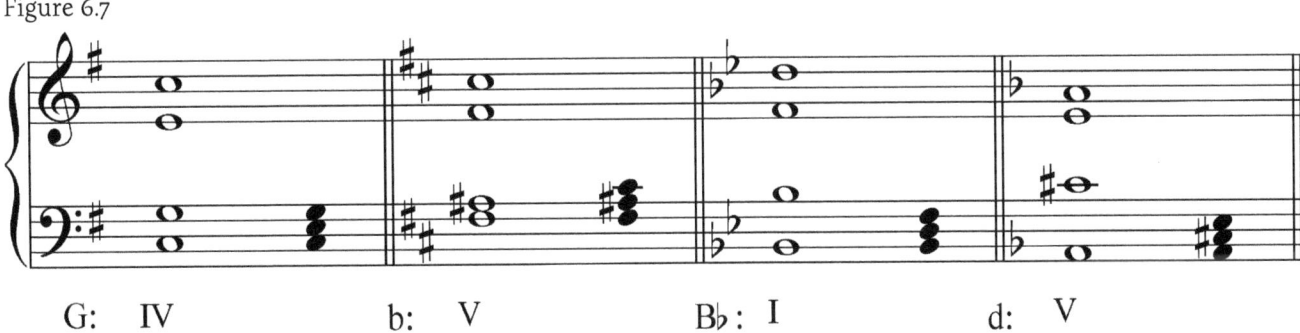

In keyboard music chords may occur in a variety of patterns in the left hand or may be spread out over both hands in broken chord patterns. To identify chords in keyboard texture, collect all the pitches for one chord together including the melody notes and stack them in thirds to find out the identity of the chord. Figure 6.8, 6.9, and 6.10 illustrate various piano accompaniment patterns in the left hand.

Figure 6.8

Johann Baptist Vaňhal
Sonatina, Op. 41, 4

Figure 6.9

Muzio Clementi
Sonatina, Op. 36, No. 6

Figure 6.10

Frédéric Chopin
Fantaisie-Impromptu Op. 66

Figure 6.11 is an example of a string quartet score. In order to provide a functional chord analysis for this work, collect all the notes on each beat or in each measure to determine the chord structure. The first complete measure contains all the notes of the I chord (B♭-D-F). The 2nd measure is made up of all the notes of the IV chord (E♭-G-B♭). The chord symbol V is assigned to the two pickup notes (F-F). This is considered *implied harmony*. We don't have a full chord here, but the two F's are implying or suggesting the V chord. Pickup notes often imply V or I.

Figure 6.11

Joseph Haydn
String Quartet, Op. 74, No. 3

Occasionally segments of the music you are analyzing may not contain all of the notes required to make a complete chord. In this case you must state the implied harmony. This is the logical harmony outlined by the notes that are available. Figure 6.12 consists of only two voices. Drawing on knowledge of chord progressions and harmony we can arrive at the implied harmony.

Figure 6.12

F: I —————   IV —————   V —————   I

Figure 6.13 is the opening of a piano piece. To analyze it, the first thing we do is name the key. Here, it is C major. Then we analyze each chord and provide functional chord symbols (Roman numerals) within that key. We can see that this example consists of the I and V chord in C major. There are a number of notes in the treble clef in measures three and four that have to be explained, and that is what we will do in this section.

Jan Baptist Vaňhal
Sonatina, Op. 41, No. 1

Figure 6.13

C: I   V   I   I ———————————————————— V I V I

Notes that are not part of the underlying harmony are called *nonchord tones* or *nonharmonic tones*. The underlying harmony in measures three and four of Figure 6.13 is I in C major, or the C major chord (C-E-G). In these measures, any note that is not part of the C major chord, that is, not a C, E, or a G is considered a nonchord tone and must be identified. When we analyze a composition every note must be explained. If a note is not a chord tone it must be labelled as a nonchord tone and its function identified.

Nonchord tones help to create smoother lines by reducing the number of leaps in a melody. Although leaps are necessary in a melody, too few leaps and the melody is monotonous, but too many and the melody sounds disjunct. Nonchord tones also create movement and increase rhythmic activity.

Nonchord tones are called different names by different writers in music theory. They can also be called: *foreign tones, bytones, accessory tones,* and *nonharmonic tones*. We will stick to the name: *nonchord tones*.

The Passing Tone

Nonchord tones are identified by how they are approached and left. There are several types of nonchord tones and we will begin by studying a few in this chapter.

A nonchord tone that is approached and left by step in the same direction is called a *passing tone*. Identified by the symbol: **PT**. Passing tones fill in the gap (usually a third) between two chord tones. Figure 6.14 (a) illustrates the passing tone D between two chord tones, E and C. The underlying harmony is C major and since the D is not part of that harmony, it must be labelled as a nonchord tone. Its function is as a passing tone. 6.14(b) contains the passing tone (F) filling in the third between E and G. Passing tones may occur simultaneously in two voices. These are known as *double passing tones* and usually move in parallel 6ths 6.14(c), 3rds (d), or contrary motion (e). When analyzing a passing tone in a score, it is circled and the symbol PT is placed next to it.

Figure 6.14

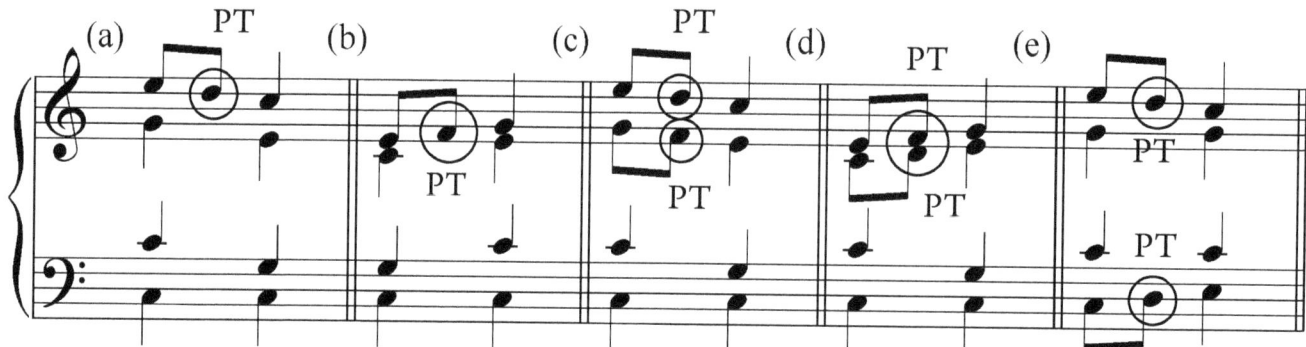

Two passing tones may fill in the interval of a 4th as shown in the tenor in Figure 6.15 (a). A *chromatic passing tone* (symbol: **Chr. PT**) fills in a whole step with two half steps. The D♯ circled in the soprano in ex. (b) is a chromatic passing tone between the notes D and E. An *accented passing tone* (symbol: **APT**) is a passing tone that falls on a strong beat or part of the beat. 6.15(c) shows an unaccented passing tone, as studied above. In 6.15(d) the passing tone is shifted to a stronger beat and becomes an accented passing tone. 6.15(e) illustrates an error that can occur when using passing tones. Here the addition of a passing tone creates faulty parallel 5ths between the alto and soprano. This passing tone should not be used.

Figure 6.15

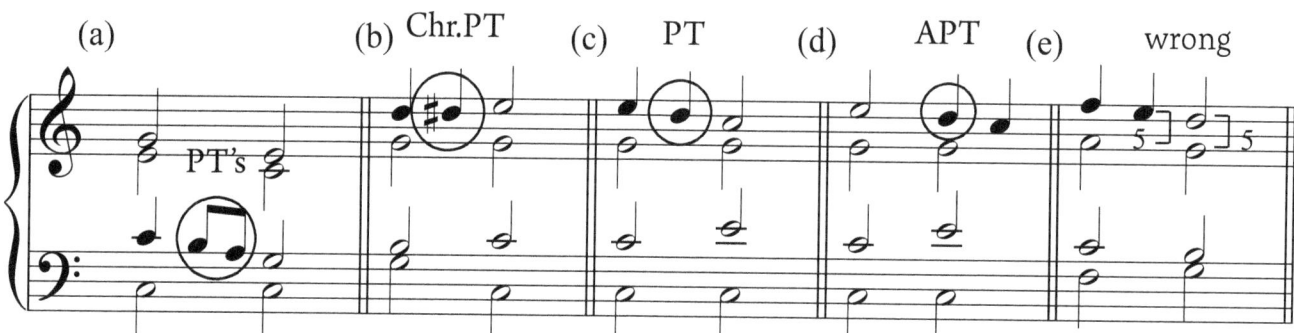

Examine Figure 6.16. We can now fully analyze the earlier Sonatina opening. All the notes that are not part of the C major chord in measure three and four are passing tones.

Jan Baptist Vaňhal
Sonatina, Op. 41, No. 1

6. Complete the analysis of the following excerpt by circling and identifying the nonchord tones in the right hand.

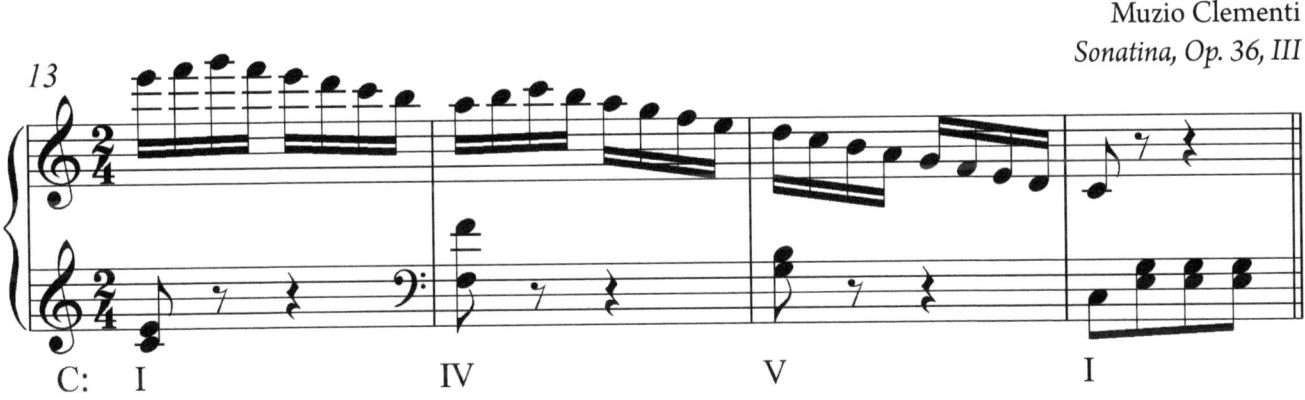

Muzio Clementi
Sonatina, Op. 36, III

7. Name the key and provide a harmonic analysis of the following excerpts using functional chord symbols. Circle and label any nonchord tones.

The Neighbor Note

A *neighbor note* (symbol: **NN**) is a nonchord tone that steps away from a chord tone and then steps back to it. The upper neighbor, Figure 6.17 (a), is a step above the chord tone and the lower neighbor (b), is a step below the chord tone. More than one neighbor can occur as the same time. In Figure 6.17 (c) and (d) two neighbors move by the interval of a sixth.

Figure 6.17

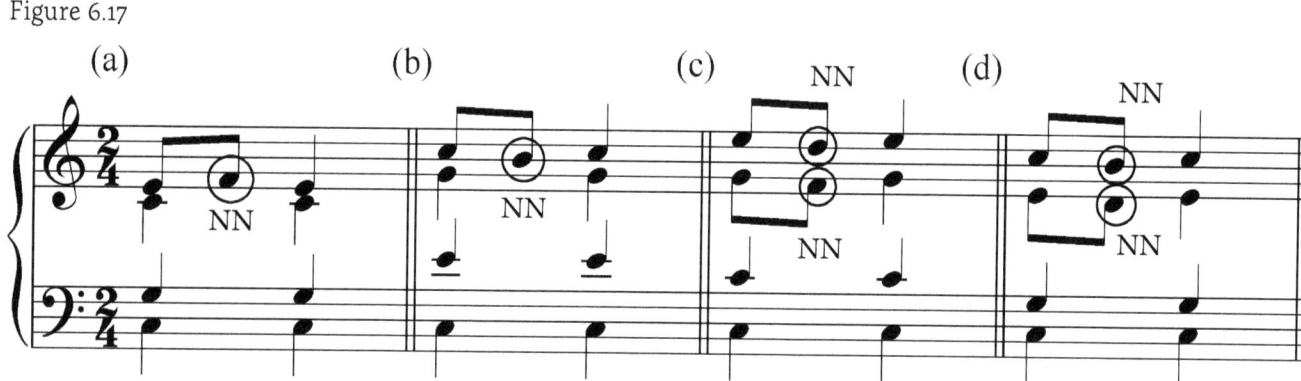

Neighbor notes usually fall on weak beats or weak parts of a beat. However, if a neighbor falls on a strong beat or stronger part of a beat it is considered an *accented neighbor note* (symbol: **Acc. NN**). Figure 6.18 (a) and (b) contain accented neighbor notes in the soprano and tenor. Double neighbor notes, known as *a neighbor group* (symbol: **NG**) are a combination of two neighbor notes, an upper neighbor and a lower neighbor, or vice versa. The notes of a neighbor group move by step, skip and step as in 6.18(c) and (d).

Figure 6.18

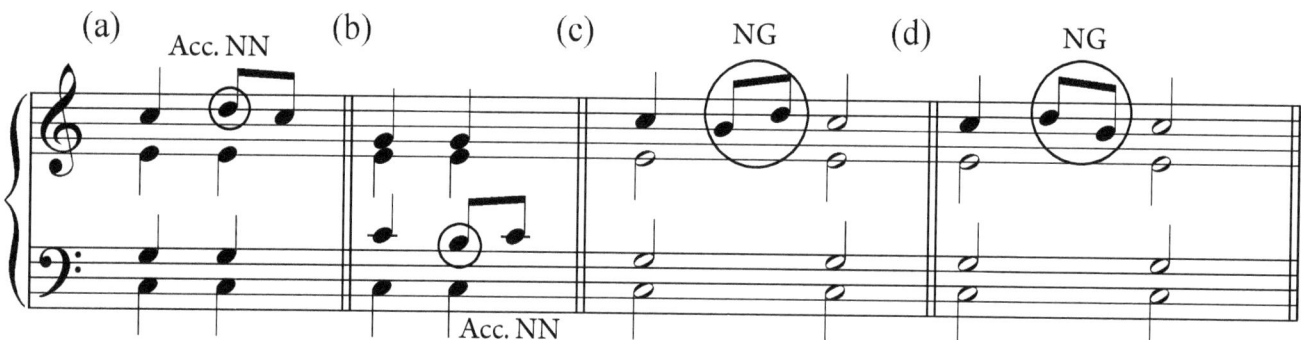

Chapter 6: The Subdominant

8. Name the key and provide a harmonic analysis of the following excerpts using functional chord symbols. Circle and label any nonchord tones.

Johann Sebastian Bach
Two Part Invention No. 8

Luigi Boccherini
Violincello Concerto

Chapter 6: The Subdominant

7
First Inversion Chords

The bass or lowest note of a triad determines its position. Having the root, third, or fifth in the bass determines if a triad is in root position, first inversion or second inversion. Inversions are used to create smoother bass lines and produce a variety of effects in an harmonic progression. When a triad is in root position, the root is the lowest note. If the root is not the lowest note, the triad is *inverted*. A *first inversion triad* has the third in the bass. Compare the chords in Figure 7.1.

Figure 7.1

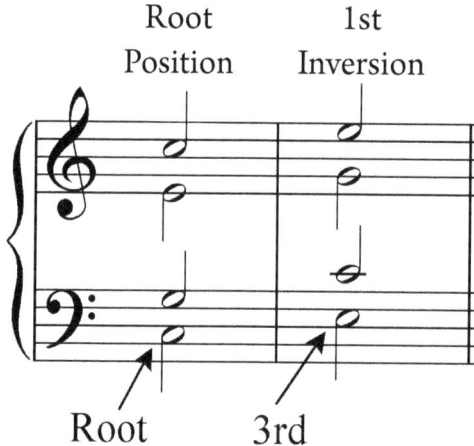

Figured bass is a system of indicating notes above the bass. This system can be used in conjunction with functional chord symbols in harmonic analysis and chord identification. We use figured bass symbols to indicate the position of a chord. Figured bass symbols are a listing of the intervals that occur above the lowest note of a chord. Figure 7.2 contains a C major triad in root position and 1st inversion. The figured bass symbol of a root position triad is 5 with a 3 under it. This indicates that there is the interval of a 5th (C to G) and a 3rd (C to E) above the lowest note. The figured bass symbols for a 1st inversion chord are a 6 with a 3 underneath. This indicates the interval of a 6th (E to C) and 3rd (E to G) above the lowest note. When notating chords with functional chord symbols (Roman numerals), a root positon chord gets the Roman numeral only and no figures are necessary (eg. I, IV, V). A 1st inversion chord gets the Roman numeral with a 6 beside it to indicate that the chord is in 1st inversion (eg. I^6, IV^6, V^6).

Figure 7.2

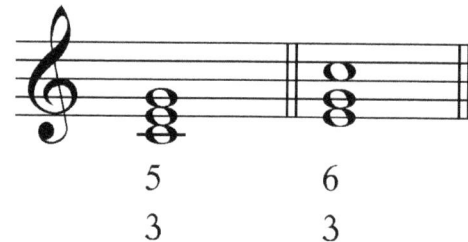

Figure 7.3 contains three first inversion chords in C minor. In each case, the 3rd is in the bass and the root is doubled. We will explore other possibilities for chord doubling later. Since i and iv are minor chords, they use lowercase Roman numerals with a 6 to indicate the first inversion. The root/quality chord symbols consist of the root, the chord quality, a slash and the bass note.

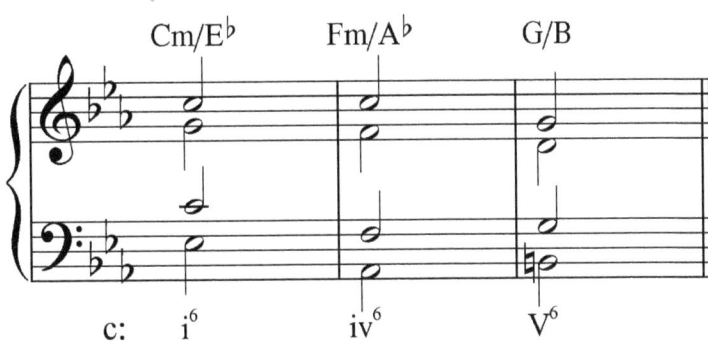

Figure 7.3

1. Write the following first inversion chords in four parts. Double the root in each one.

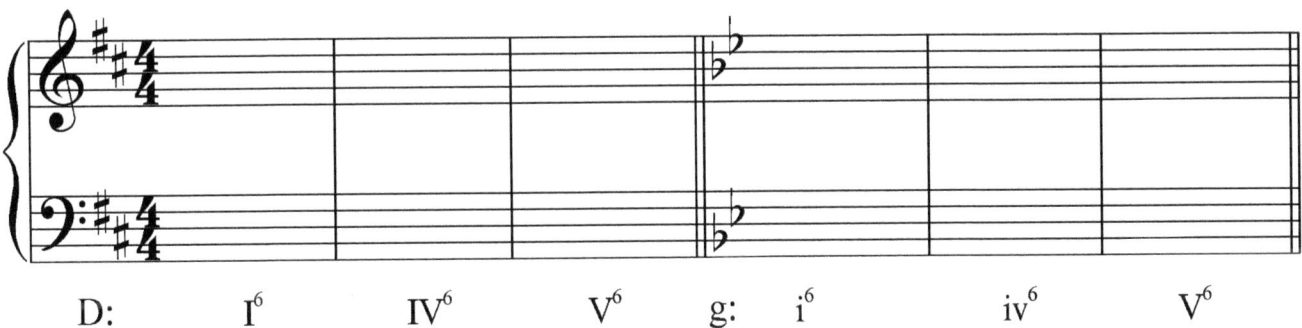

D: I⁶   IV⁶   V⁶   g: i⁶   iv⁶   V⁶

Triads in first inversion are less stable than root position chords. Composers use them for voice leading or expressive reasons. In a perfect authentic cadence both chords must be in root position with the soprano ending on the tonic. If a composer wants a less final cadence, one of the chords may be written in first inversion. In this case V⁶ - I or V - I⁶ is considered an imperfect authentic cadence. In Figure 7.4 the first cadence ends with the tonic in the soprano. However, since the V is in first inversion (V⁶), it is not a perfect authentic cadence. It is an imperfect authentic cadence.

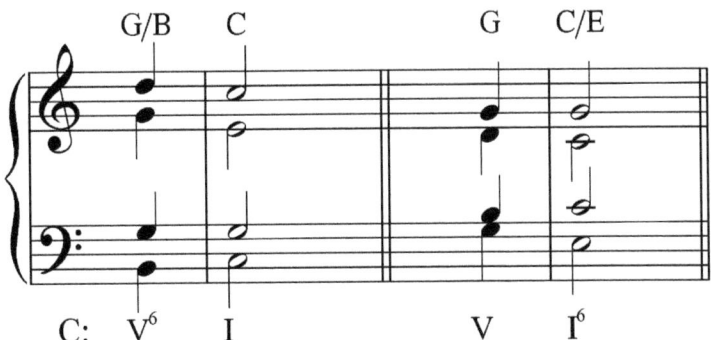

Figure 7.4

Chapter 7: First Inversion Chords

2. Name the keys and write the following imperfect authentic cadences in four parts.

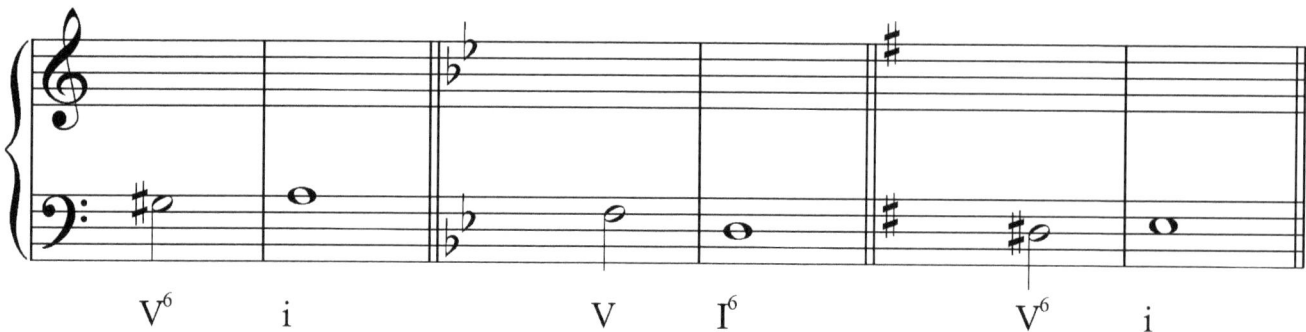

    V⁶   i   V   I⁶   V⁶   i

First Inversion Chords in Prolongation

First inversion chords can be used to prolong or expand an area of harmonization. This is a common function of these chords. In Figure 7.5 (a),(b), and (c), I is prolonged with I⁶. The chord does not change, only the chord position. This progression could be used to prolong the beginning tonic. A technique called *voice exchange* is used in 7.5(a). Here, the bass and soprano exchange pitches (C-E and E-C). Voice exchange also works for the reverse of this progression (I⁶ - I). Another way to write this progression is to write parallel tenths between the bass and soprano 7.5(b). Smoother voice leading can be achieved in this progression if the fifth is doubled in I⁶ (c). 7.5(d) and (e) show a prolongation of predominant harmony (IV) using IV⁶. 7.5(d) uses voices exchange and (e) uses motion in parallel tenths.

Figure 7.5

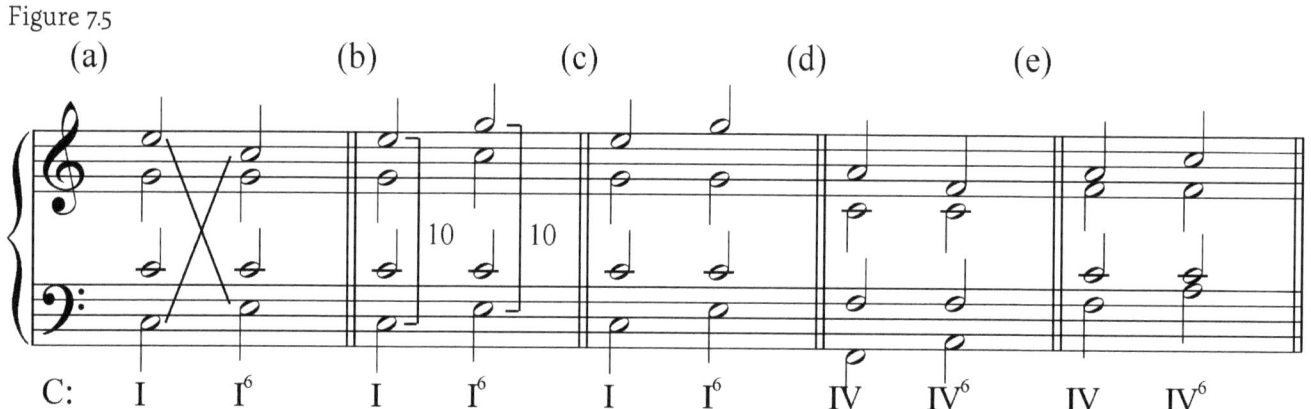

C: I   I⁶   I   I⁶   I   I⁶   IV IV⁶   IV IV⁶

First inversion chords can be used to prolong the first two areas of harmonization:

        Beginning Tonic   Predominant   Dominant   Ending Tonic
            I - I⁶   IV - IV⁶   V   I

The above areas outline a typical chord progression. However, there may be exceptions to this, and not every harmonic progression will fit so neatly into this formula. For example, if the phrase ends on V for a half cadence, the progression will look different.

3. Name the keys and write the following progressions using voice exchange.

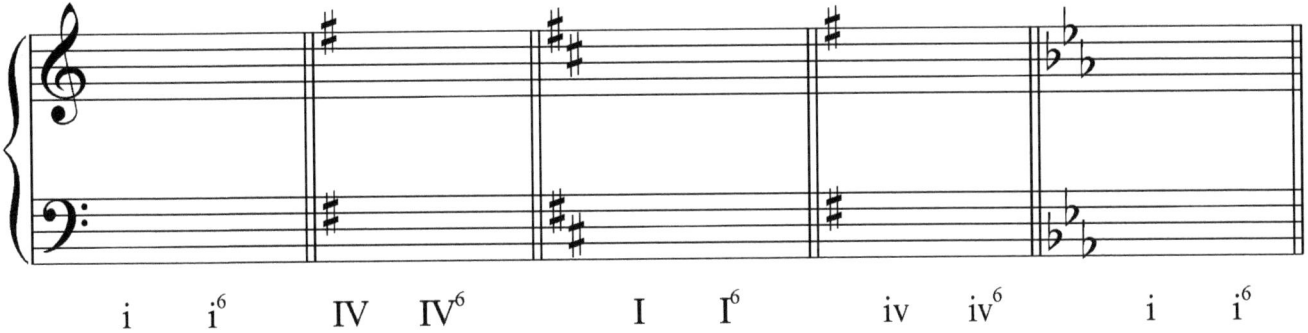

4. Name the keys and write the following progressions using parallel motion in tenths. Double the 5th in the first inversion chords.

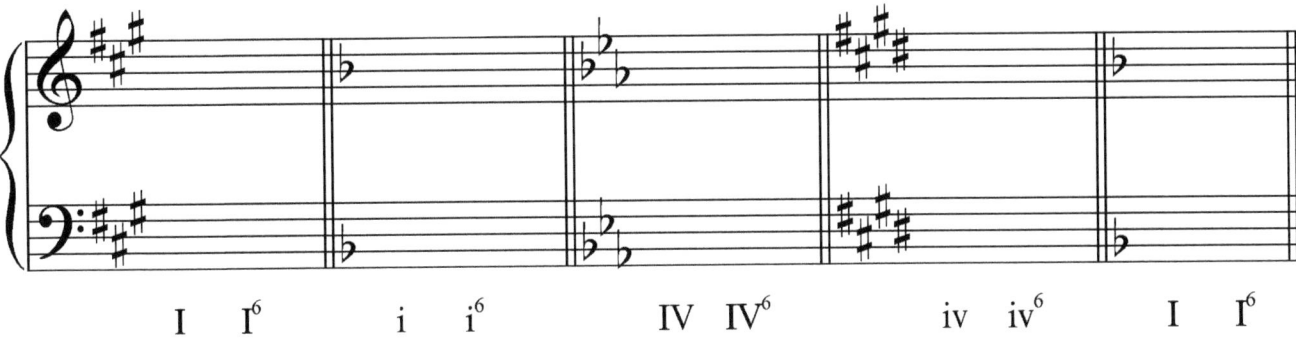

V^6 in Tonic Prolongation

V^6 may act as a neighbor chord between two statements of I to prolong tonic harmony in the progression: I - V^6 - I. Figure 7.6 (a) and (b) prolong the tonic with neighbor notes. One voice in each progression repeats the common tone, and the others move in neighbor motion. An alternative and common voice leading for this progression can be found in 7.6(c). The neighbor motion in two of the upper voices is replaced with voice exchange between $\hat{1}$-$\hat{2}$-$\hat{3}$ and $\hat{3}$-$\hat{2}$-$\hat{1}$. These progressions work well to prolong the beginning tonic area.

Figure 7.6

5. Name the keys and add the bass, tenor and alto to complete the following progressions.

i   V⁶   i   I   V⁶   I   i   V⁶   i   I   V⁶   I

To avoid faulty parallel when moving from a first inversion chord to a root position chord approach and leave the doubled note in the first inversion chord by contrary or oblique motion. In Figure 7.7(a) the doubled A in IV⁶ is approached by oblique motion and left by contrary motion. In 7.7(b) and (c) the doubled note is approached and left by contrary motion.

Figure 7.7

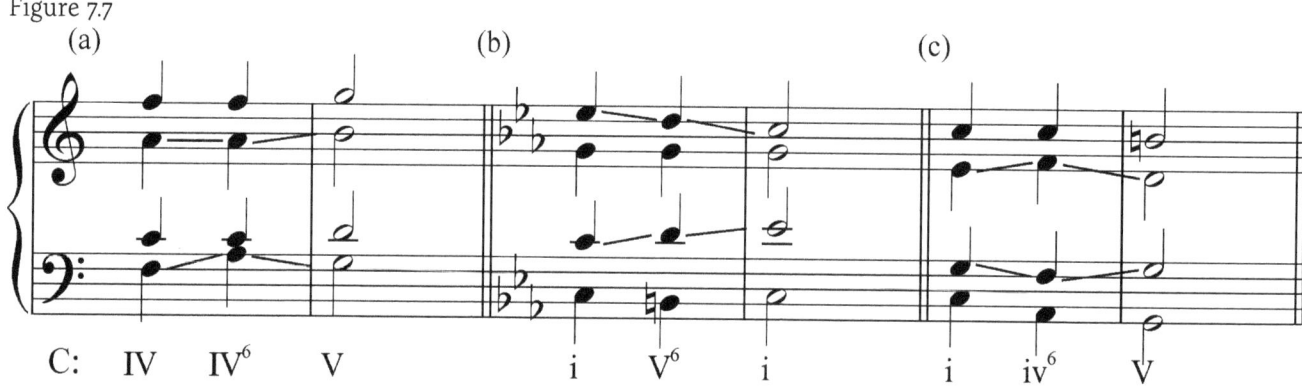

C: IV   IV⁶   V   i   V⁶   i   i   iv⁶   V

6. Complete the following progression in four parts.

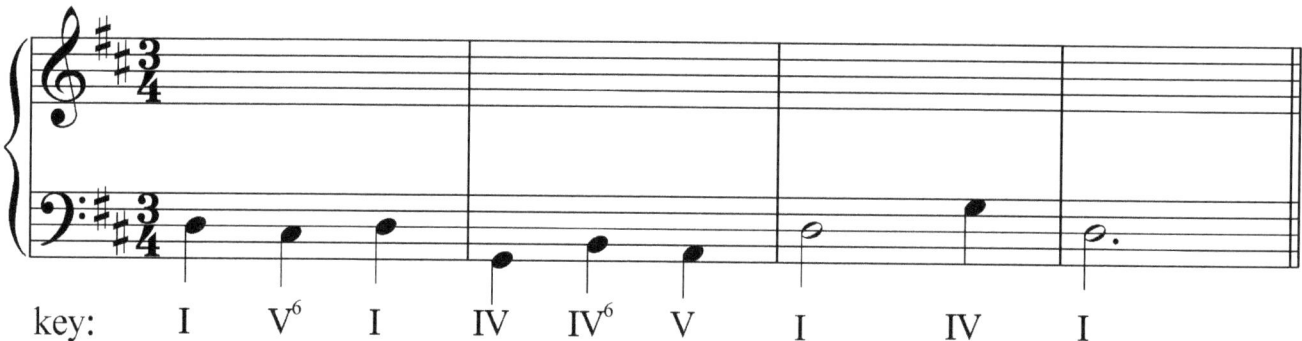

key: I   V⁶   I   IV   IV⁶   V   I   IV   I

7. Complete the following figured bass in four parts. Chords with a 6 are in first inversion. Chords without a figure are in root position. Add all functional chords symbols.

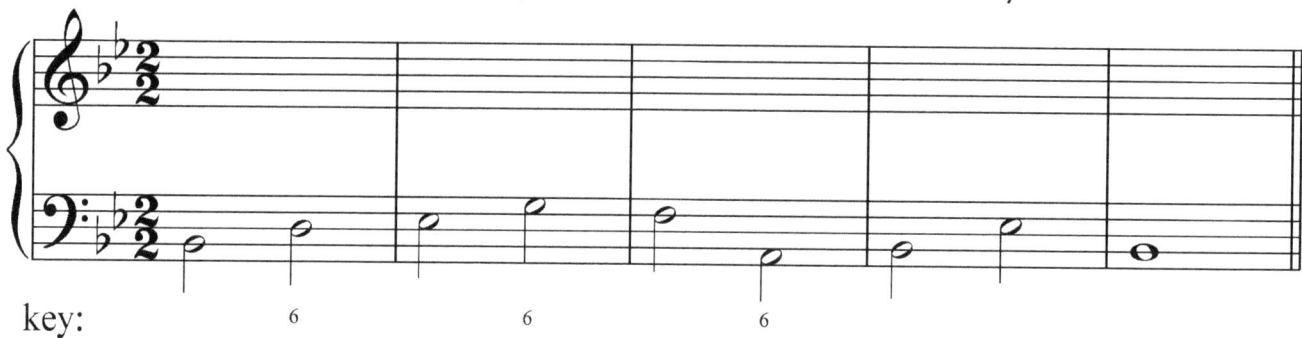

key: 6   6   6

Chapter 7: First Inversion Chords

vii°6 in Tonic Prolongation

vii°, which is the chord built on scale degree $\hat{7}$, is a diminished triad. A diminished triad in root position can sound harsh. For now, we will not use this chord in root position. In first inversion, however, it is a very effective chord in tonic prolongation (vii°6). The progressions I - vii°6 - I6 and the reverse I6 - vii°6 - I are built on $\hat{1}$-$\hat{2}$-$\hat{3}$ and $\hat{3}$-$\hat{2}$-$\hat{1}$ respectively. vii°6 functions as a *passing chord* between two different positions of I. The progressions illustrated in Figure 7.8 contain voice exchange between the bass and one other voice. (C-D-E and E-D-C). The other voices move in neighbor motion. Make note of the parallel 5ths that occur between the tenor and alto in 7.8(a). These are not considered faulty because they are not parallel perfect fifths. C to G is a perfect fifth, but B to F is a diminished fifth. This progression works in both major and minor keys, but vii°6 requires a raised leading tone in the minor key.

- ***It is important to note that the root of vii°6 is the leading tone, and the leading tone is not doubled. Here, we always double the third of vii°6, which is in the bass.***

Figure 7.8

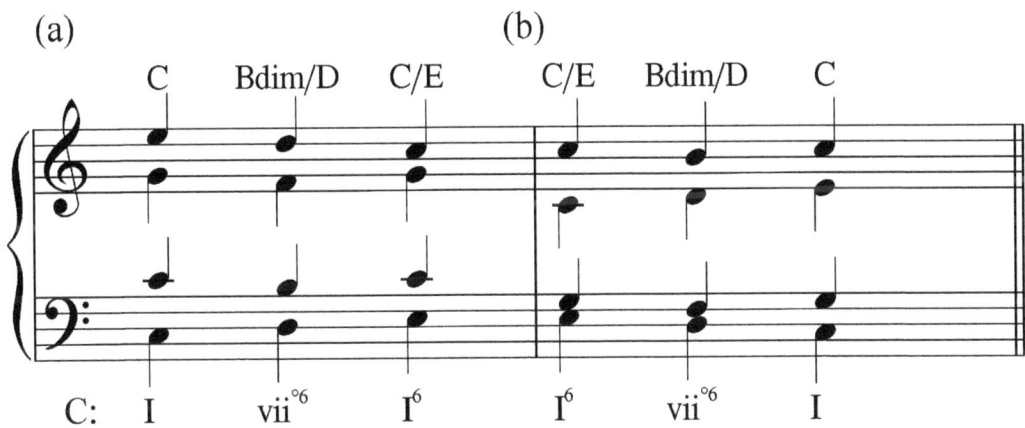

8. Name the keys and complete the following progressions.

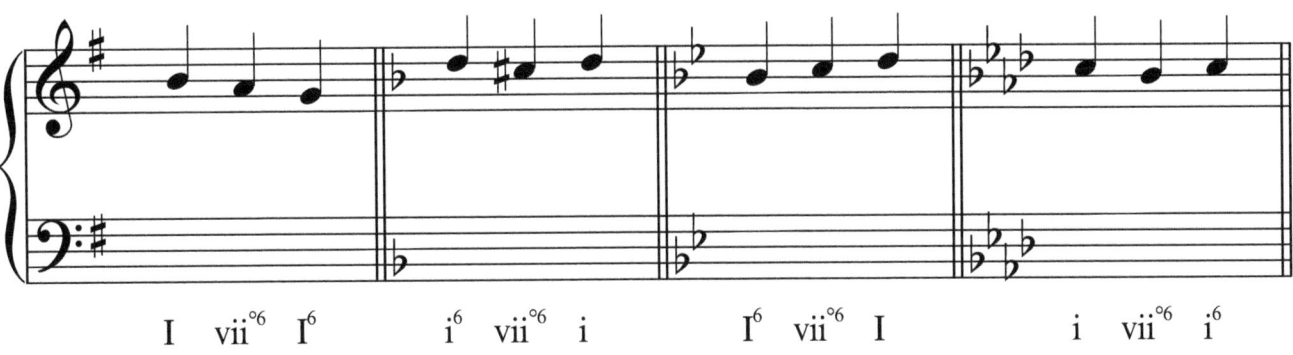

vii°⁶ may be used as a neighbor chord between two statements of I to prolong tonic harmony. In this progression all voices move in neighbor motion (Figure 7.9). The third is doubled in vii°⁶.

Figure 7.9

9. Complete the following progressions in four parts.

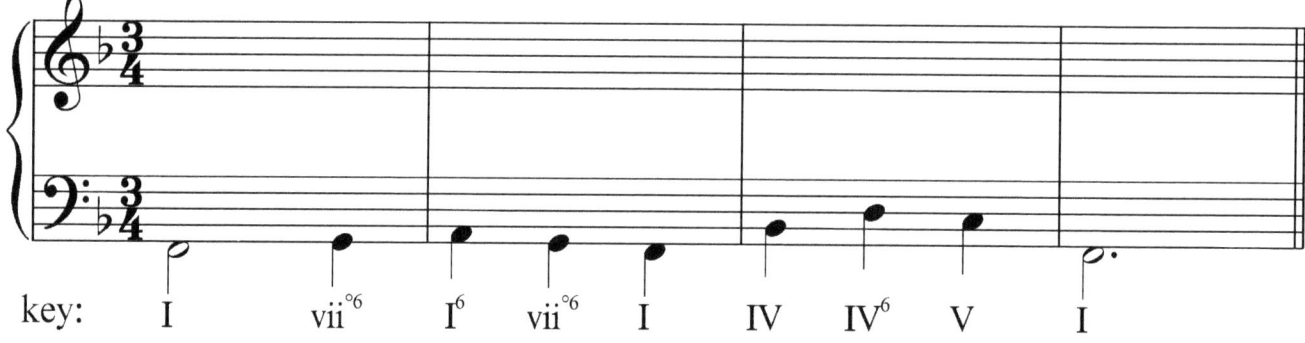

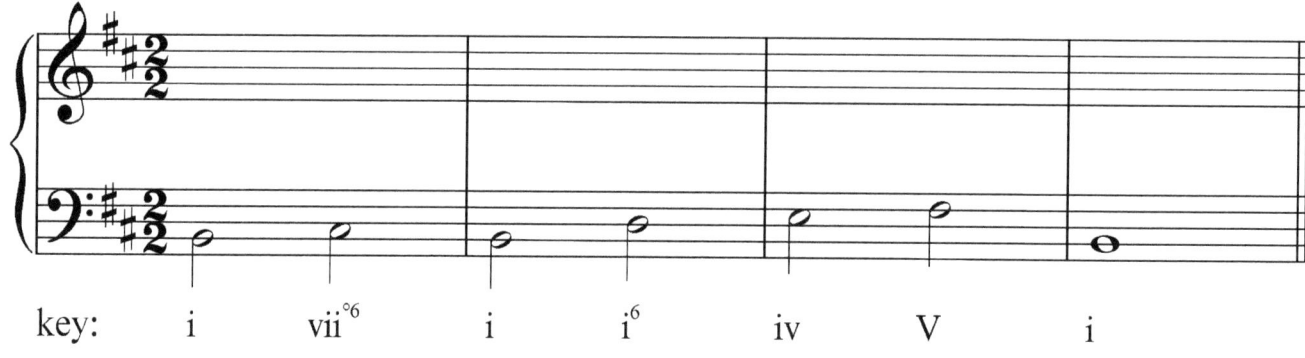

The Phrygian Cadence

A cadence that ends on V is a half cadence. In minor keys iv⁶ - V is a half cadence called a *Phrygian cadence*. The bass of this cadence moves by a half step. The soprano usually moves in contrary motion to the bass on scale degrees $\hat{4}$-$\hat{5}$. It gets its name from the Phrygian mode which has half steps between $\hat{1}$-$\hat{2}$ and $\hat{5}$-$\hat{6}$ and resembles a cadence that occurs in compositions written in this mode. iv⁶ may be written with a doubled 5th as in Figure 7.10(a) or doubled root as in 7.10 (b).

Figure 7.10

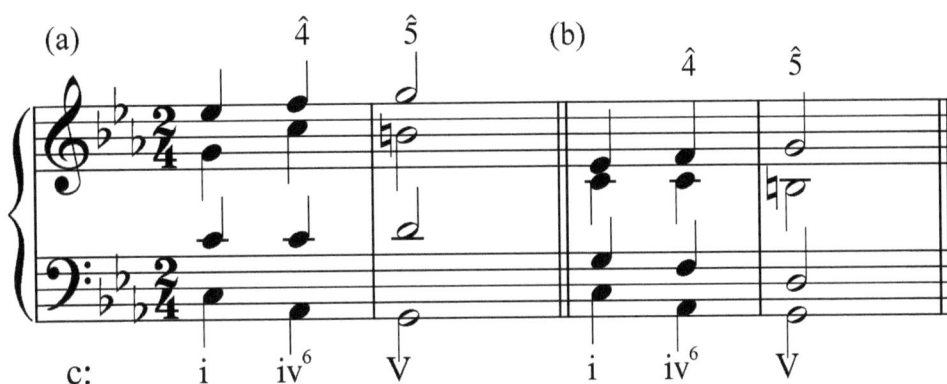

10. Complete the following progression in four parts.

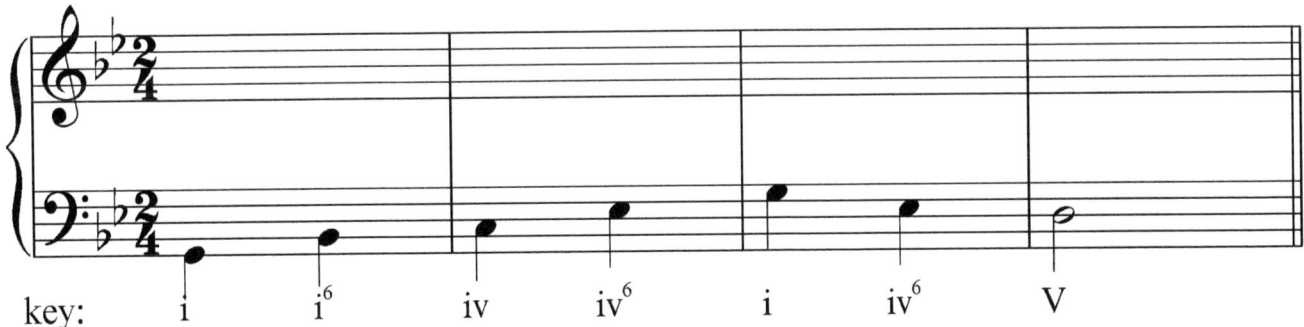

Harmonic Analysis

11. Provide a harmonic analysis of the following using functional chord symbols. Circle and identify any nonchord tones.

Muzio Clementi
Sonatina, Op. 36, No. 2, III

Muzio Clementi
Sonatina, Op. 36, No. 3, II

8

Harmonizing a Melody

Harmonizing a melody allows us to use our knowledge of harmony and voice leading. So far, we have harmonized bass lines according to functional chords symbols. In this chapter we will learn to choose the chords, bass line, and the melodic figuration of the inner voices for a given melody in the soprano.

For now, our melody harmonizations will begin and end on the tonic. The first step is to look at the melody and try to identify harmonic patterns that will fit with it. It is helpful to identify the notes of the melody with scale degrees. Figure 8.1 has a couple of familiar patterns in the soprano $\hat{3}$-$\hat{2}$-$\hat{1}$, and $\hat{1}$-$\hat{2}$-$\hat{3}$, which can be harmonized with harmonic patterns we have studied.

Figure 8.1

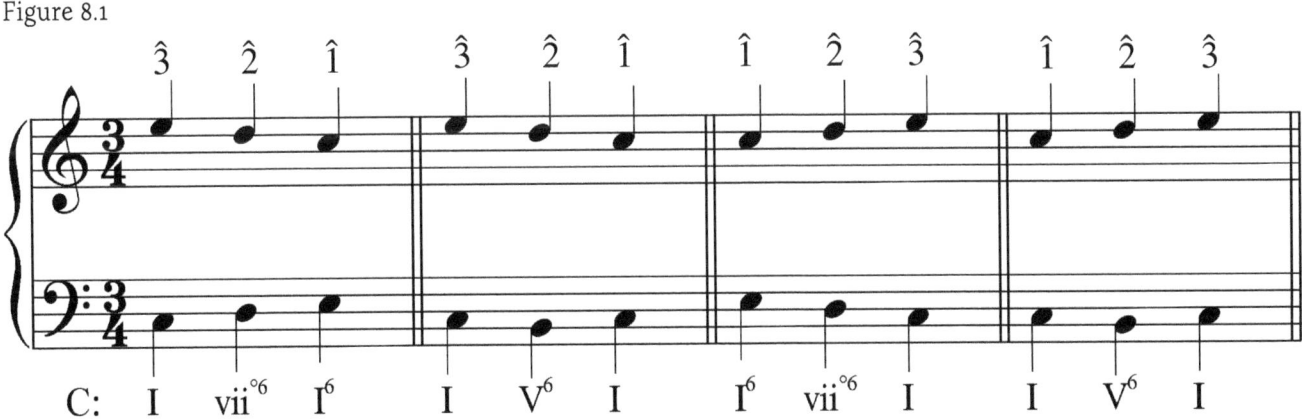

Sometimes each note of the melody will have a chord. Sometimes two notes may be harmonized by one chord as in Figure 8.2 (a). 8.2 (b) contains a change of chord position (I - I⁶) and adds interest to the bass line. 8.2 (c) shows a I - IV - I prolongation over one held note. The melody $\hat{4}$-$\hat{2}$-$\hat{1}$ can be harmonized with IV - V - I as in 8.2 (d). Here we have a predominant followed by a perfect authentic cadence.

Figure 8.2

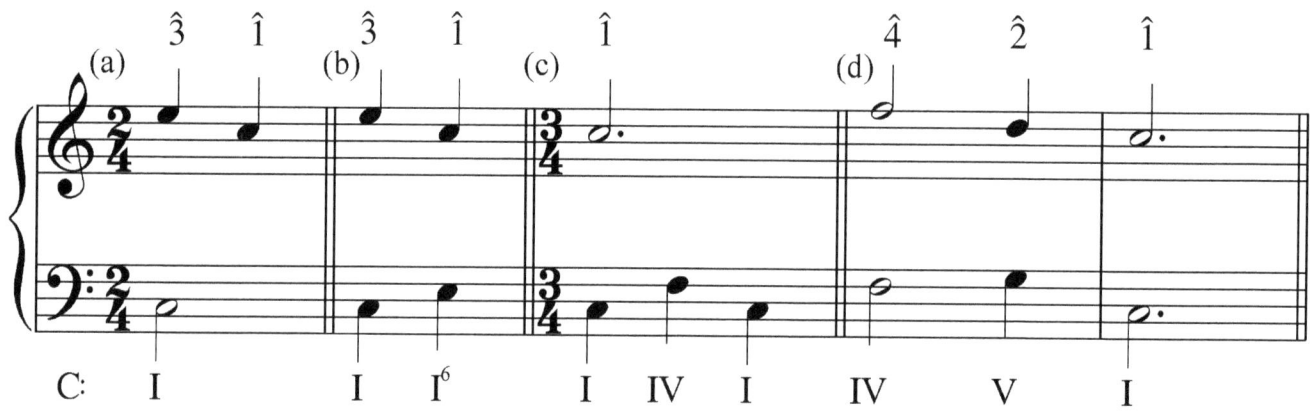

Steps for Harmonizing a Melody

Lets examine a melody and go through the steps in completing it for four parts. The first step is to analyze the melody and decide the key. Sing or play the melody to understand its shape and contour. The melody is Figure 8.3 consists of one four measure phrase.

Figure 8.3

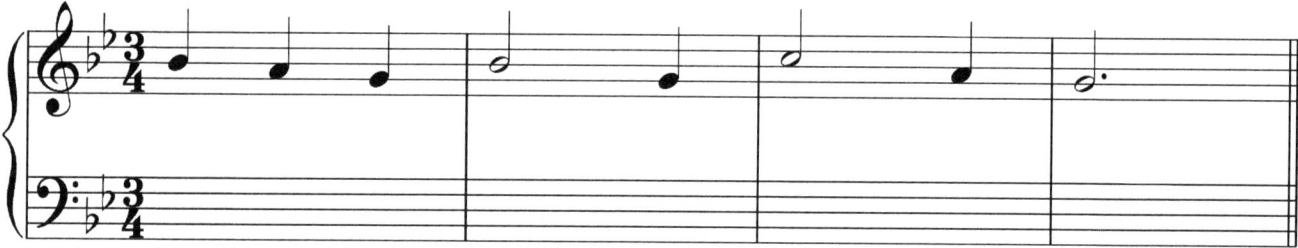

The key of this melody is g minor. In Figure 8.4 we added scale degrees to the melody notes and chose a cadence for the end of the phrase. Each phrase must end in a cadence, so this is a good place to start. The melody ends on $\hat{2}$ -$\hat{1}$, which supports a perfect authentic cadence in g minor.

Figure 8.4

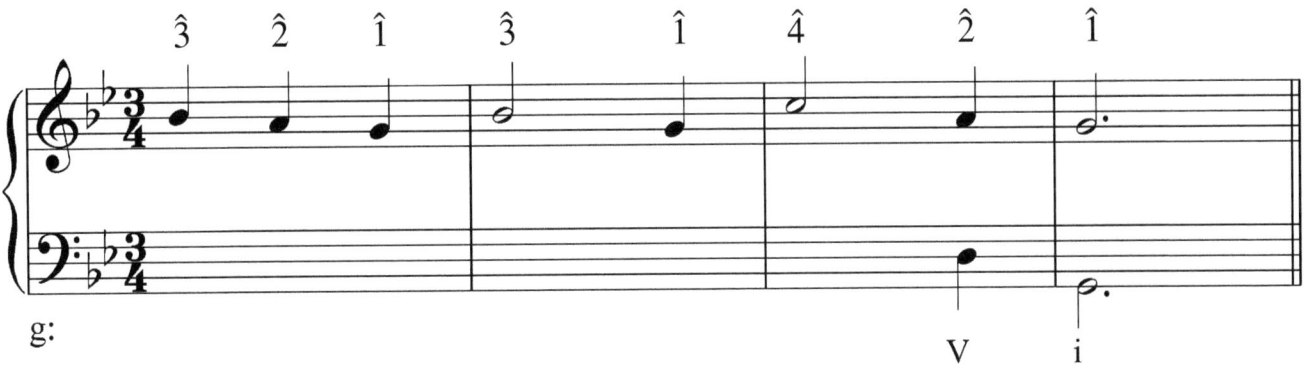

In Figure 8.5 we chose the predominant harmony which comes just before the V of the cadence. Here, the melody is $\hat{4}$ (C) which supports the predominant chord iv. Sometimes the predominant chord may be i or i^6. It depends on the melody note and what harmony it will support.

Figure 8.5

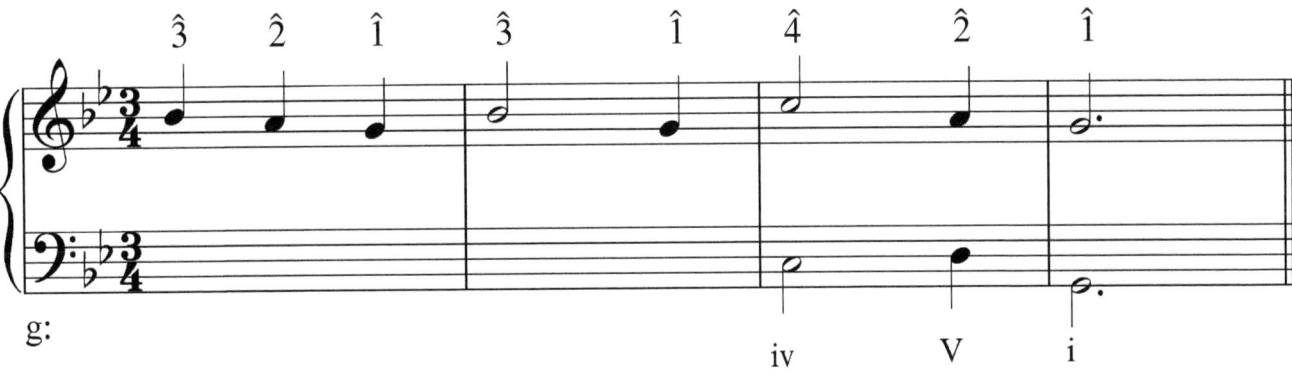

The next step is to look at the opening and decide what chords can be used with the given notes. The opening measure of Figure 8.6 ($\hat{3}$-$\hat{2}$-$\hat{1}$) supports the progression i-vii°⁶-i⁶, but you could use i-V⁶-i or i-V-i here too. The melody in measure two ($\hat{3}$-$\hat{1}$) supports i-i⁶ but you could also use a i chord for the whole measure. i-i⁶ provides bass movement and voice exchange between the outer voices. Upon completing this step, check the bass and soprano for correct voice leading. Make sure there is no faulty parallel motion between these two voices before moving on.

Figure 8.6

The final step is to add the alto and tenor. This is where your knowledge of voice leading is essential. Check your work carefully for incorrect spacing, faulty parallel motion, etc. Follow the voice leading rules we have studied so far. Try to repeat the common tone whenever possible. If you cannot do this, move to the nearest available chord tones avoiding faulty parallels. Try not to leap more than a fourth in the inner voices. Aim for smooth voice leading whenever you can.

Figure 8.7

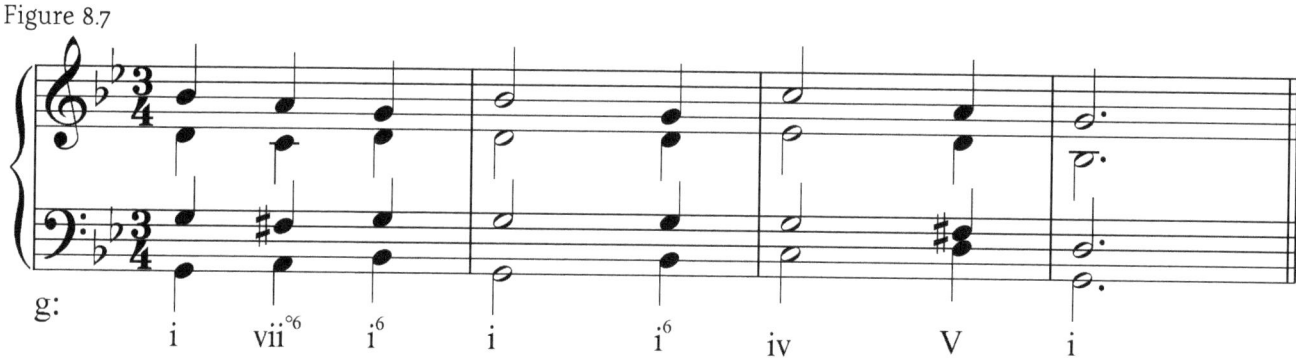

Chapter 8: Harmonizing a Melody

1. Harmonize the following melodies in four parts.

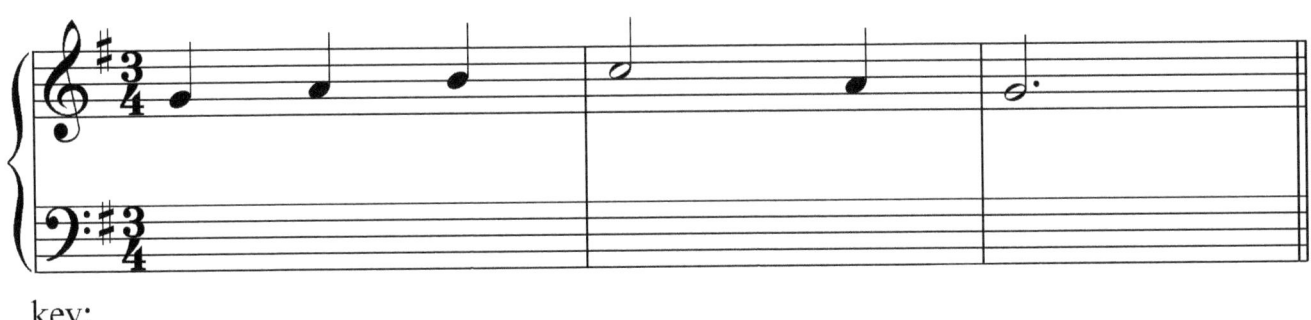

key:

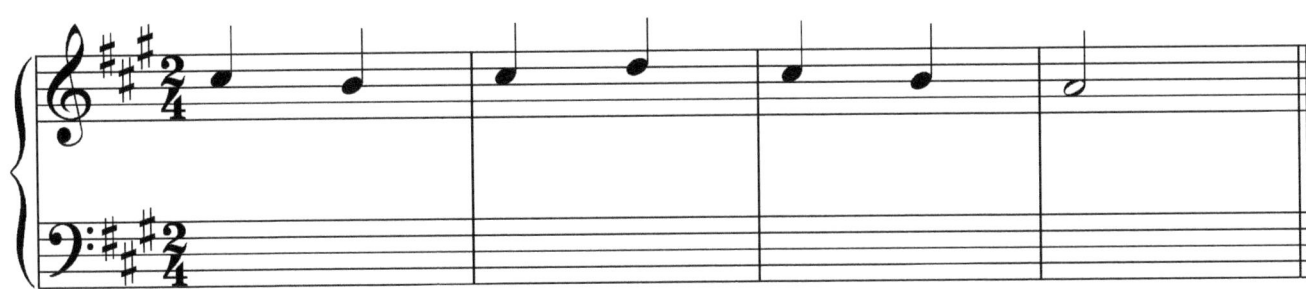

key:

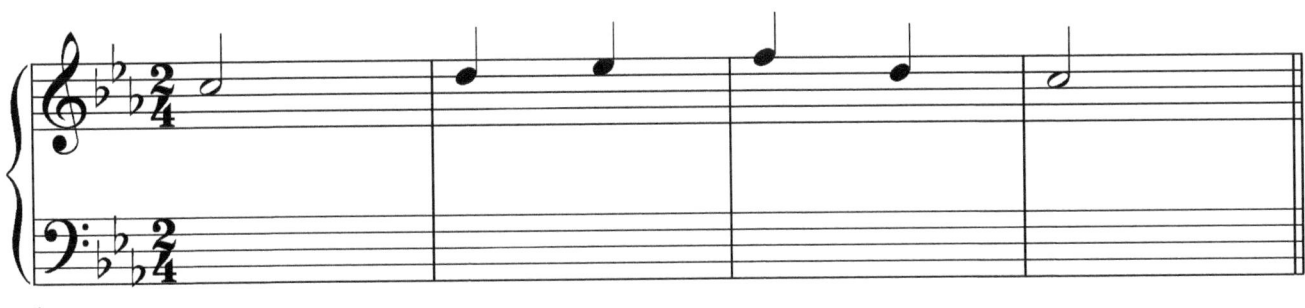

key:

key:

Chapter 8: Harmonizing a Melody

9
V⁷ and Its Inversions

In this chapter we will continue to expand our harmonic vocabulary by introducing the *dominant seventh chord* (V⁷) and its inversions.

V⁷ in Root Position

The seventh chord built on scale degree $\hat{5}$, or the dominant, frequently acts as a substitute for V in our dominant area of harmonization. The dominant seventh is a major-minor seventh chord in both major and minor keys. It consists of a major triad with a minor seventh above the root. Study the V⁷ chords in Figure 9.1. Make note of the chord symbols for these chords. The functional chord symbol is an uppercase Roman numeral (V) with a 7. The root/quality chord symbol consists of the root of the chord with a 7. Note that V⁷ in a minor key contains raised scale degree $\hat{7}$, the leading tone.

Figure 9.1

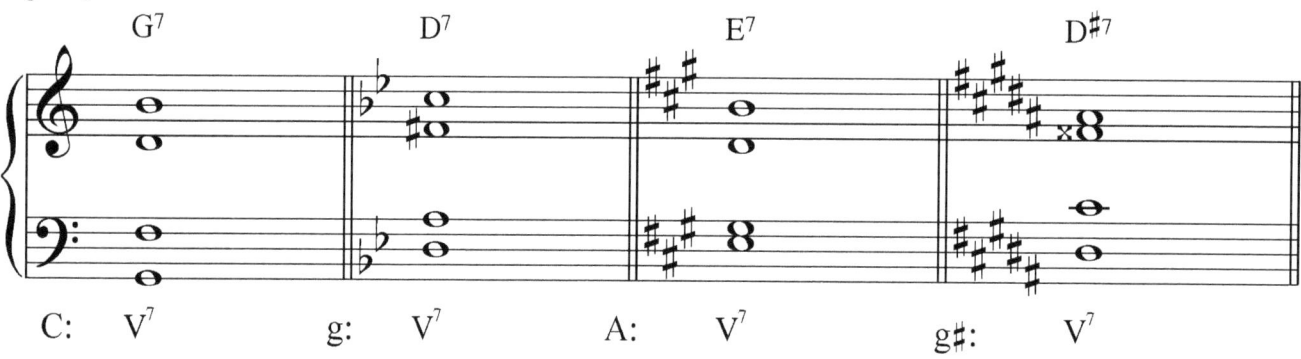

1. Using key signatures, write V⁷ chords in four parts in the following keys. Add root/quality chord symbols.

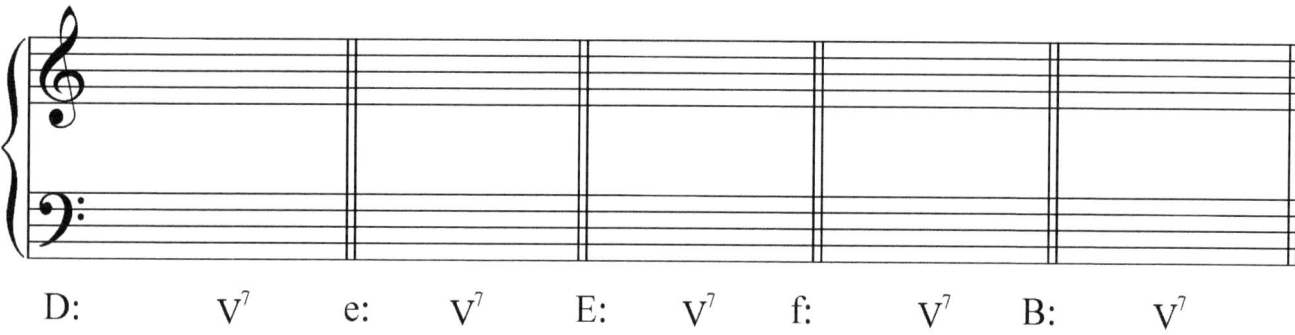

Doubling Notes in V⁷

Because V⁷ is a four note chord the doubling of notes should not be an issue. However, V⁷ often occurs as an incomplete chord with the root doubled and the fifth omitted (root, root, 3rd, 7th). The fifth is the only note of a 7th chord that may be omitted. The root and third of every chord must be present, and since V⁷ is a 7th chord the 7th must also be present. Certain notes of V⁷ are tendency tones that must not be doubled, and that leaves us the root to double. Incomplete V⁷ chords always resolve to complete I chords which contain the doubled root, third and fifth. A complete V⁷ may resolve to an incomplete I chord made up of a tripled root and a third.

Approaching and Resolving V⁷

There are a couple of important points to consider with the V⁷ chord. The first is the 7th of the chord, which is scale degree $\hat{4}$. This forms a dissonant interval with the root of the chord and must be treated carefully. The 7th may be approached in a number of ways. It can be approached with common tone motion from the previous chord as seen in Figure 9.2 (a). This is called *preparing the 7th*. The 7th (F) is in the alto and is approached as a common tone. The 7th may be approached from a step above in a passing tone motion as seen in 9.2 (b) where it is part of the pattern $\hat{5}$-$\hat{4}$-$\hat{3}$. It may also be approached from a step below in a neighbor motion using scale degrees $\hat{3}$-$\hat{4}$-$\hat{3}$ as in 9.2(c). V⁷ may appear as an incomplete chord containing a doubled root, 3rd and 7th with the 5th omitted as in 9.2 (a) and (c). An incomplete V⁷ must always resolve to a complete I chord.

- *The 7th of V⁷ always resolves downward by step to the third of chord I ($\hat{4}$-$\hat{3}$).*

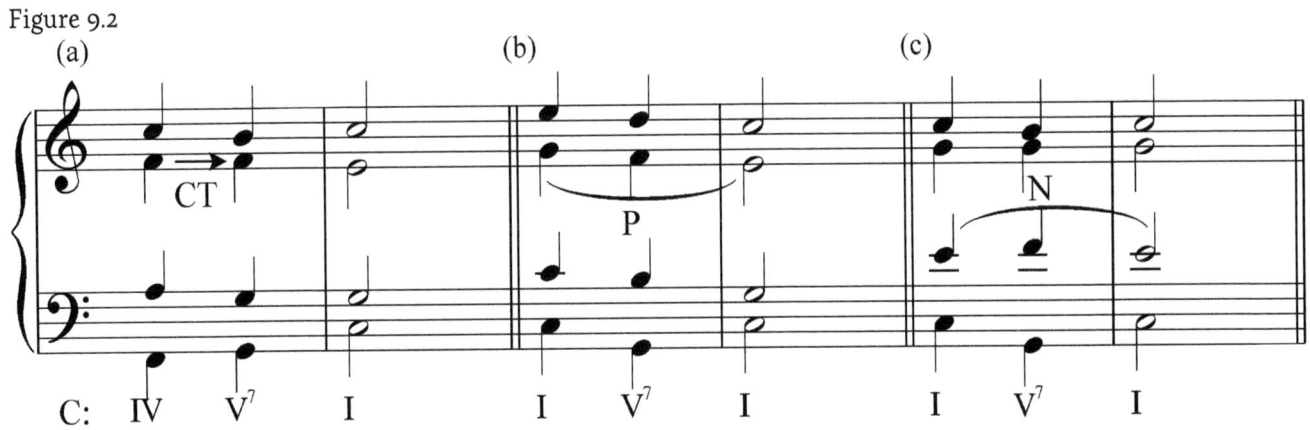

Figure 9.2

The second point involves the resolution of V⁷ to I. There is a tritone that occurs in the dominant seventh between $\hat{7}$ and $\hat{4}$. This is an unstable interval and must be resolved to a stable interval in the next chord. This interval occurs as a diminished 5th or augmented 4th depending on the arrangement of notes. The augmented 4th resolves outwardly to a 6th as in Figure 9.3 (a). The diminished 5th resolves inwardly to a 3rd as in 9.3 (b). In each case, one of the chords is incomplete. If both V⁷ and I are complete chords we cannot resolve the tritone in this way. When the leading tone occurs in an inner voice it can move down to the 5th of chord I ($\hat{7}$-$\hat{5}$) as in 9.3 (c) and (d). Here, both chords are complete. *If the leading tone occurs in an outer voice it must move to the tonic.* In 9.3 (b) the complete V⁷ resolves to an incomplete I chord made up of three roots and a 3rd. This resolution only occurs at cadence points.

Figure 9.3

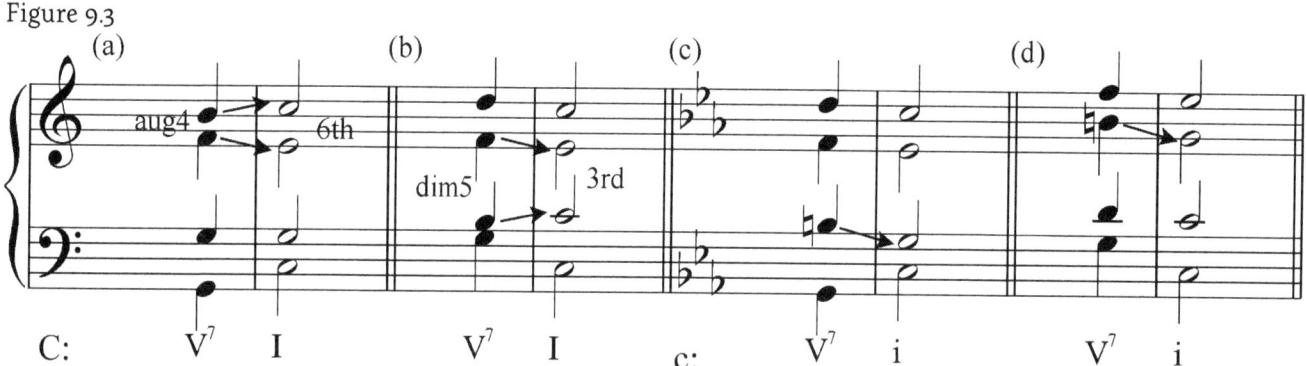

Resolving V⁷ Review

- The 7th of V⁷ always resolves downward by step to the 3rd of chord I ($\hat{4}$-$\hat{3}$).
- Incomplete V⁷ chords resolve to complete I chords.
- If V⁷ and I are both to be complete chords, the leading tone must be in an inner voice and resolve downward by skip ($\hat{7}$-$\hat{5}$).
- If the leading tone is in an outer voice it must rise to the tonic ($\hat{7}$-$\hat{1}$).

2. Name the keys and resolve the following V⁷ chords.

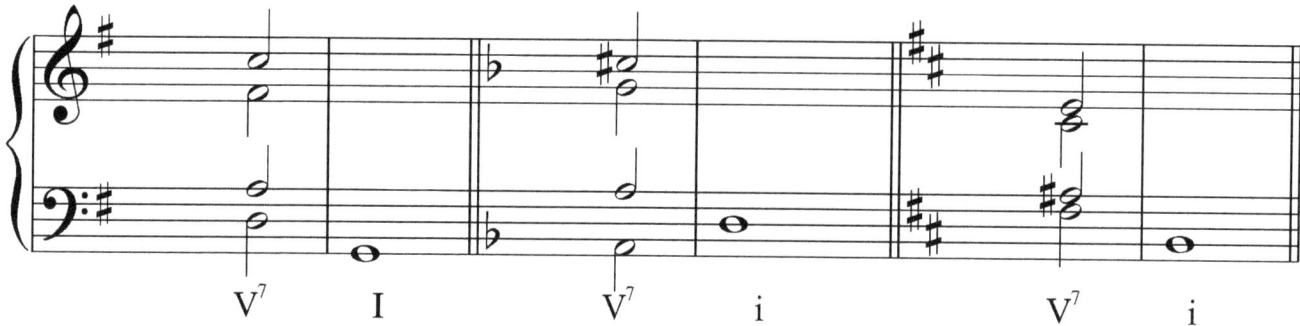

Chapter 9: V⁷ and Its Inversions

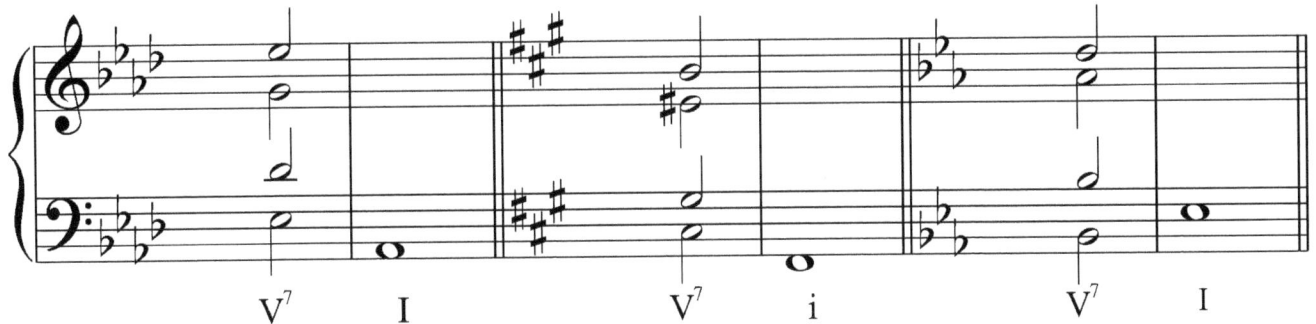

3. Name the keys and complete the following progressions in four parts.

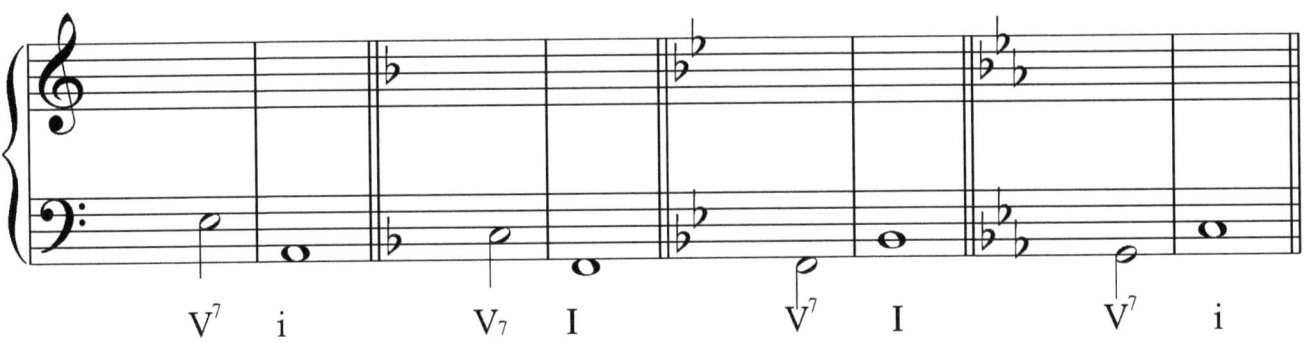

Approaching V⁷ Review

- Approach the 7th of V⁷ by common tone motion if possible.
- If there is no common tone in the previous chord, appoach the 7th from a step above or a step below if possible.
- Always resolve the 7th down a step to the 3rd of chord I ($\hat{4}$-$\hat{3}$).

4. Name the keys and complete the following progressions in four parts.

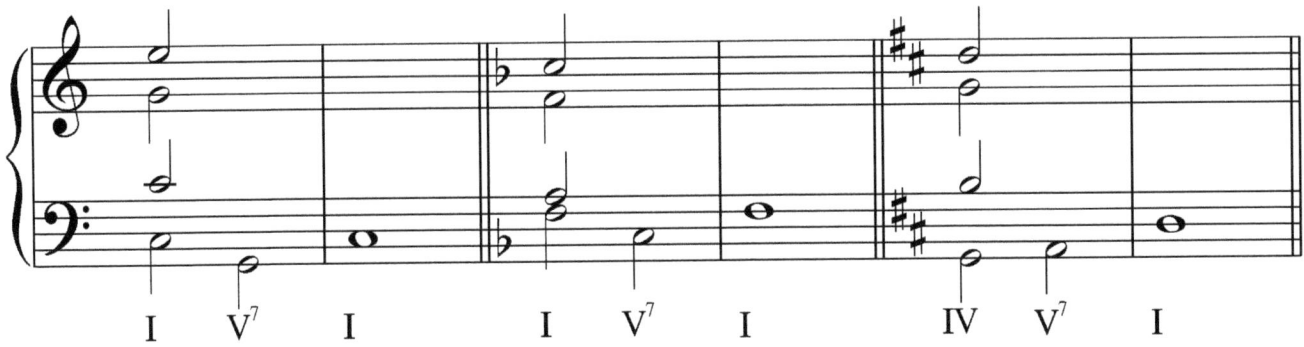

5. Name the keys and complete the following progressions in four parts.

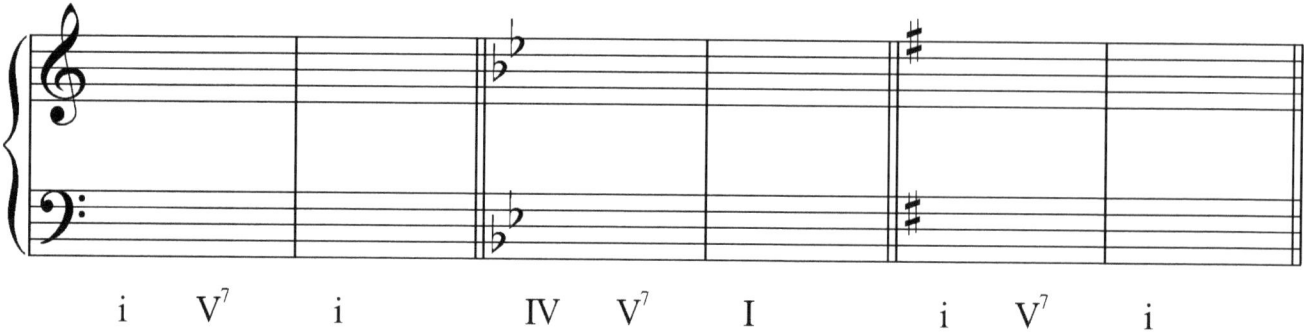

i   V⁷   i   IV   V⁷   I   i   V⁷   i

The V chord may be converted to a V⁷ chord with the addition of a passing note in one of the upper voices. This is indicated with the symbol V⁸⁻⁷. The octave above the bass moves to a 7th while the other chord voices are held. The 7th then resolves downward by step to the third of chord I (Figure 9.4).

Figure 9.4

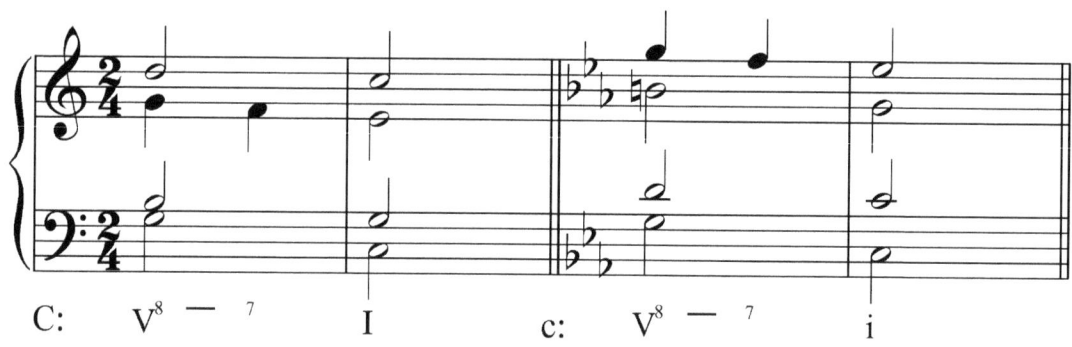

C: V⁸ — 7   I   c: V⁸ — 7   i

J.S. Bach used this technique at cadence points in many of his four part Chorales. Figure 9.5 illustrates an authentic cadence from a Bach Chorale using V⁸⁻⁷.

Figure 9.5

Johann Sebastian Bach
Chorale: Was Gott tut, das ist wohlgetan

G: I⁶   V⁸⁻⁷   I

6. Name the keys and complete the following progressions in four parts.

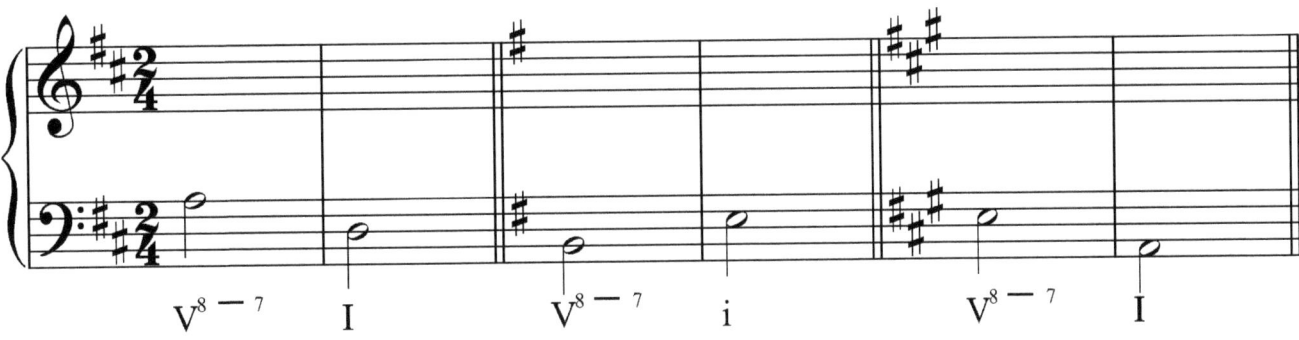

Inversions of V⁷

There are three inversions of V^7. They appear as complete chords, containing the root, 3rd, 5th and 7th and resolve to a complete tonic chord. The inversions of V^7 usually function as prolongations of one of the areas of harmonization, most commonly the beginning tonic and dominant areas.

Figure 9.6

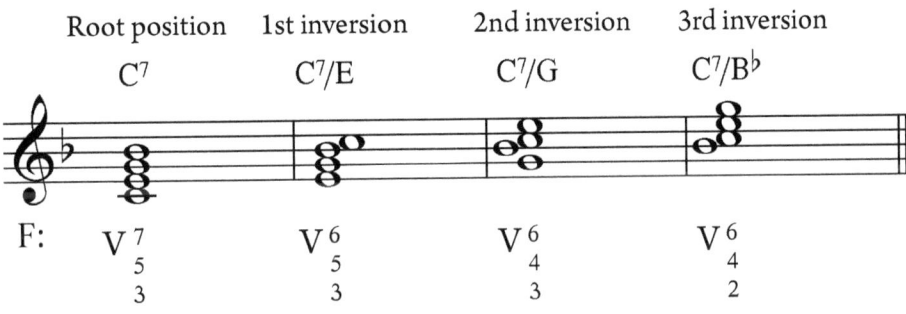

The numbers next to the Roman numeral V in Figure 9.6 are the complete figured bass symbols. However, figured bass symbols are often abbreviated. The following are the abbreviations for the figured bass symbols for the inversions of V^7.

	root position	1st inversion	2nd inversion	3rd inversion
	V^7	V^6_5	V^4_3	V^4_2

Figure 9.7 illustrates V^7 in f minor. The notes of V^7 are the same in tonic major and minor and the symbols remain the same. V^7 in root position always has the root in the bass, 1st inversion has the 3rd in the bass, 2nd inversion has the 5th, and 3rd inversion has the 7th.

Figure 9.7

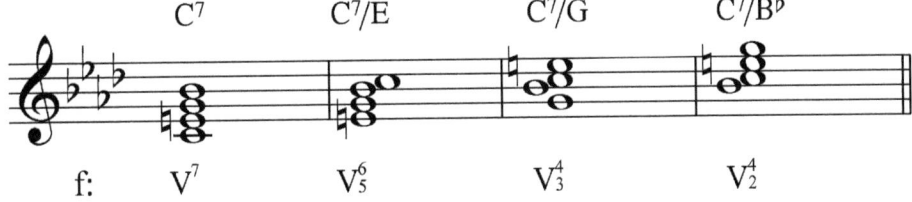

In four part writing, inversions of V⁷ are always complete chords containing the root, 3rd, 5th and 7th. Figure 9.8 contains V⁷ and its inversions written for four parts. The bass note determines the position. The root in the bass is root position, the third in the bass is 1st inversion, the fifth in the bass is 2nd inversion, and the seventh in the bass is 3rd inversion. The order of the other notes does not matter as long as you follow conventional spacing rules.

Figure 9.8

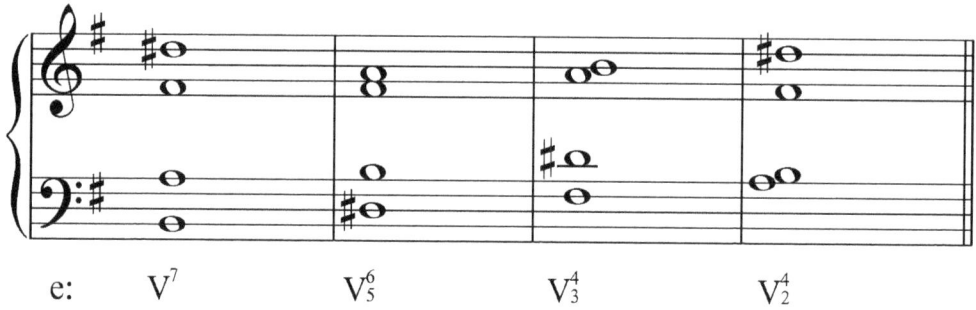

7. Write the following chords in four parts.

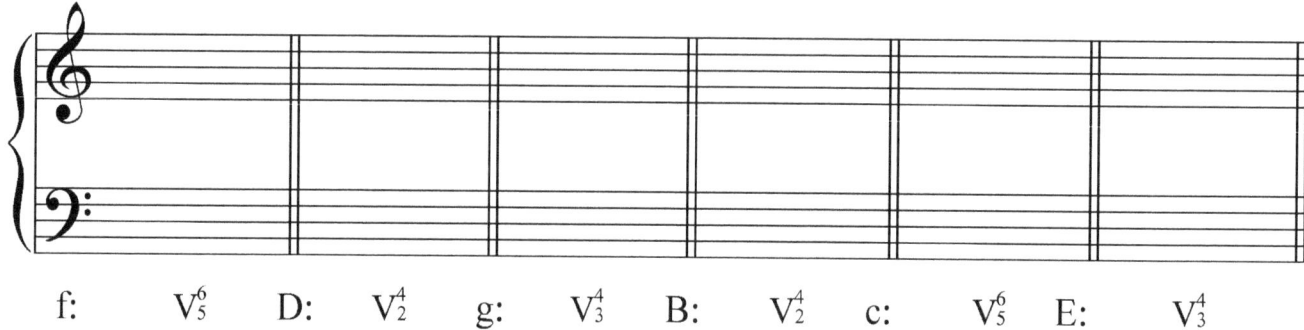

The First Inversion of V⁷

The first inversion of V⁷ has the leading note in the bass. When the leading tone is in an outer voice it moves to the tonic, so the logical resolution is to I in root position. The most common function of V^6_5 is to prolong the tonic as a neighbor chord. Figure 9.9 shows a prolongation of I with V^6_5. In this progression one voice repeats the common tone and the other voices move in neighbor motion. The leading note in the bass rises to the tonic and the 7th of the dominant 7th falls to the 3rd of I.

Figure 9.9

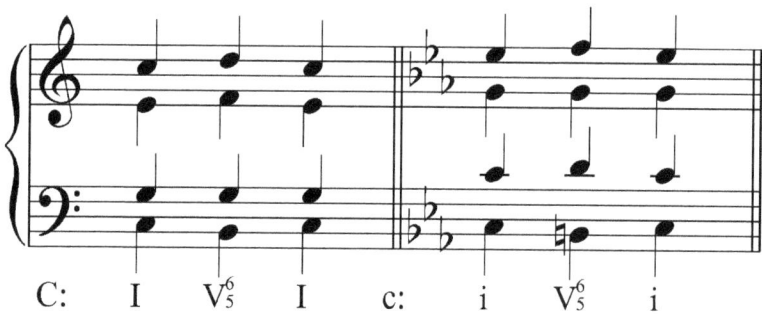

8. Complete the following progressions in four parts.

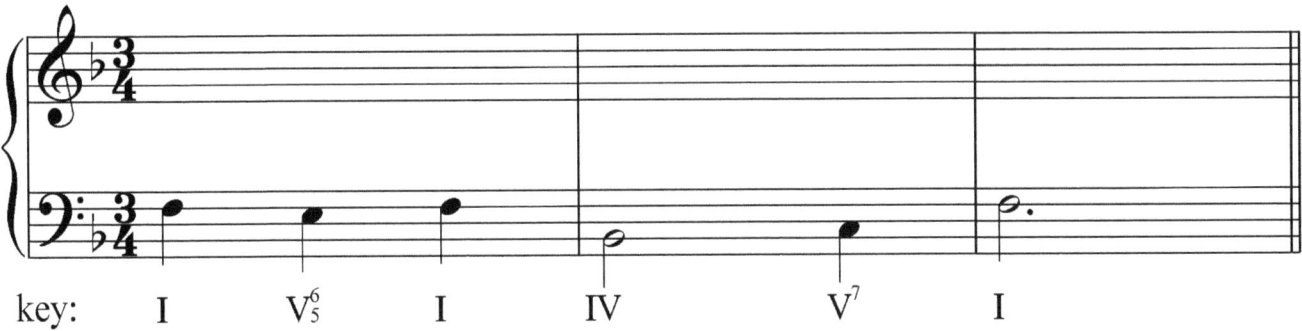

key: I   V$^6_5$ I   IV   V^7 I

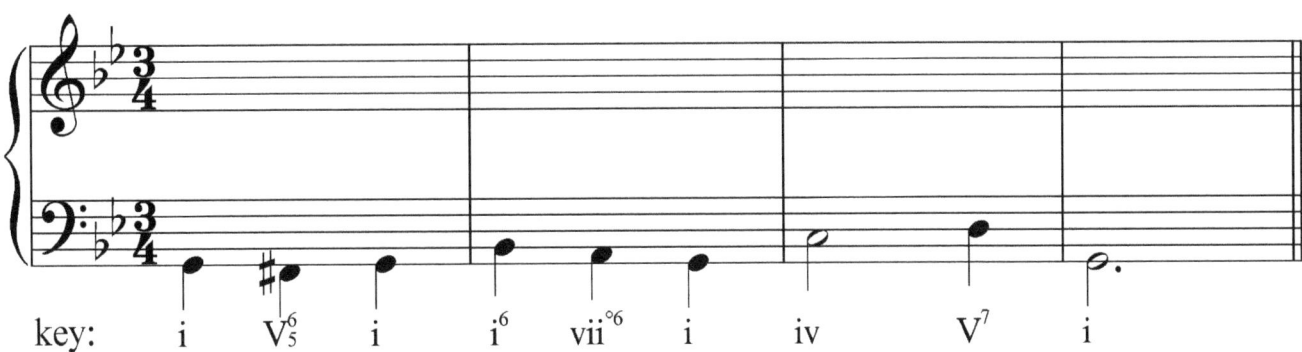

key: i   V$^6_5$ i   i^6 vii$^{°6}$ i   iv   V^7 i

V$^6_5$ may also be used in a progression which prolongs I: I - IV^6 - V$^6_5$ - I as shown in Figure 9.10. Special consideration must be given when writing this progression in the minor key. Here, the bass contains $\hat{6}$ followed by $\hat{7}$. In this progression scale degree $\hat{6}$ must be raised along with scale degree $\hat{7}$, as in a melodic minor scale to avoid the interval of a melodic augmented second (A♭ - B♮). Melodic augmented seconds are considered wrong and must be avoided. When $\hat{6}$ and $\hat{7}$ occur together melodically in the minor key, both must be raised in order to avoid this interval. It is fine to have an A♭ in one chord and then a B♮ in the next, as long as they are not in the same voice.

Figure 9.10

C: I   IV^6 V$^6_5$ I   c: i   iv^6 V$^6_5$ i

Chapter 9: V^7 and Its Inversions

The Second Inversion of V⁷

The second inversion of V^7 has the 5th in the bass. This chord can resolve in two ways: down to chord I in root position, and up to chord I in first inversion. The function of this inversion is to prolong the tonic chord either as a neighbor chord as in Figure 9.11 (a) or as a passing chord 9.11(b). The latter has a doubled third in I^6. This is necessary since the bass is rising to the third, and the 7th in the alto must resolve downward by step to the third. Example (c) deserves special attention. This is the only time that the 7th of V^7 does not fall. Here, the attention is on the parallel 10ths between the bass and alto and not the rising 7th. This progression only occurs between V^4_3 and I^6 and is referred to as a ***rising resolution.***

Figure 9.11

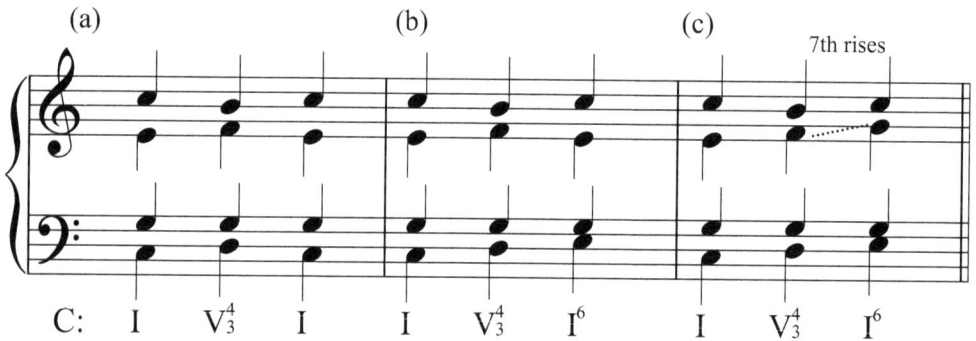

9. Complete the following progression in four parts.

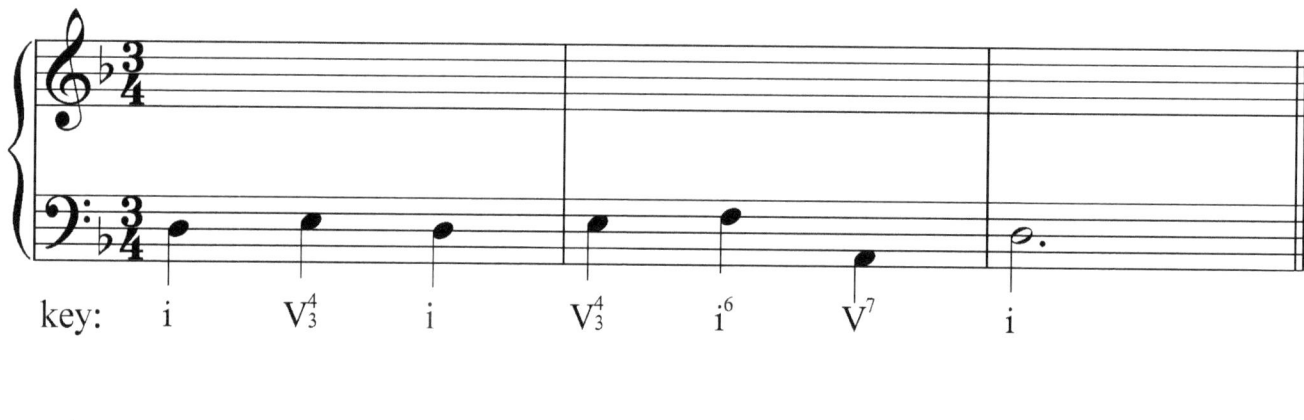

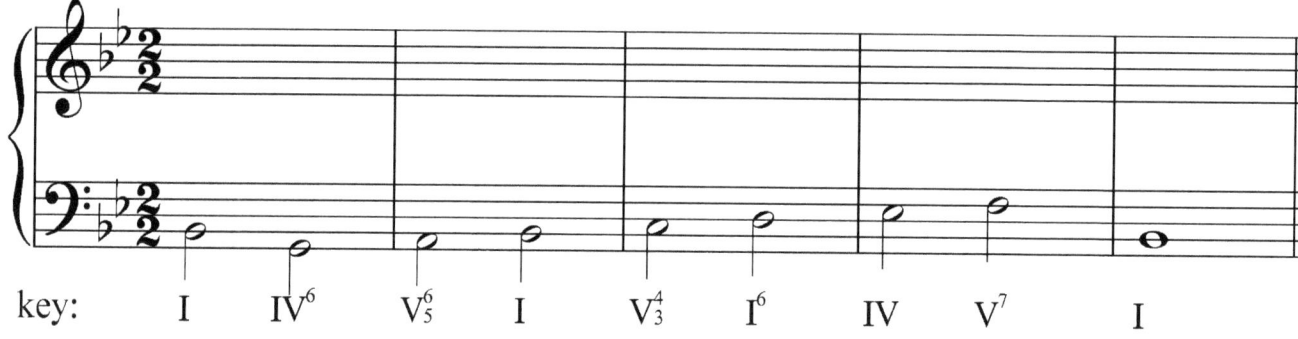

The Third Inversion of V⁷

The third inversion of V⁷ has the 7th in the bass. Since the 7th must always resolve downward by step it always moves to I⁶. A common function of V_2^4 is to prolong dominant harmony with passing motion in the bass ($\hat{5}$-$\hat{4}$-$\hat{3}$) as in Figure 9.12 (a). A predominant chord with $\hat{4}$ in the bass often precedes V_2^4 before it resolves to I⁶ as in 9.12 (b). Here, IV has $\hat{4}$ in the bass which prepares the 7th of V_2^4. V_2^4 may occur as a neighbor chord between two statements of I⁶ to prolong tonic harmony as in 9.12 (c).

Figure 9.12

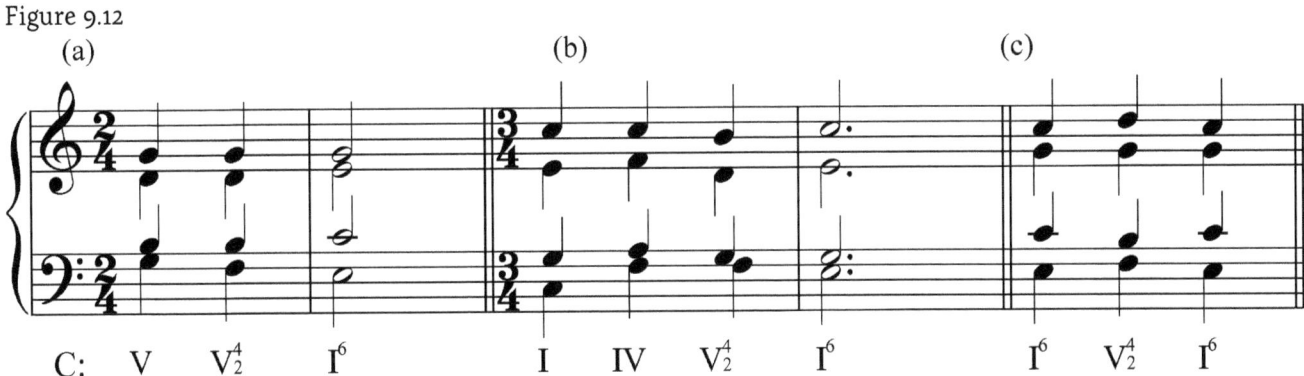

10. Complete the following progressions in four parts.

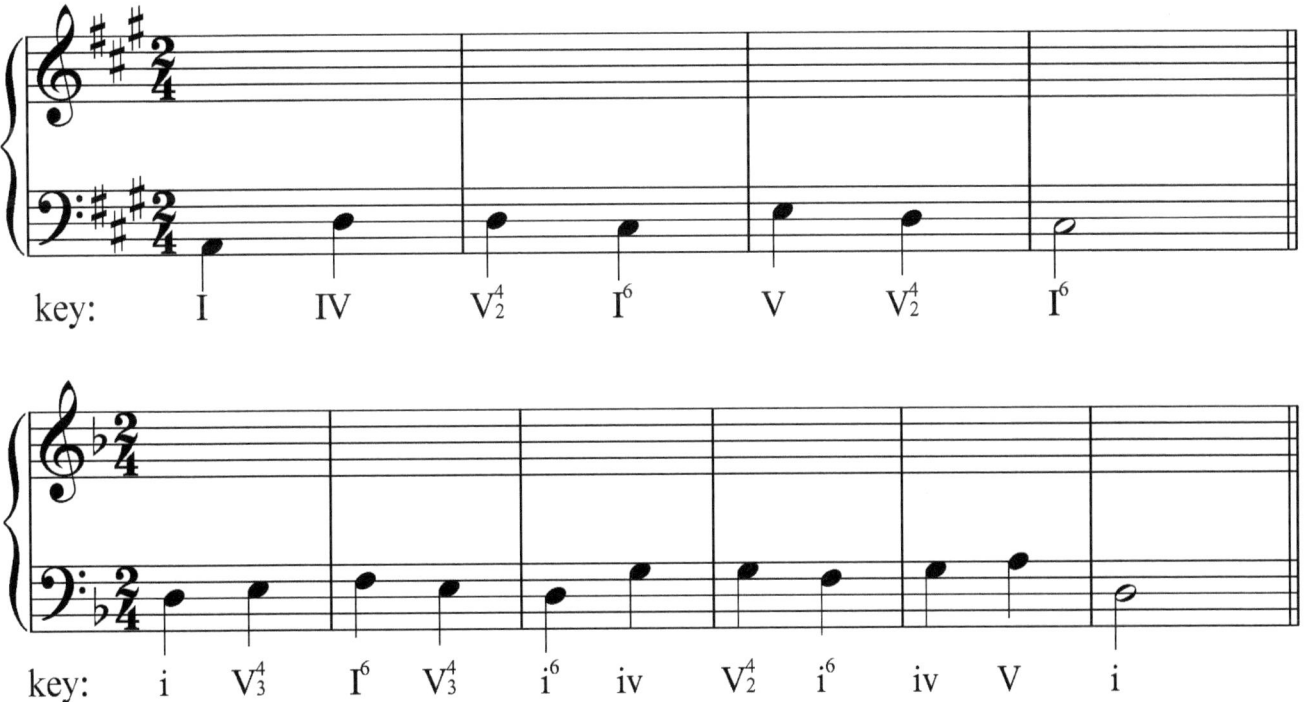

- Resolve the 7th of V⁷ and its inversions downward by step.
- When the leading note is in an outer voice it must rise to the tonic ($\hat{7}$ - $\hat{1}$).
- When both V⁷ and I are complete chords $\hat{7}$ must be in an inner voice and move to $\hat{5}$ in order to avoid faulty parallel 5ths.
- V_2^4 always resolves to I⁶.

Harmonic Analysis - The Anticipation

An *anticipation* (symbol: Ant.) is a non chord tone that anticipates a note of the next chord. Non-chord tones are classified by how they are approached and left. An anticipation is approached by step and left by repetition. It occurs on a weak beat or weak part of the beat. Figure 9.13 illustrates an anticipation in the soprano. The C is approached by step and is left by repetition. It anticipates the chord tone C.

Figure 9.13

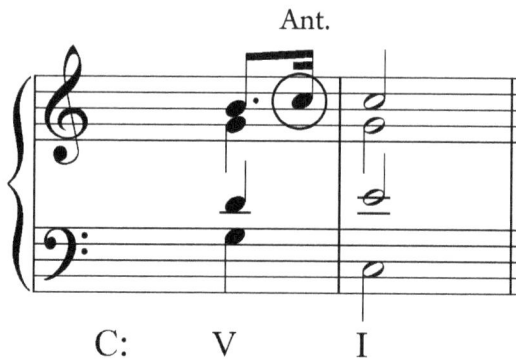

The Incomplete Neighbor

The *incomplete neighbor note* is a nonchord tone that occurs in three different forms.
- An *incomplete neighbor* (symbol: IN) seen in Figure 9.14 (a), is a nonchord tone that occurs on a weak beat and is approached by leap and left by step. Here, the A in the tenor is a neighbor only to the B. Hence the name incomplete neighbor.
- An *escape tone* (symbol: ET), which is another type of incomplete neighbor, can be seen in 9.14 (b). An escape tone occurs on a weak beat or weaker part of a beat and is approached by step and left by leap.
- An *appoggiatura* (symbol: App.) seen in 9.14 (c), occurs on a strong beat or stronger part of the beat and is approached by leap and left by step. It differs from the incomplete neighbor (IN) by its metrical placement. The App. is on a strong beat while the IN is on a weak beat.

Figure 9.14

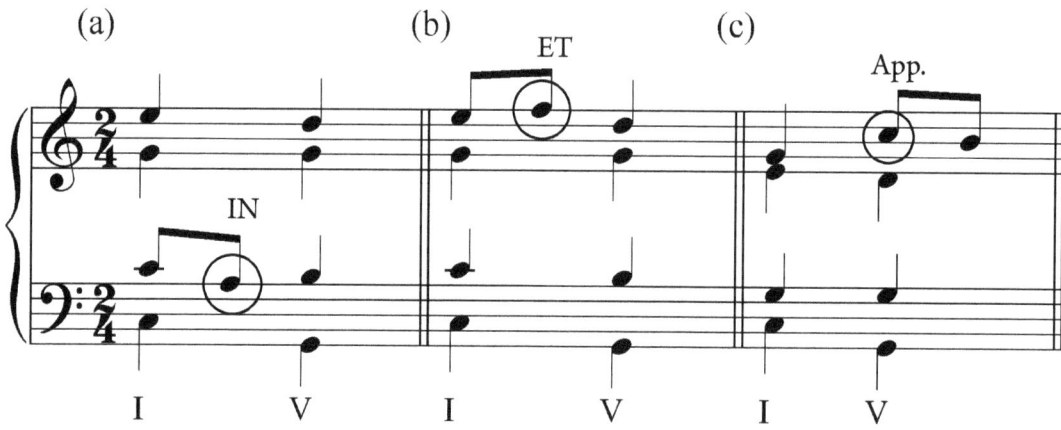

11. Define the three different incomplete neighbors:

Incomplete neighbor: _____

_____

Escape tone: _____

_____

Appoggiatura: _____

_____

12. Provide a harmonic analysis of the following. Circle and label all nonchord tones.

Joseph Haydn
Quartet, Op. 76, No. 4

key:

Ludwig van Beethoven
Sonata, Op.10, No. 1

key:

Johann Sebastian Bach
Chorale: Nicht so traurig, nicht so sehr

key:

George Frideric Handel
Suite in D minor (Sarabande)

key:

Ludwig van Beethoven
Sonata, Op.13

key:

Wolfgang Amadeus Mozart
Fantasia in D minor, K.397

D:

10
The Supertonic

The *supertonic chord* functions almost exclusively as a predominant chord. This chord, ii in major and ii° in minor is built on $\hat{2}$ and consists of scale degrees $\hat{2}$, $\hat{4}$, and $\hat{6}$.

The Supertonic in Root Position

The supertonic chord is used in root position in major keys only. In minor keys it is a diminished chord. We rarely use diminished chords in root position because they contain a diminished 5th and are dissonant. We will not use it in the minor key.

There is a fifth relationship between ii and V (like V and I), and because of this, these two chords have a strong connection. As a result, ii is a very strong predominant chord. In fact, the best chord to follow ii is V.

ii - V - I can be used to harmonize $\hat{2}$-$\hat{2}$-$\hat{1}$ or $\hat{2}$-$\hat{7}$-$\hat{1}$ as seen in Figure 10.1 (a) and (b). Note the voice leading between ii and V in these progressions. It is the typical voice leading for fifth related chords:

- *When connecting chords whose roots are a fifth apart (ii - V), repeat the common tone in the same voice and move the remaining voices to the nearest chord tones using correct doubling and spacing. Maintain either open or closed spacing for both chords 10.1(a). or:*

- *When connecting these chords and the common tone is not repeated in the same voice, move all voices to the nearest chord tones using correct doubling and spacing. Maintain either open or closed spacing for both chords 10.1(b).*

The supertonic chord is very effective before V^7. ii contains $\hat{4}$, which is the 7th of V^7. It can be used to prepare the 7th of V^7 with common tone motion as shown in Figure 10.1(c).

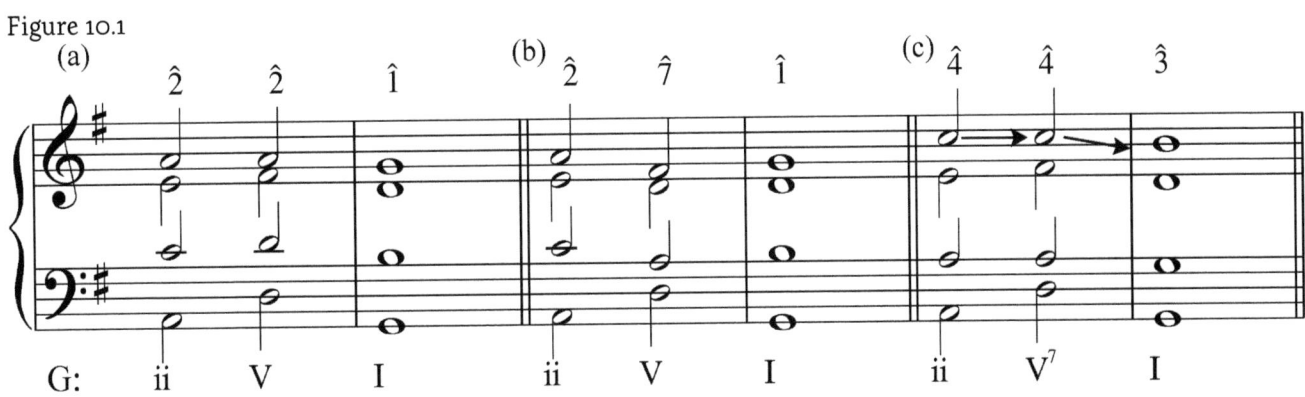

Figure 10.1

IV and ii have two common tones. IV often precedes ii as a prolongation of the predominant as in Figure 10.2 (a). **However, IV never follows ii in a harmonic progression**. When IV moves to ii, it is best to repeat the two common tones and move the other voice by step.

10.2 (b) contains the progression I-ii-V-I. Although I can move to ii in a progression, and is correct, it is relatively rare. When writing this progression remember to move the three upper notes in contrary motion to the bass, like the progression IV - V. This will avoid faulty parallel fifths and octaves. ii is more commonly preceded by I^6 as in 10.2 (c). I^6-ii does not present the same voice leading challenges as I-ii. There are no common tones. Move to the nearest available chord tones avoiding faulty parallels.

Figure 10.2

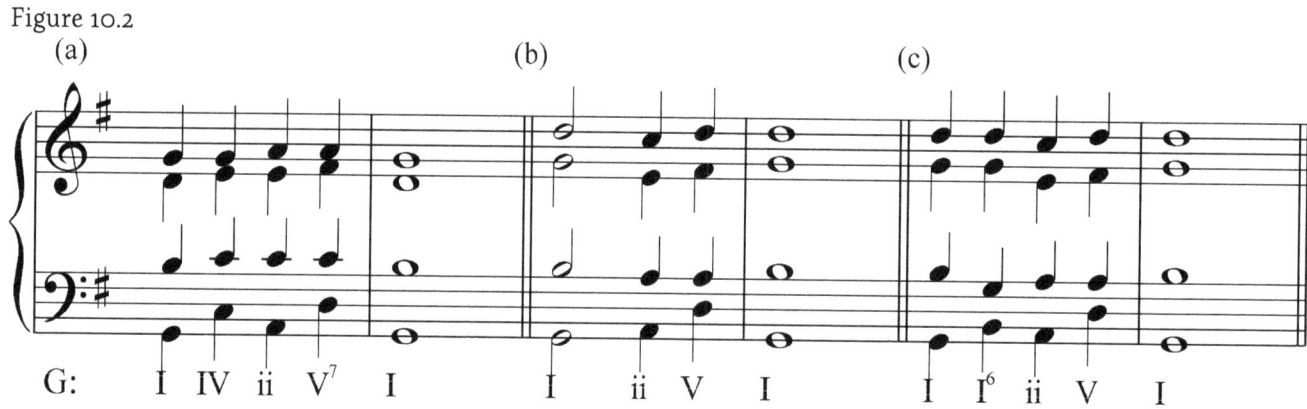

1. Name the keys and complete the following progressions in four parts.

85

Chapter 10: The Supertonic

2. Harmonize the following melodies containing ii. Provide functional chord symbols.

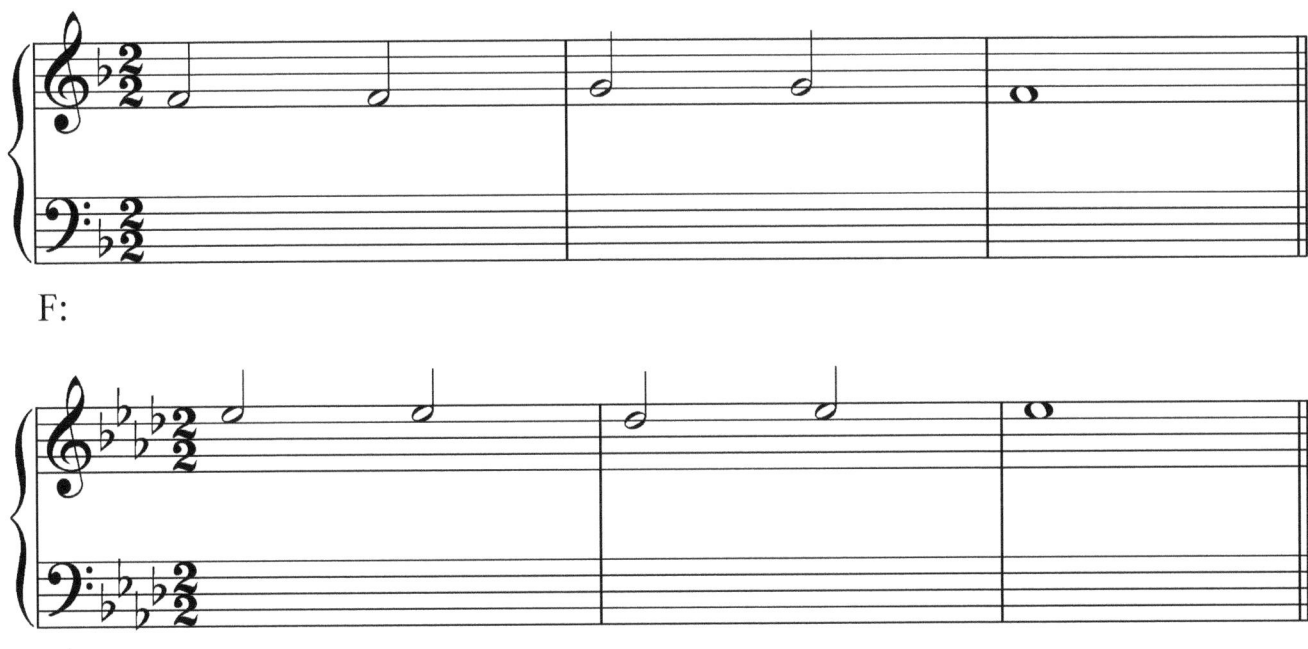

F:

Ab:

The Supertonic in First Inversion

The supertonic chord is seen most often in first inversion as a predominant chord. In major keys, it is a minor chord (ii⁶), and in minor keys, it is a diminished chord (ii°⁶). We do not use ii root position in minor keys, but ii°⁶ is an effective chord to use in minor.

ii⁶ has $\hat{4}$ in the bass so ii⁶ - V has only one pitch difference than the progression IV - V. Figure 10.3 (b) shows how a IV can become a ii⁶ with a change of one pitch. The movement here in the alto from G to A transforms the IV chord into ii⁶.

The most common tone to double in ii⁶ is the 3rd as shown in 10.3 (c), but it is perfectly acceptable to double the root as in 10.3 (d). Doubling the 5th, shown in 10.3 (e) is seen less frequently.

Figure 10.3

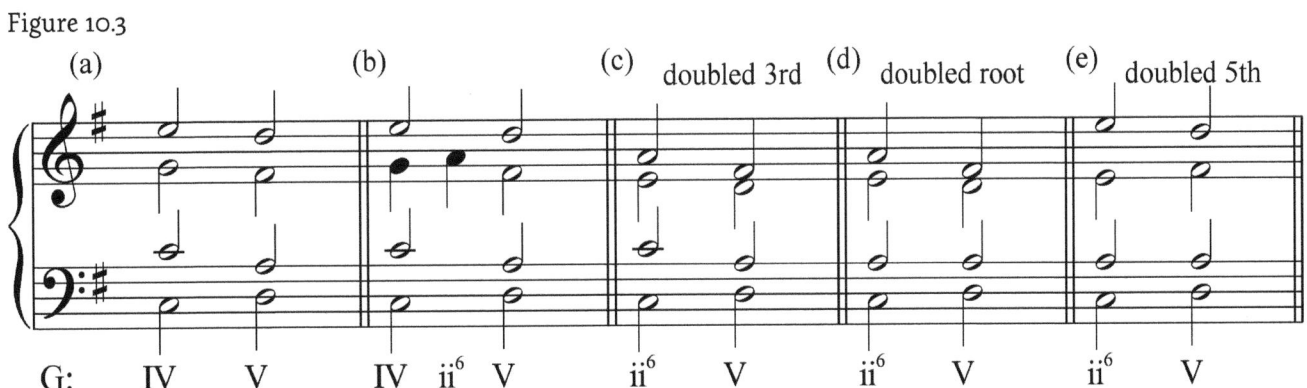

Chapter 10: The Supertonic

ii°⁶ in Minor Keys

In minor keys, the best note to double in ii°⁶ is the 3rd as shown in Figure 10.4 (a). Doubling the root is also possible. Doubling the 5th can be problematic because an augmented 2nd can result as in 10.4 (b). Here, either do not double the 5th, or raise $\hat{6}$ along with $\hat{7}$ to avoid the augmented 2nd. The progression ii⁶ - V - I or ii°⁶ - V - i (in minor) is an extremely common and effective formula at cadences with ii⁶ acting as a predominant chord.

In the progression I - ii⁶ faulty parallel 5ths can occur if the root is doubled in I shown in 10.4 (c). This can be avoided by doubling the 3rd of chord I. This error occurs in major keys, but is not a problem in minor keys since the 5ths are a perfect 5th and a diminished 5th. Only parallel perfect 5ths are faulty. A phrase ending on ii⁶ - V is a half cadence.

Figure 10.4

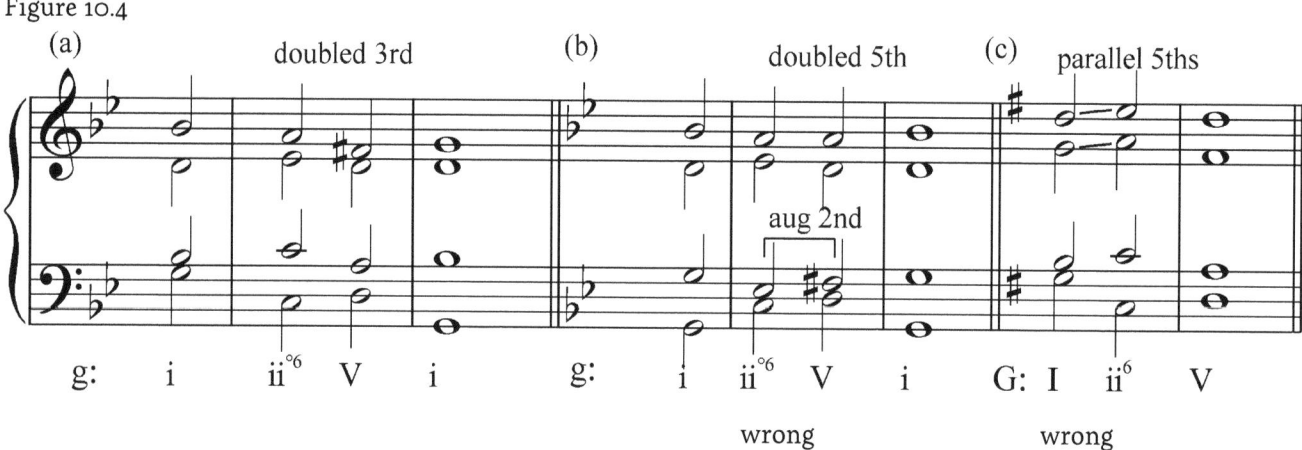

3. Complete the following progressions in four parts.

Chapter 10: The Supertonic

ii⁶ is an excellent chord to precede V⁷. ii⁶ contains scale degree $\hat{4}$, which is the 7th of V⁷. It is good to prepare the 7th with common tone motion from ii⁶ to V⁷ before resolving the 7th downward by step as in Figure 10.5 (a). In this progression it is possible to have scale degrees $\hat{6}$-$\hat{7}$-$\hat{1}$ in one voice. This works well in major keys as seen in 10.5 (c). The same progression in minor keys may result in a melodic augmented 2nd (D♭ - E♮) as in 10.5 (b). Here, scale degree $\hat{6}$ should be raised along with scale degree $\hat{7}$ (D♮ - E♮), eliminating the faulty melodic interval.

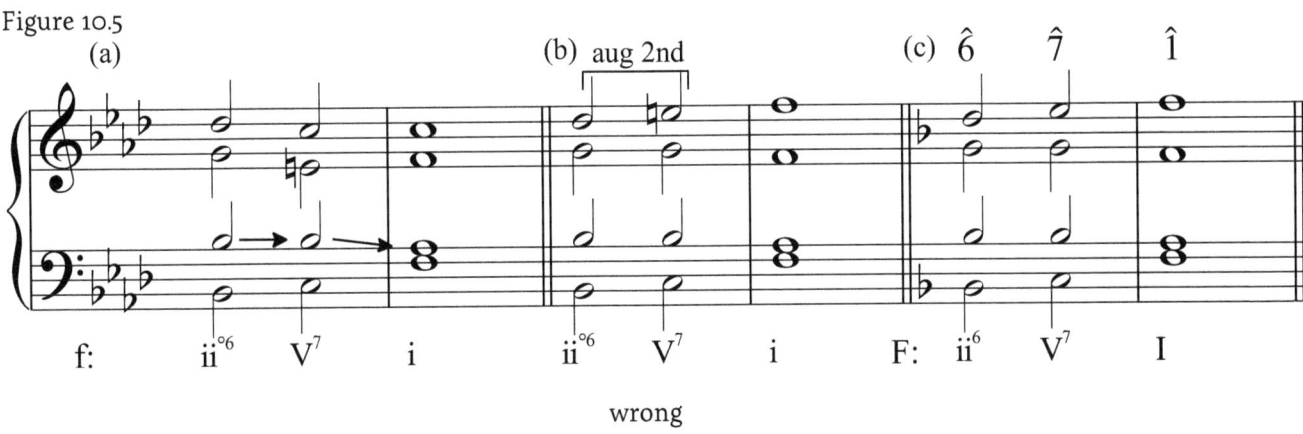

Figure 10.5

4. Complete the following progressions in four parts.

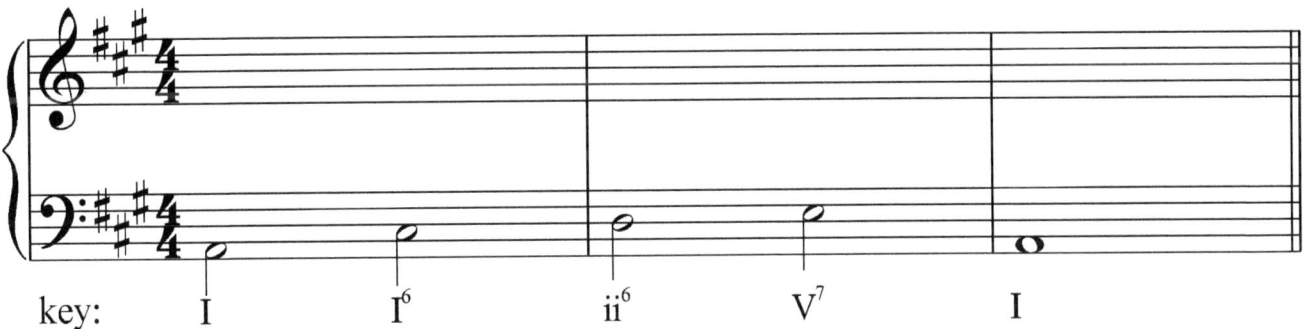

5. Add functional chord symbols and complete the following in four parts. Use ii⁶ and V⁷.

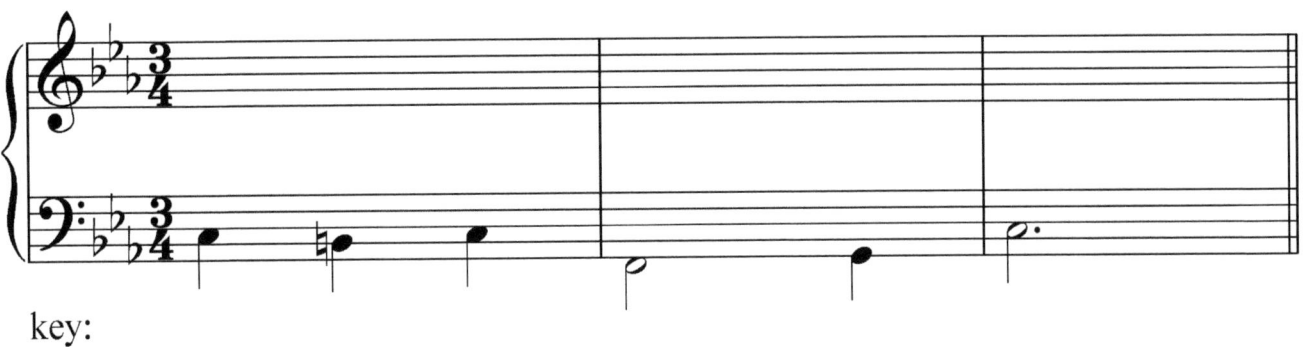

6. Complete the following progression in four parts.

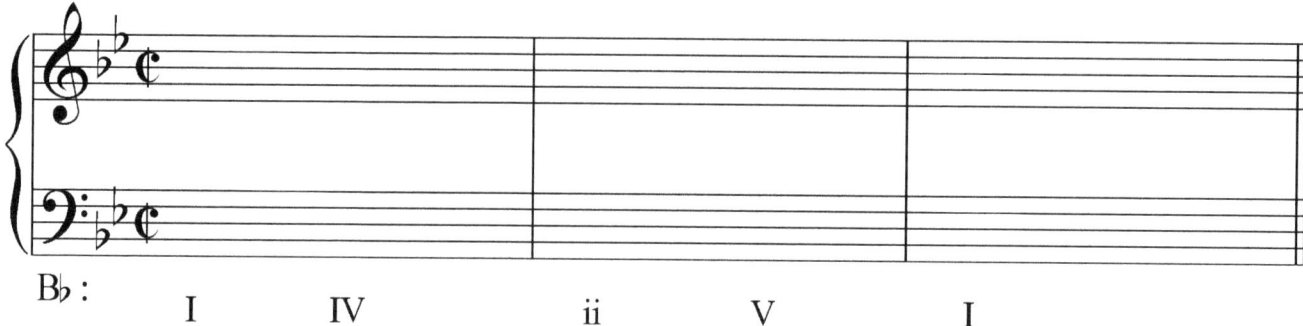

B♭: I   IV   ii   V   I

7. Realize the following figured basses in four parts. All notes without figures are in root position.

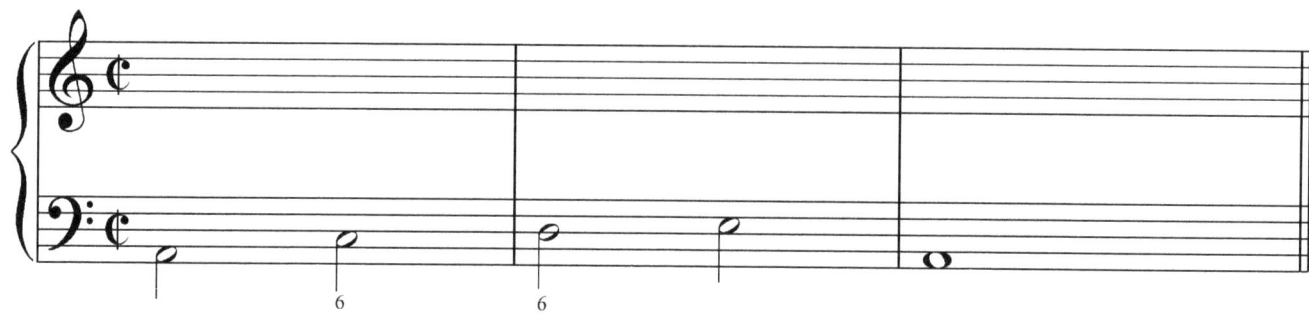

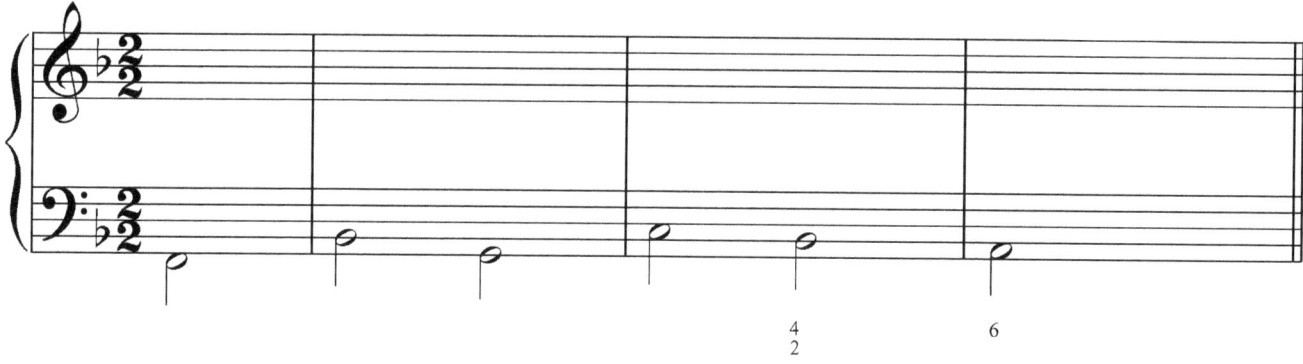

8. Harmonize the following melody.

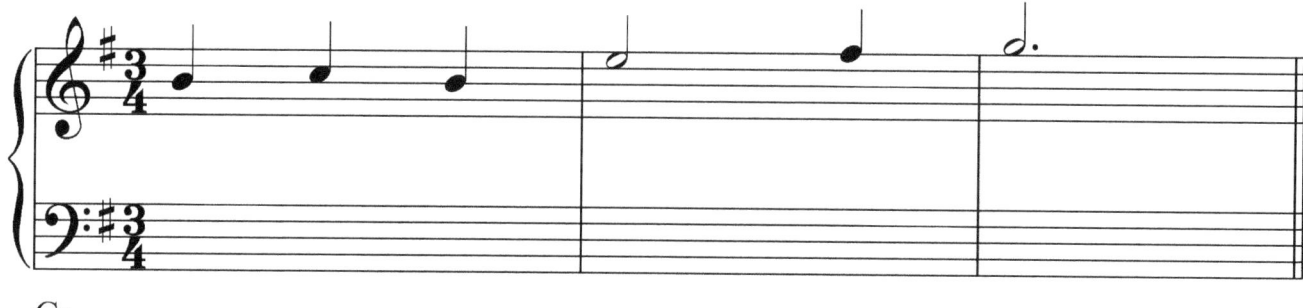

G:

Harmonic Analysis

9. Provide a harmonic analysis of the following using functional chord symbols. Identify and label all nonchord tones.

key:

key:

key:

11

The Cadential Six Four Chord

Figured Bass

The chords in Figure 11.1 illustrate the complete figured bass symbols for a triad and its inversions. These numbers indicate intervals above the bass or lowest note. The second inversion chord contains the intervals of a 6th and a 4th above the lowest note. Second inversion chords are known as *six four chords*.

Figure 11.1

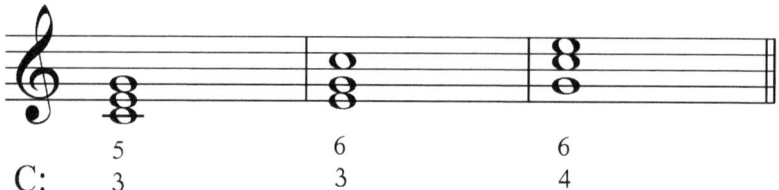

A six four chord, $^6_4$ has the fifth in the bass. The intervals of a 6th and a 4th occur above the bass note in this chord. Not all six four chords function as second inversion triads. Most of the time these chords are linear chords and function as prolongations or decorations of other chords. These chords contain a dissonance between the bass and an upper voice, the perfect 4th. This requires resolution. As a result, some six four chords are considered dissonant chords. Two six four chords are considered consonant: the *arpeggio six four* and the *oscillating six four*. Six four chords always have a function, and are only used in specific situations. These chords cannot be used unless they follow one of these specific functions. This chapter focuses on the *cadential six four chord*.

Consonant Six Four Chords

Most six four chords function as prolongations of other harmonies. The consonant six four chords are heard as second inversion chords not as prolongations of another chord. Since they sound like chord inversions they are not considered dissonant.

If the notes of a chord are played one after the other they create an arpeggio. The *arpeggio six four* occurs as a result of a bass arpeggiation. Figure 11.2 illustrates an arpeggio six four chord. The progression here is I - I^6 - I$^6_4$ - I. Here, the six four is used to extend a consonant harmony as part of a series of inversions of the I chord.

Figure 11.2

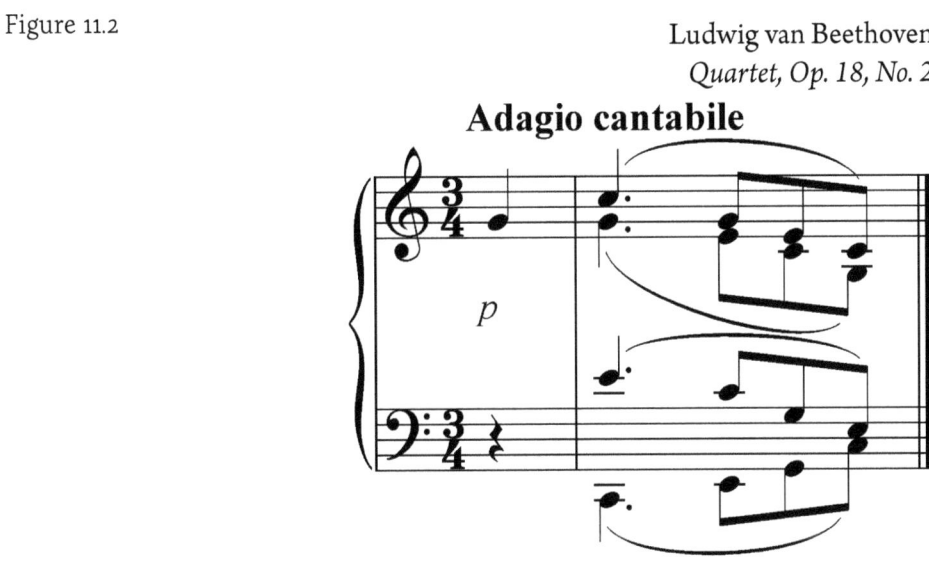

Figure 11.3 illustrates an *oscillating six four*. This type of consonant six four is often found as a result of an oscillating accompaniment pattern found in marches and waltzes. Here, the bass moves back and forth between $\hat{1}$ and $\hat{5}$.

Figure 11.3

Chapter 11: Cadential Six-Four

The Cadential Six Four Chord

One of the most common six four chords is the *cadential six four*. This is a dissonant six four chord, and requires resolution and often preparation. Its function is to embellish and prolong the dominant. Unlike the consonant six four chords, it is heard in a linear way as an extension of dominant harmony, not as a second inversion triad. As its name implies, it occurs at or near a cadence. Figure 11.4 shows two different analysis of the same progression. However, 11.4 (a) is not an accurate representation of the function of this progression. Although this chord looks like a I^6_4, it does not function as a tonic. It is a linear chord that occurs on scale degree $\hat{5}$. Its function is to decorate and prolong the dominant to which it resolves. The correct functional analysis is seen in 11.4 (b). We will examine this chord, the cadential six four, and its voice leading in four part writing.

Figure 11.4

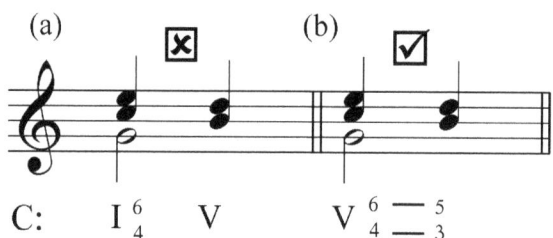

The Cadential Six Four in Four Part Harmony

The examples in Figure 11.5 demonstrate the normal voice leading for a six four chord written in four parts. *The bass note of the six four chord is always doubled.* The 6th above the bass moves to the 5th and the 4th moves to the 3rd. In 11.5 (a), the 6th above the bass is E and it moves to the 5th, D, in the soprano. The 4th is C and it moves to the 3rd, B, in the tenor. The doubled G is repeated as a common tone in the alto. This voice leading is the same in the minor key as shown in 11.5 (b). The cadential six four may also resolve to a V^7 chord as is 11.5 (c). In this case, the 6th moves to the 5th, the 4th to the 3rd. In this resolution the 8th moves to the 7th instead of remaining a common tone. Take note of the functional and the root/quality chord symbols for this progression.

Figure 11.5

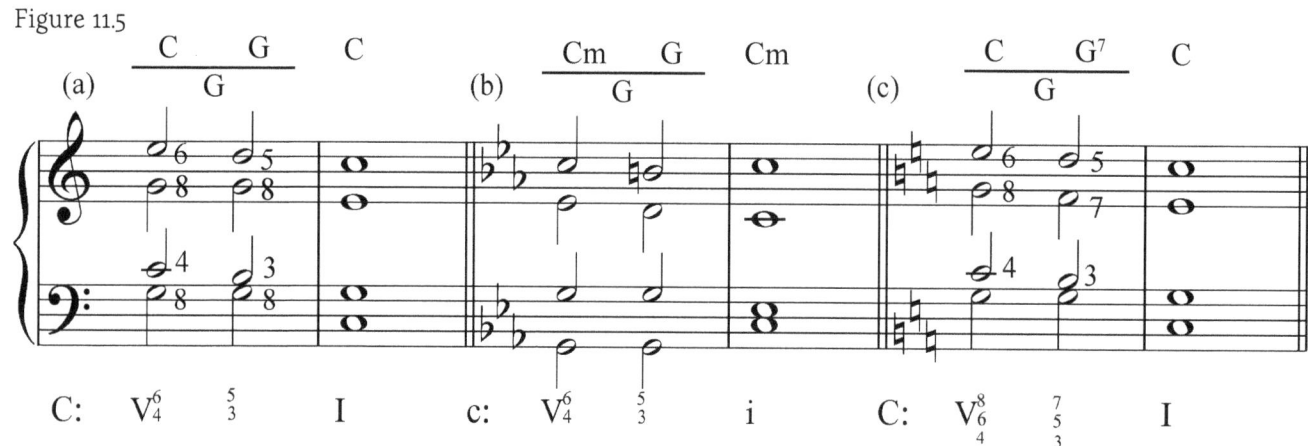

1. Resolve the following six four chords in four parts.

2. Complete the following progressions in four parts.

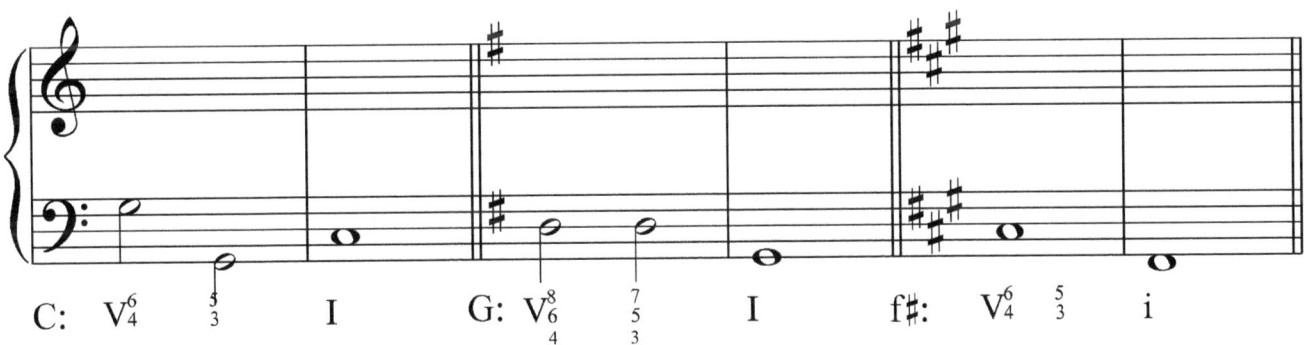

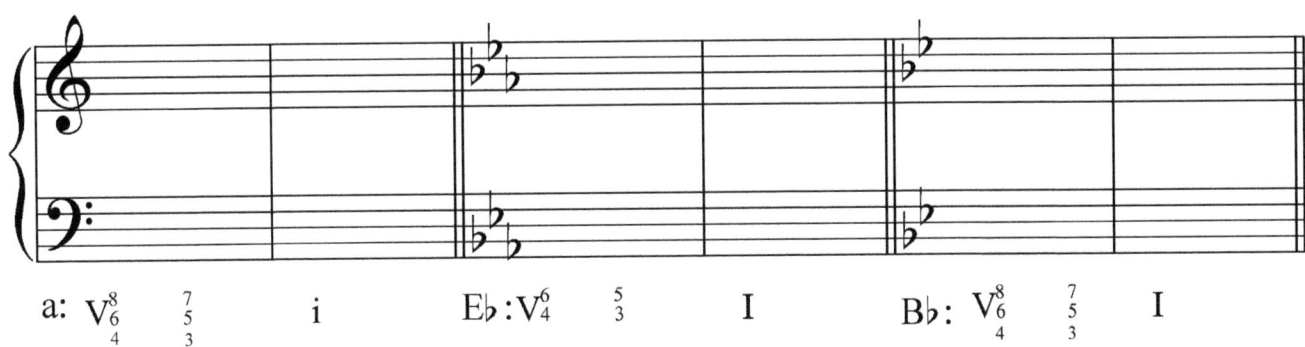

Chapter 11: Cadential Six-Four

Approaching Cadential Six Four

When cadential six four is preceded by IV, the 6th above the bass acts as an accented passing tone. This is illustrated in Figure 11.6 (a) in the alto, which moves $\hat{4}$-$\hat{3}$-$\hat{2}$ (F-E-D). The 4th above the bass is prepared with common tone motion in the tenor, and resolves down to the 3rd (C-C-B). The soprano repeats the doubled bass note (G). The same voice leading is used in the minor key as shown in 11.6 (b).

Figure 11.6

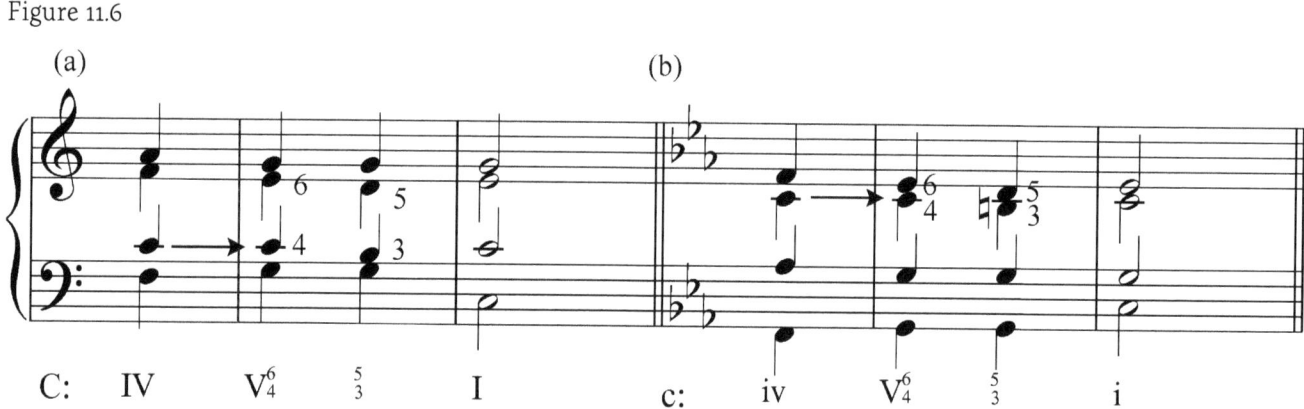

ii is a predominant chord and often precedes cadential six four. There are no common tones between ii and cadential six four. The correct movement from ii or ii⁶ is to approach the 6th and the 4th by step from above as in Figure 11.7 (a) and (b). Here, the 6 and 4 act like accented passing tones in the progression. Faulty parallel 5ths can occur when writing this progression as shown in 11.7 (c). The easiest way to avoid this is to switch the voices so they become parallel 4ths.

Figure 11.7

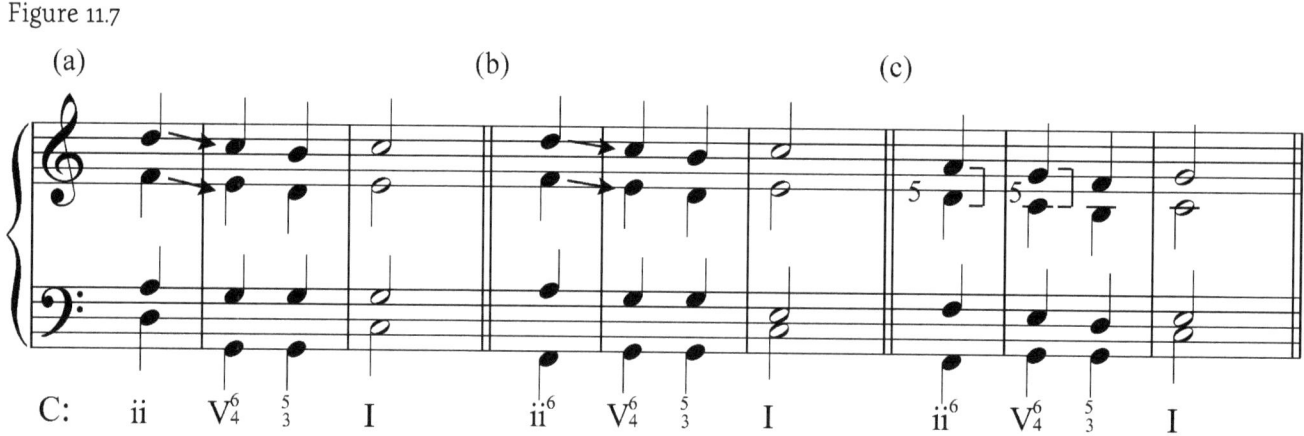

In this progression scale degree $\hat{5}$ in the bass gives the cadential six four a dominant function, not a tonic function. This is the reason for figuring it V_4^6 $_3^5$ instead of I_4^6 - V. The voice leading here indicates a V chord with increasing tension, not a I chord in second inversion.

3. Complete the following progressions in four parts.

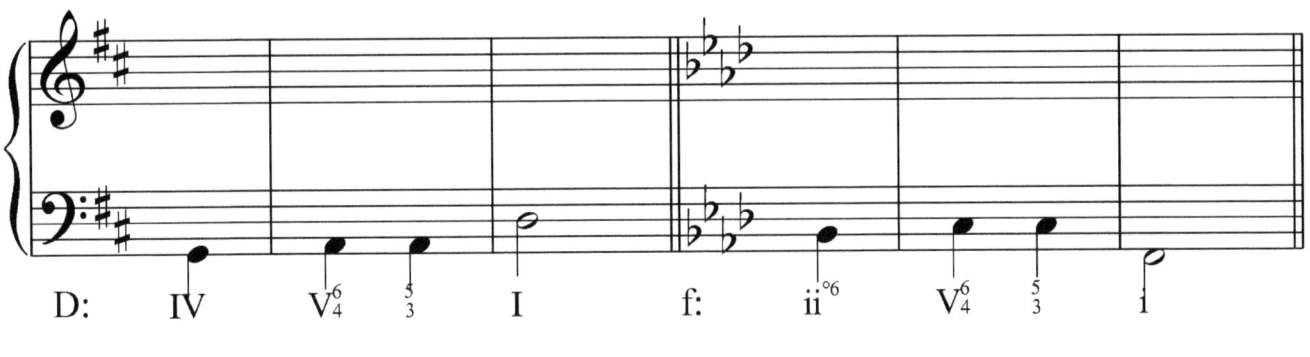

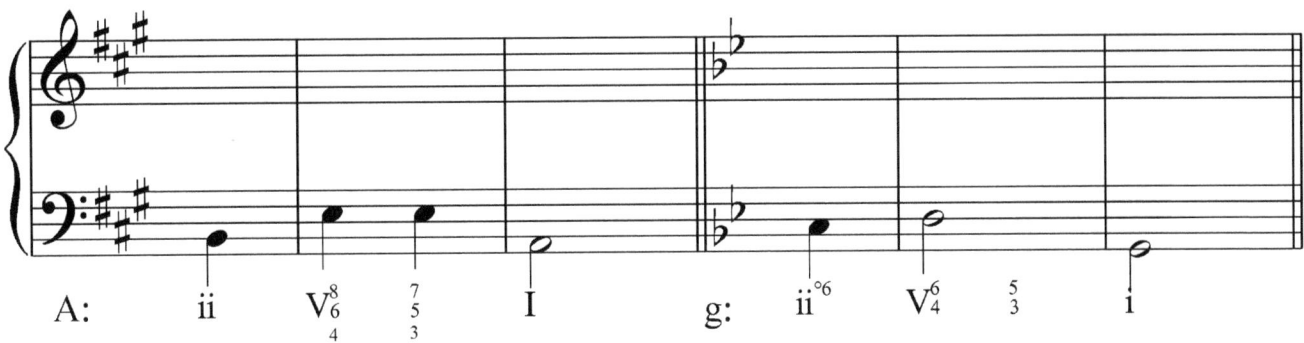

4. Add functional chord symbols and complete the following bass lines in four parts. Use a cadential six four in each.

The Cadential Six Four and Implied Harmony

The cadential six four prolongs and embellishes the dominant (V). It can occur at the end of a phrase to form a half cadence. Any chord that can precede V can precede the cadential six four in this cadence. Study Figure 11.8. At the end of the first phrase the cadential six four prolongs the dominant in a half cadence. At the end of the second phrase it prolongs the dominant in a perfect authentic cadence.

Figure 11.8

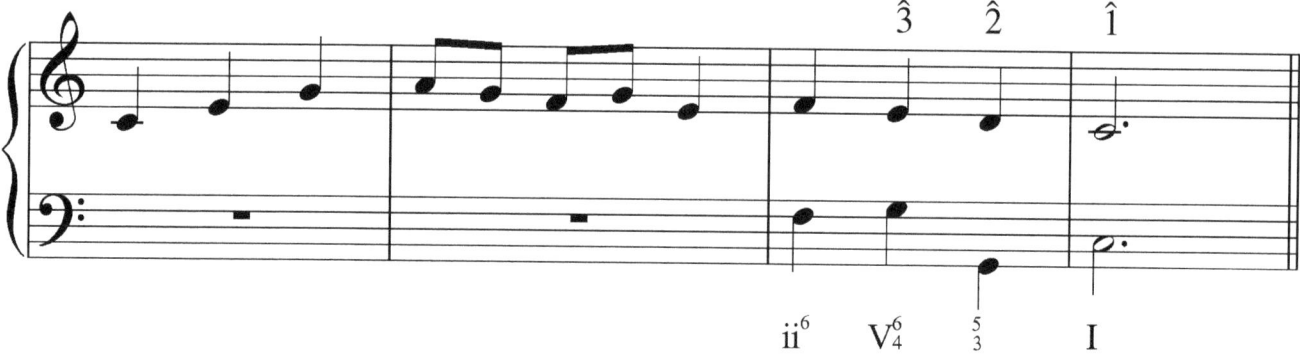

Certain melodic patterns can imply a cadential six four. The scale degrees in Figure 11.9 (a) and (b) can imply a cadential six four at half cadences. The scale degrees in 11.9 (c) and (d) can imply a cadential six four at authentic cadences.

Figure 11.9

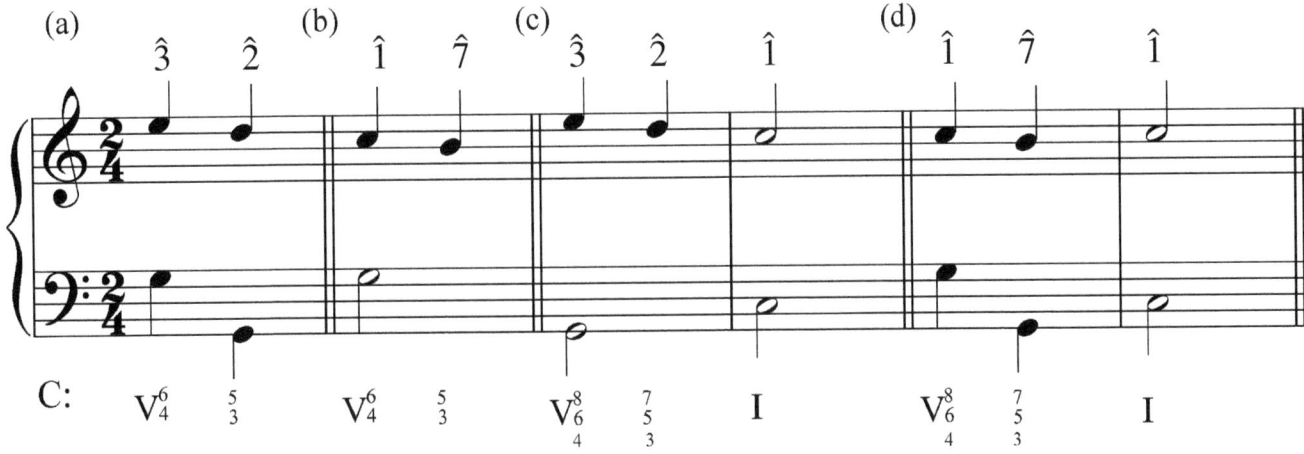

5. Harmonize the following melody. Use a cadential six four chord where appropriate.

Harmonic Analysis - The Suspension

A *suspension* is a nonchord tone that is approached by repetition and left by step. It occurs on a strong beat or a strong part of the beat. The suspension consists of three parts:

- *The Preparation.* The note of preparation is a chord tone in the chord that occurs before the suspension. It appears in the same voice as the suspension. It may be tied to the suspension, but not always.

- *The Suspension.* The note of preparation is held into the second chord where it becomes the suspension, which is a nonchord tone that creates a dissonance. This note falls on a strong beat and is as long or longer than the note of preparation.

- *The Resolution.* The suspension resolves downward to a chord tone of the second chord. This chord tone is the resolution.

Figure 11.10 illustrates a I - V - I progression without a suspension. Then, the same progression with a suspension in the soprano. The preparation occurs as a chord tone of the first I chord (C). It is held over and becomes a nonchord tone with V, becoming the suspension. It then resolves downward by step to the 3rd of V, becoming the resolution (B). The suspension and resolution create the intervals of a 4th and 3rd above the bass. This is notated in the functional chord symbols with two Arabic numbers, 4 - 3. The 4 refers to the interval between the bass and the suspension and the 3 refers to the interval between the bass and resolution.

Figure 11.10

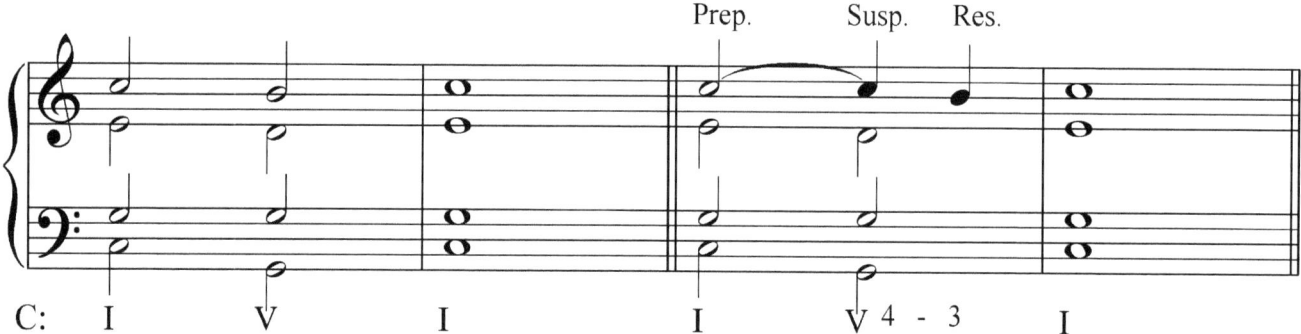

Suspension Types

There are various types of suspensions that occur in four part writing. They are classified according to the intervals formed between the bass and the suspension and its resolution.

1. In a *4-3 suspension* (Figure 11.10), the suspended note forms a 4th with the bass and resolves downward to a 3rd.

2. In a *7-6 suspension* (Figure 11.11(a)) the suspension is a 7th above the bass and resolves down to a 6th. Since the chord of resolution contains a 6, it will be a first inversion chord.

3. A *9-8 suspension* (11.11(b)) involves a suspended 9th resolving down to an 8ve.

4. A *2-3 suspension* (11.11(c)) occurs in the bass. Here, the C is suspended in the bass and creates a 2nd (or 9th) with the alto. This resolves down a step to form a 3rd with the alto. This creates the intervals 2-3 when counted upward from the bass. This suspension resolves to a first inversion chord. The alternate figuration $\genfrac{}{}{0pt}{}{5\text{-}6}{2\text{-}3}$ indicates that A in the tenor is suspended over the bass and creates a 5-6 between the bass and tenor when the suspension resolves.

5. A suspension may occur in two or more voices at the same time (11.11(d)). In this example, the soprano has a 9-8 suspension and the alto has a 4-3 suspension at the same time. This is considered a double suspension.

Figure 11.11

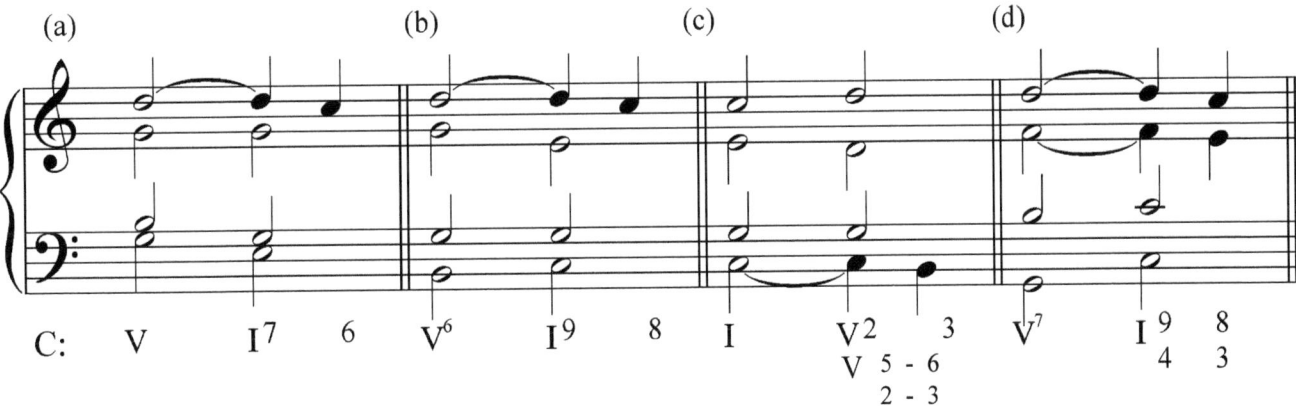

A different type of suspension is the 6-5 suspension (Figure 11.12). Sometimes it is not considered a real suspension because it is a consonant suspension. Both the note of suspension and the note of resolution are chord tones. It is less effective than a dissonant suspension.

Figure 11.12

The Ornamental Resolution

Suspensions may be decorated with various figurations. A suspension embellished with other nonchord tones is considered to have an *ornamental resolution*. The suspension in Figure 11.13(a) has been decorated with an incomplete neighbor before the note of resolution. In 11.13 (b) there is an anticipation between the suspension and resolution. In 11.13(c) the suspension resolves by step and is decorated with a lower neighbor. 11.13 (d) inserts an escape tone between the suspension and its resolution.

Figure 11.13

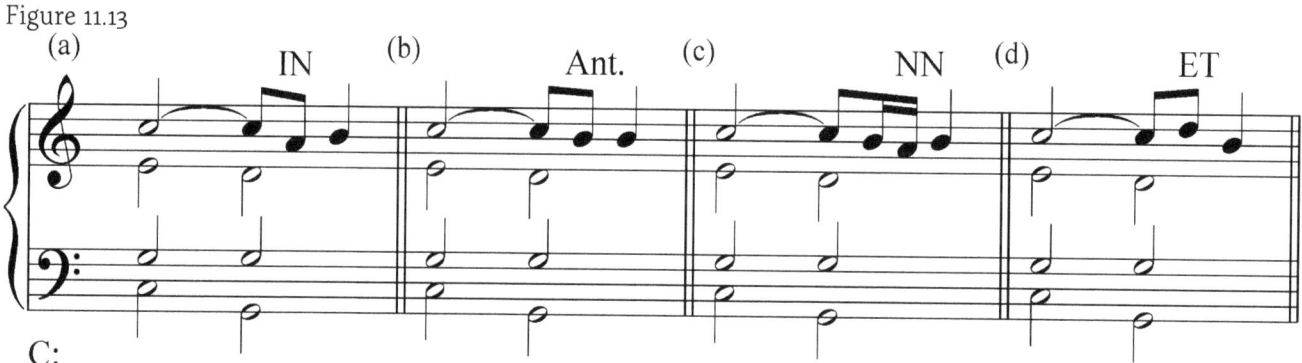

A Chain of Suspensions

Composers often wrote a series of suspensions in a row. This creates a *chain of suspensions*. Figure 11.14 contains a chain of suspensions that is part of a melodic sequence. A *sequence* is a repetition of a musical pattern at a higher or lower pitch. The preparation, sequence and resolution are marked on the score.

Figure 11.14

6. Identify and label, using Arabic numbers, suspensions in the following progressions. Label any ornamental resolutions.

7. Complete the following progressions with suspensions.

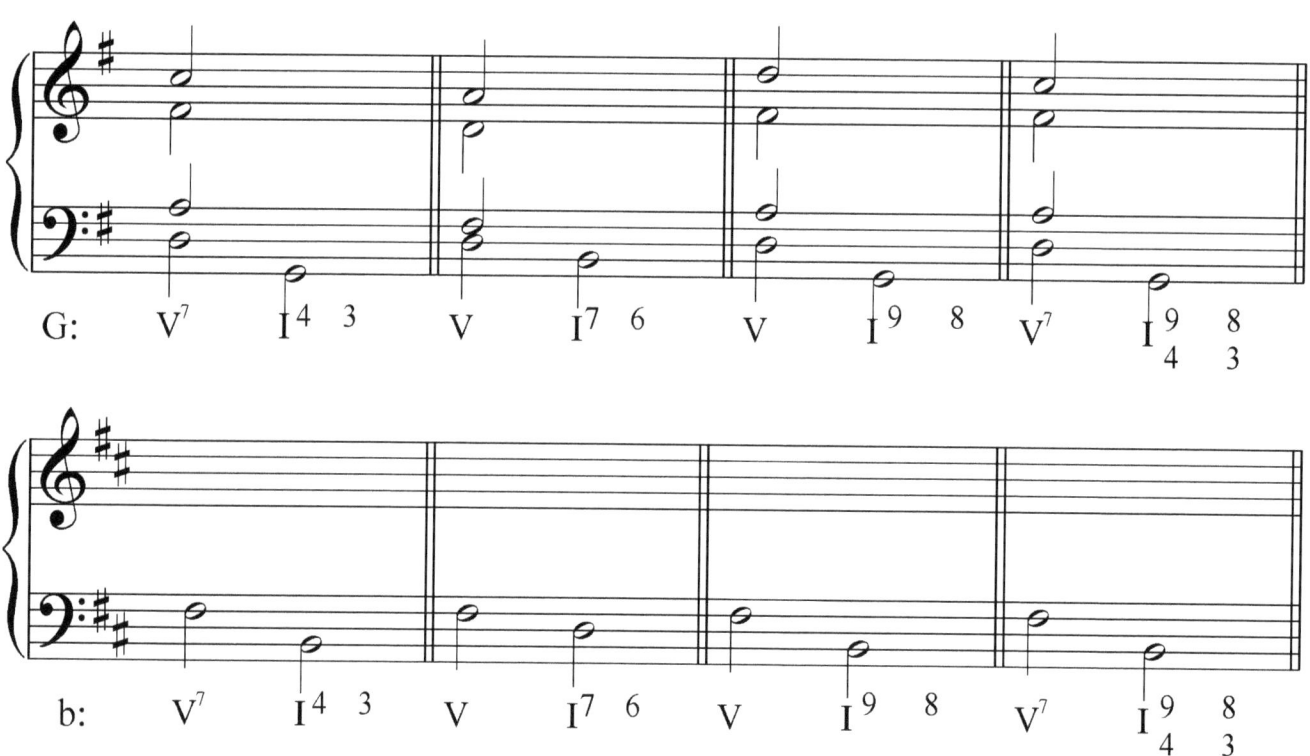

8. Provide a harmonic analysis of the following examples. Use functional chord symbols and circle and identify any nonchord tones.

George Frideric Handel
Sonata No. 1 for Oboe and Harpsichord

key:

key:

12

The Leading Tone Chord

vii°6 as a Prolongation of I

In Chapter 7 we discussed vii°6 as a passing chord between I and I6. This is its most common function. It works in a linear fashion as a prolongation of tonic harmony. Examine the voice leading in Figure 12.1. This progression has $\hat{1}$-$\hat{2}$-$\hat{3}$ or $\hat{3}$-$\hat{2}$-$\hat{1}$ in the bass. In 12.1 (a) the outer voices feature voice exchange (C-D-E and E-D-C). The tenor uses the $\hat{1}$-$\hat{7}$-$\hat{1}$ leading tone figure. This progression can be used to harmonize a $\hat{1}$-$\hat{2}$-$\hat{3}$ or $\hat{3}$-$\hat{2}$-$\hat{1}$ bass line and various melodic patterns including $\hat{3}$-$\hat{2}$-$\hat{1}$, $\hat{1}$-$\hat{2}$-$\hat{3}$, $\hat{1}$-$\hat{7}$-$\hat{1}$ and $\hat{5}$-$\hat{4}$-$\hat{5}$.

It is important to note that the root of vii°6 is the leading tone, and the leading tone is not doubled. Here, we always double the third of vii°6, which is in the bass.

Figure 12.1

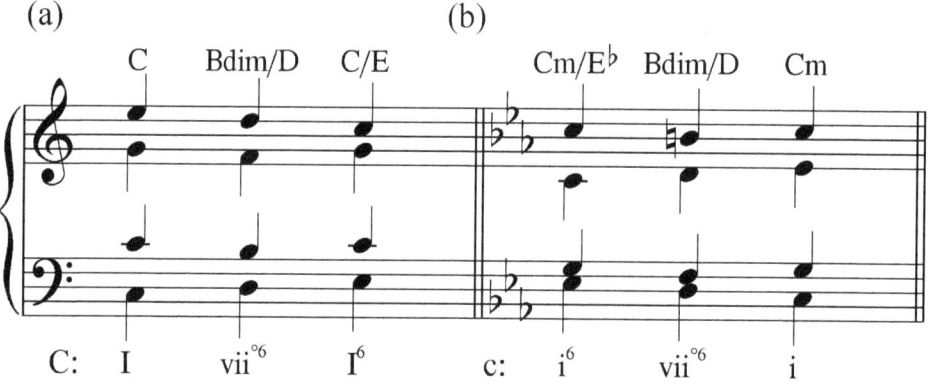

1. Harmonize the following melodic fragments with passing vii°6 chords. Add functional and root/quality chord symbols.

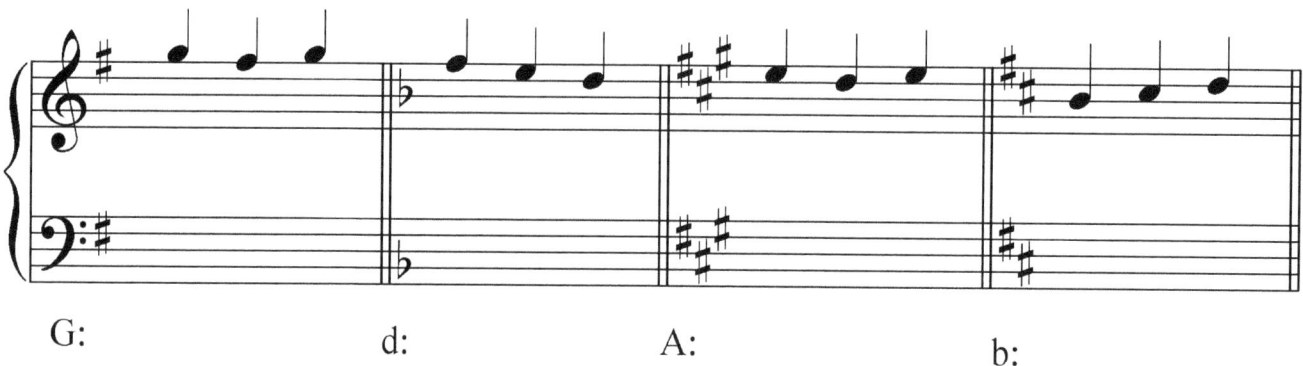

vii°6 may appear between two statements of I to prolong tonic harmony. This role is often described as a "neighboring chord" because the pattern involves voices that step away and step back again. In Figure 12.2 all the voices move in neighbor motion.

Figure 12.2

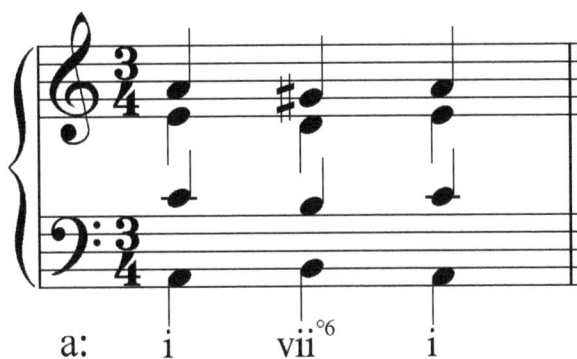

Voice Leading

The leading tone chord is diminished. It is rarely used in root position and nearly always occurs in first inversion. The leading tone is the root of this chord. For now, we do not double the leading tone in any chord. Double the third of vii°6, which is the bass. Like V7, vii°6 contains a dim 5th (or aug 4th) when written in four parts. The resolution of this tritone is the same as in V7. The diminished 5th resolves inwardly to a 3rd as in Figure 12.3 (a) and the augmented 4th resolves outwardly to a 6th as in 12.3 (b). In both of these cases the chord of resolution (i) is incomplete containing a doubled root and doubled 3rd. vii°6 may also resolve to the tonic in first inversion as in 12.3 (c). Although this is the best resolution of vii°6 there are other options. It is not absolutely necessary to resolve the tritone in this manner. In 12.3 (d) and (e) both $\hat{7}$ and $\hat{4}$ rise a step. The 5ths in (d) are not faulty parallel 5ths because one is diminished and one is perfect. This resolution is common and results in a complete tonic chord. $\hat{2}$ may move up to $\hat{3}$ or down to $\hat{1}$. These resolutions apply in both major and minor keys.

Figure 12.3

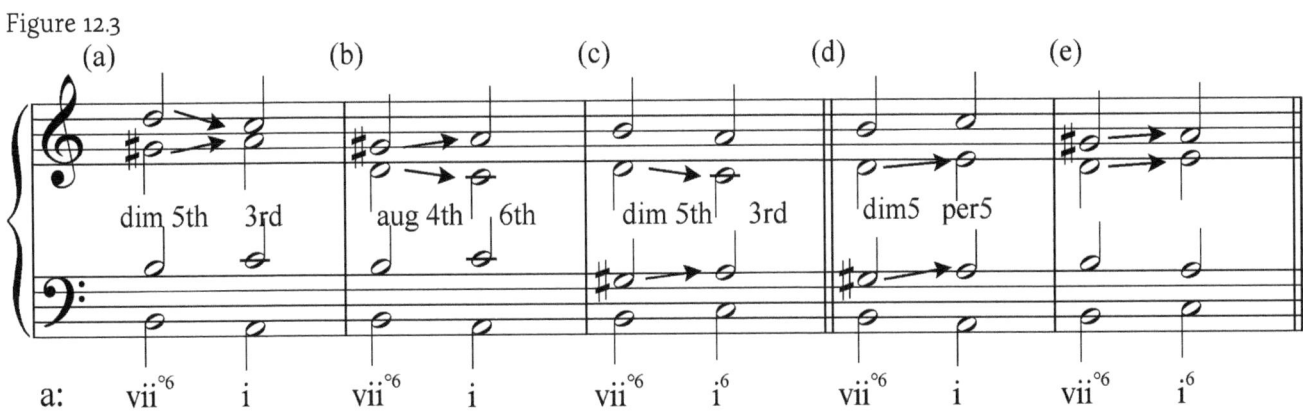

2. Name the keys and add the inner voices to complete the following progressions.

Dominant Functioning vii°⁶

vii°⁶ shares three notes in common the V⁷. vii°⁶ can act as a substitute for V in our basic harmonic progression:

Beginning tonic - Predominant - Dominant - Ending Tonic
I   IV   vii°⁶   I

The IV - vii°⁶ - I portion of this progression commonly harmonizes a melody made up of $\hat{6}$-$\hat{7}$-$\hat{1}$ or $\hat{1}$-$\hat{2}$-$\hat{3}$ as in Figure 12.4 (a) and (b). When writing this progression in the minor key, if $\hat{6}$ and $\hat{7}$ occur in the same voice, you must use the melodic form of the minor scale and raise $\hat{6}$ along with $\hat{7}$ in order to avoid a melodic augmented 2nd as shown in 12.4 (c).

Figure 12.4

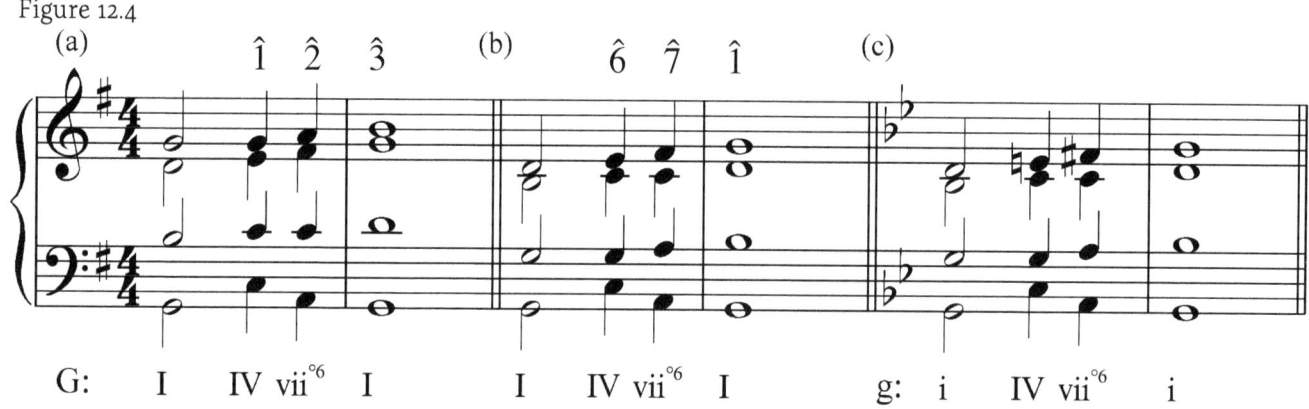

107   Chapter 12: The Leading Tone Chord

The Leading Tone Cadence

vii°6 is like V7 without the root. This weak dominant function makes it ideal for leading to the tonic chord (either in root position or in first inversion) in the middle of a phrase, but inappropriate for a strong cadence. Although this cadence is not used frequently today, it was common in the 15th and 16th centuries. When it is used at the end of a phrase it is called a *leading tone cadence*. Some music theorists consider this cadence an imperfect authentic cadence. Figure 12.5 is an example of a leading tone cadence.

Figure 12.5

George Frideric Handel
Chorale: Ach Gott und Herr, wie gross und schwer

C: I6   IV   vii°6   I

3. Complete the following progressions in four parts.

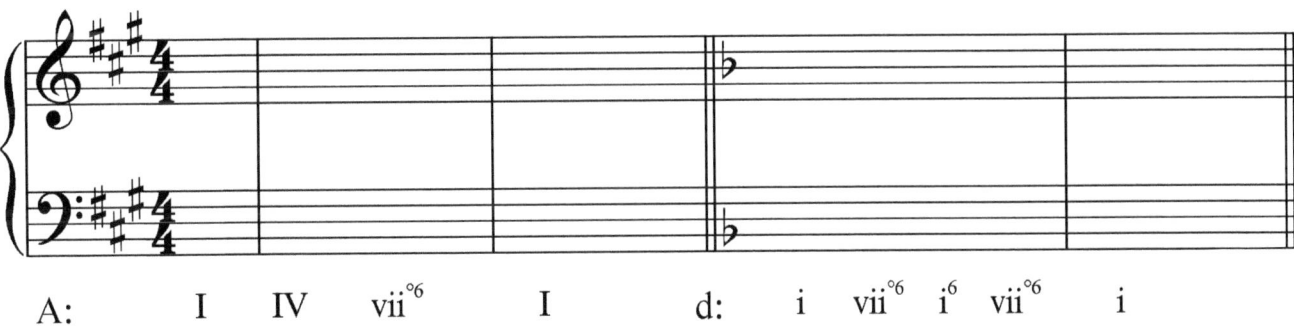

A: I   IV   vii°6   I   d: i   vii°6   i6   vii°6   i

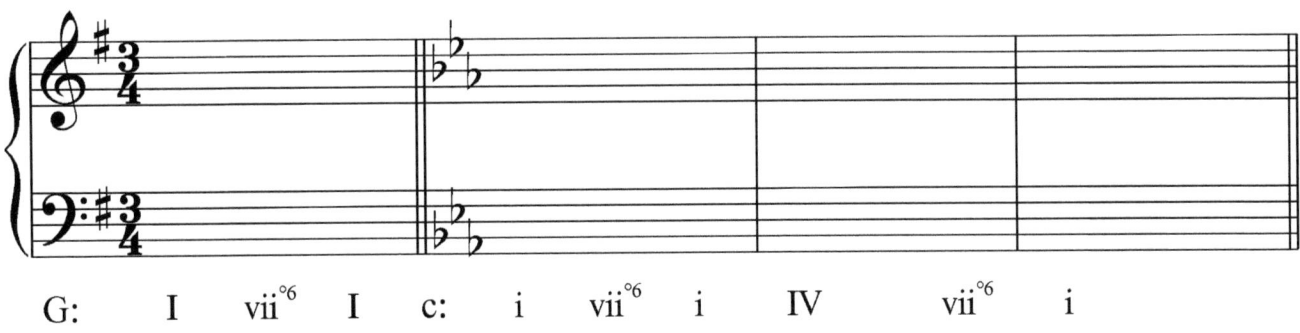

G: I   vii°6   I   c: i   vii°6   i   IV   vii°6   i

Harmonic Analysis - The Pedal Point

A *pedal point* is a note that is held, usually in the bass, under a number of changing harmonies. Most of the time the pedal point is the tonic ($\hat{1}$) or the dominant ($\hat{5}$) and functions as a prolongation of one of these two chords.

The piece in Figure 12.6 begins with what is called a *tonic pedal*. It gets this name because the pedal point is the tonic of the key. There is an chord progression above the pedal which is an elaborated I IV V I. Throughout this progression the bass maintains an F. The F is a chord tone of IV, but it is a completely foreign pitch in the V^7 chord. The functional chord symbols are shown in root position. The repeated F masks the sound of the chord inversions written above it. Inversions may be indicated if the pedal point is written in one of the upper voices.

Figure 12.6 — Wolfgang Amadeus Mozart, *Piano Sonata K280, I*

4. Provide a harmonic analysis using functional chord symbols. Circle and identify all nonchord tones.

Johann Sebastian Bach
9 Kleine Präludien, No. 3 BWV 926

key:

5. Provide a harmonic analysis using functional chord symbols. Circle and identify all nonchord tones.

Johann Sebastian Bach
Chorale No. 26: O Ewigkeit, du Donnerwort

key:

Johann Sebastian Bach
Chorale No. 103: Nun ruhen alle Wälder

key:

Franz Joseph Haydn
Piano Sonata Hob. XVI: 37, III

Presto ma non troppo

key:

13

More Six Four Chords

The Passing Six Four Chord

Dissonant six four chords occur as a result of linear motion and do not function as independent chords. They are always part of a harmonic idea that prolongs or decorates and embellishes other chords. In Chapter 11 we learned that even though the cadential six four looks like I in second inversion, it functions as a decoration and prolongation of V, not as a tonic chord.

Another chord that occurs as a result of linear motion is the *passing six four*. This functions as a passing chord linking and prolonging tonic or predominant harmonies. Since this chord is a non-essential linear chord we will figure it with P^6_4. Most passing six four chords occur on a weak beat and connect either a triad in root position with the same triad in first inversion, or the reverse. The passing six four is most often associated with the tonic and subdominant chords. Figure 13.1 (a) contains a passing six four chord between I and I⁶. Here, it looks like V^6_4, and some texts figure it this way. However, it is not functioning as a dominant chord, so it is labelled P^6_4. 13.1 (b) contains a passing chord between iv⁶ and iv. The literal figuration of this is i^6_4, but it does not have a tonic functon so it is labelled P^6_4. Note the voice leading in these progressions. There is passing motion in the bass. Like cadential six four, the 5th of the six four chord which is in the bass, is always doubled. One voice maintains common tone motion throughout. One voice moves in neighbor motion and voice exchange occurs between the bass and another voice.
Make note of the root/quality chord symbols, which only reflect the root and quality of a chord and do not state its function.

Figure 13.1

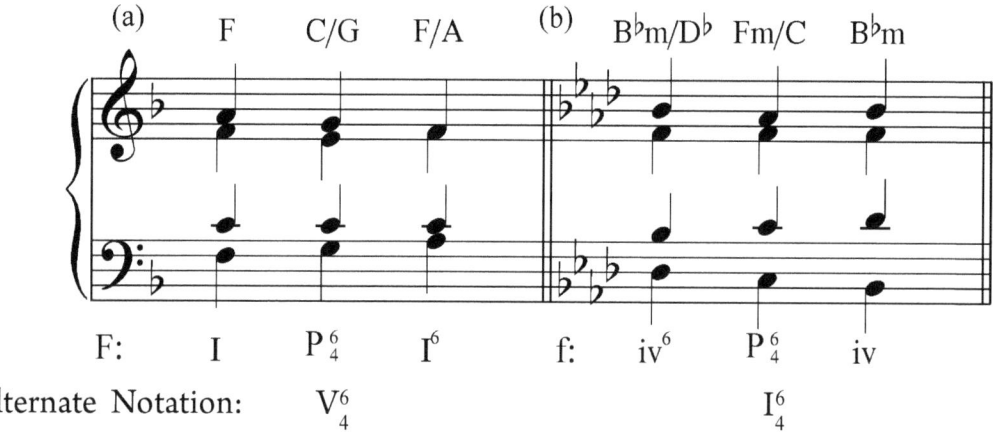

1. Name the keys and complete the following progressions by adding the alto and tenor.

2. Complete the following figured basses in four parts.

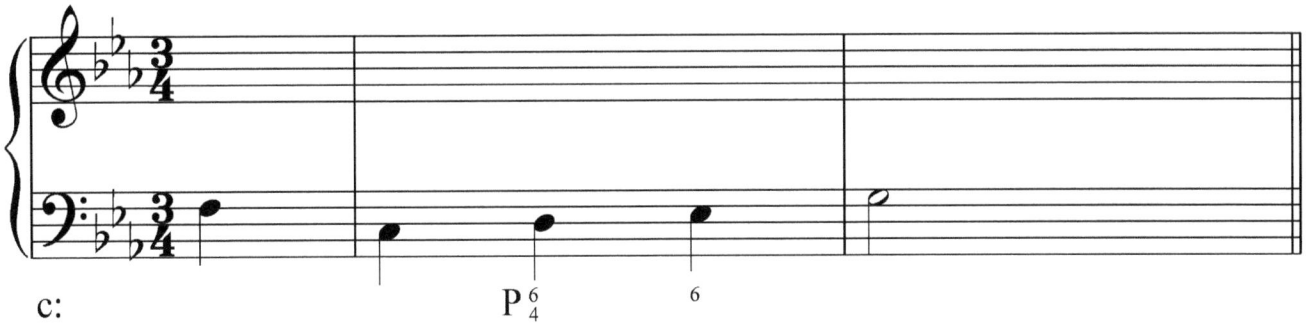

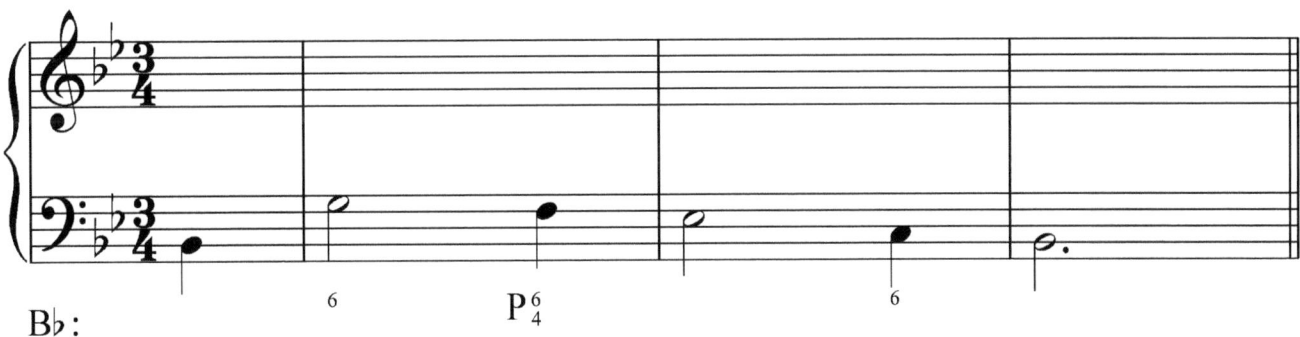

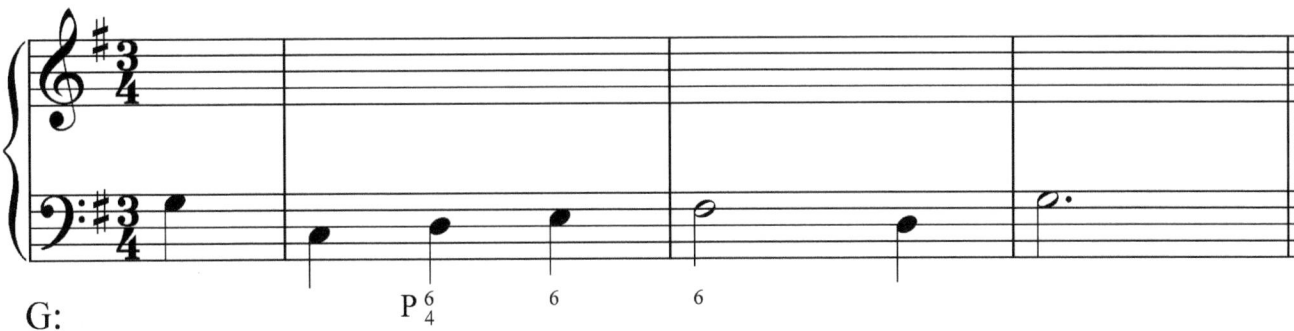

The Neighbor Six Four Chord

A six four chord may outline an upper neighbor figure over a root position triad. This chord is known as a *neighboring six four chord*. It is sometimes called a *pedal six four* because the bass remains stationary like a pedal point. This chord is designated in the functional chord symbols as: N_4^6. Figure 13.2 contains two neighboring six four chords in the bass clef. The first embellishes I and the second embellishes V. The neighboring six four acts as a linear double neighbor decorating i and V.

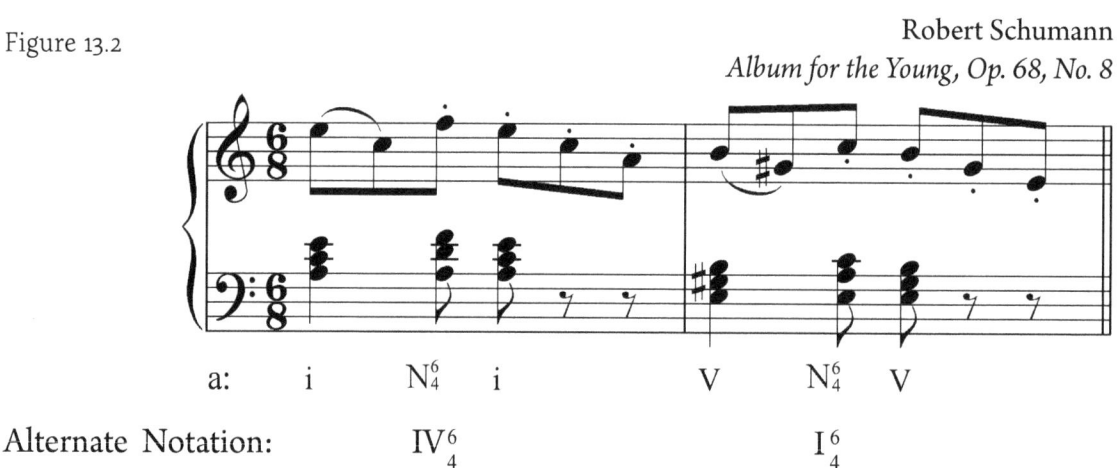

Figure 13.2

Robert Schumann
Album for the Young, Op. 68, No. 8

The neighboring six four occurs most commonly as an prolongation of the tonic. In Figure 13.3 (a) $\hat{1}$ is repeated throughout the bass acting like a pedal point. It is usually doubled in another voice (here the tenor), while the other two voices move in neighbor motion. This is the most common voice leading for this progresson. 13.3 (b) contains a neighboring six four prolonging the dominant. The voice leading here is the same as (a).

The literal analysis of these prolongations is I - IV_4^6 - I and V - I_4^6 - V respectively. However, the IV_4^6 is not functioning as the subdominant and I_4^6 is not functioning as the tonic. They result from linear motion and function as neighbor chords to I and V. As a result these chords are labelled with the symbol N_4^6.

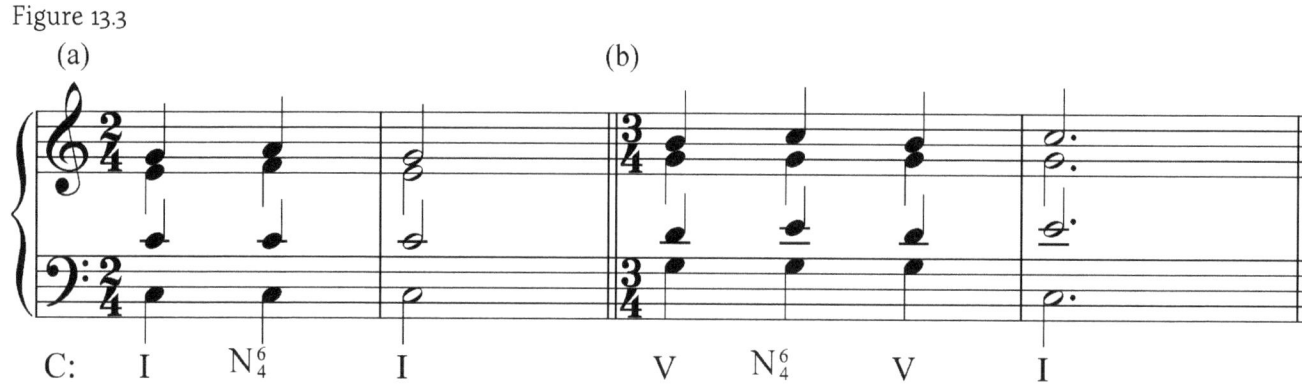

Figure 13.3

Chapter 13: More Six-Four Chords

3. Complete the following progressions in four parts.

4. Add the alto and tenor to complete the following progressions.

5. Complete the following figured bass in four parts.

Figure 13.4 illustrates four different six four chords. Cadential, passing and neighbor six four chords are dissonant and occur as a result of linear motion. Their function is to prolong and decorate other harmonies. The arpeggio six four is a consonant six four. Consonant six four chords are heard as the second inversion of a triad and do not have a linear function. Note that the 5th, which is in the bass, is always doubled in a six four chord.

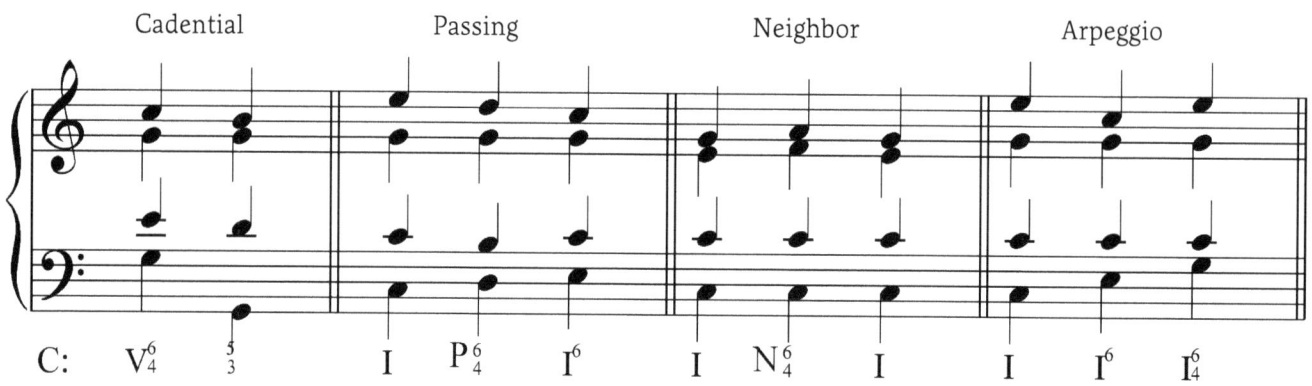

Harmonic Analysis

6. Provide a harmonic analysis of the following examples. Use functional chord symbols. Circle and identify any nonchord tones.

Wolfgang Amadeus Mozart
Sonata, K545

key:

Robert Schumann
Album for the Young, Op. 68, No. 11

Allegretto

key:

Felix Mendelssohn
Song Without Words, Op. 38, No. 3

Presto e molto vivace

key:

Ludwig van Beethoven
Quartet, Op. 18, No. 2

Adagio cantabile

key:

14

The Submediant and Mediant Chords

The *submediant triad* is built on $\hat{6}$ and is a third below the tonic. The *mediant triad* is built on $\hat{3}$ and is a third above the tonic. These chords are not as functionally strong as the previous chords we have studied. This chapter examines their use and function in a chord progression.

VI as a Prolongation of I

The submediant triad, built on $\hat{6}$, consists of scale degrees $\hat{6}$-$\hat{1}$-$\hat{3}$. In major keys it is a minor triad (vi), and in minor keys it is a major triad (VI)

Figure 14.1

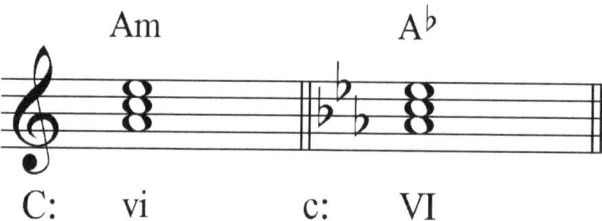

The submediant may prolong the tonic in a progression where the bass decends in thirds. This is a common progression and often occurs as I - vi - IV - V - I or I - vi - ii⁶ - V - I. The bass note of vi is scale degree $\hat{6}$ and it divides a downward leap from $\hat{1}$ to $\hat{4}$ into thirds. In third related chord progressions like I - vi there are two common tones. The best voice leading opton is to retain these common tones in the same voices. In Figure 14.2 the common tones are repeated in the soprano and tenor in both progressions. In 14.2 (a), there are two common tones between vi and IV and they are repeated in the same voices (alto and tenor). In 14.2 (b) there is one common tone between VI and ii°⁶ and it is retained in the alto. The root of VI is doubled. These progressions are effective in major and minor keys.

Figure 14.2

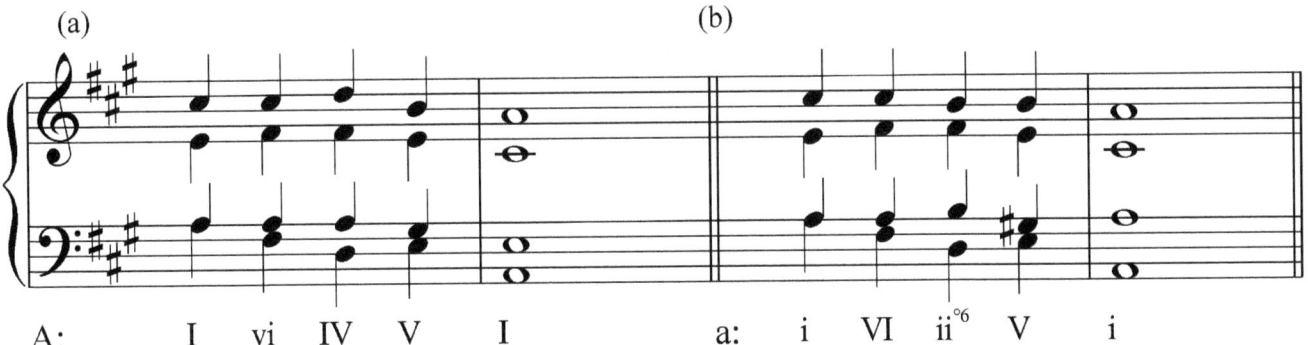

1. Complete the following progressions in four parts.

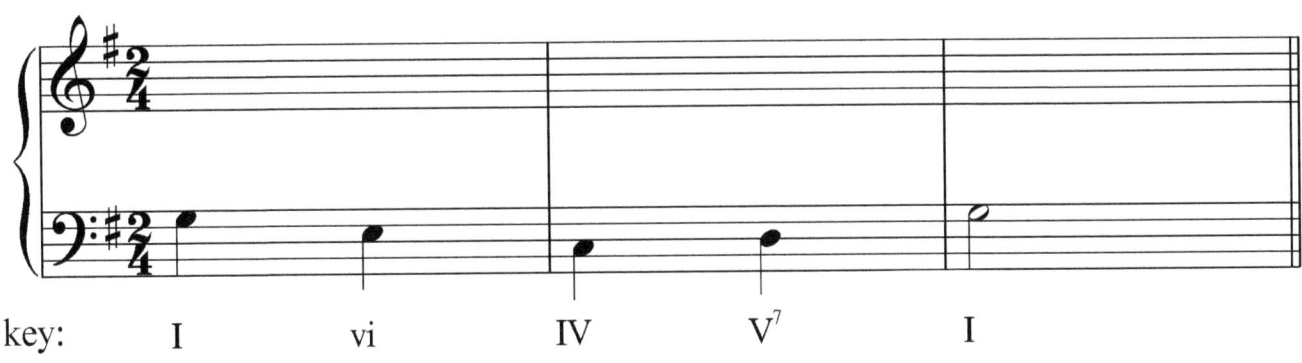

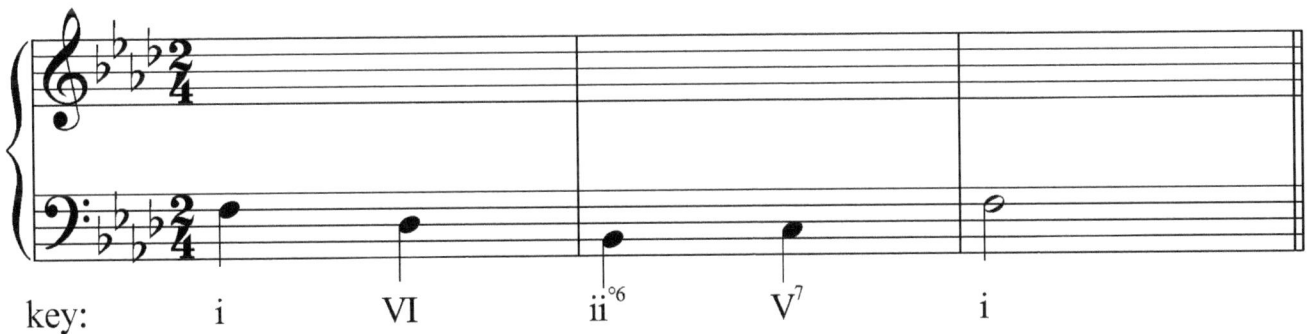

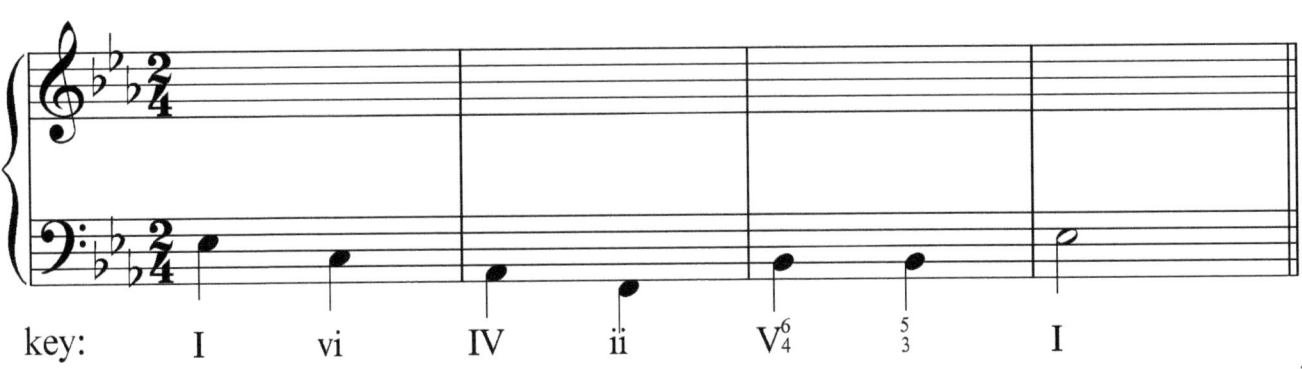

The Submediant Chord as a Predominant

The submediant may be used as a predominant immediately preceding V in a harmonic progression. In major keys the general voice leading rule in this progression is to move the three upper voices in contrary motion to the bass to the nearest available chord tones as seen in Figure 14.3 (a). In minor keys, however, if all voices move in contrary motion to the bass a melodic augmented second results as shown in 14.3 (b). The solution to this error is shown in 14.3 (c). In minor keys this progression requires a doubled 3rd in chord VI. **Two voices rise, two voices fall, and the 3rd is doubled in VI.**

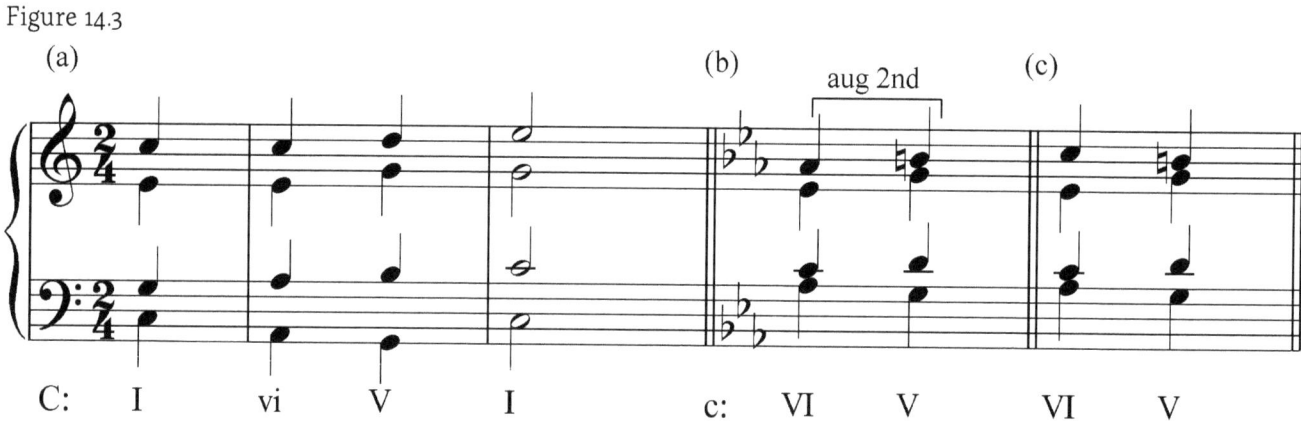

Figure 14.3

2. Name the keys and complete the following in four parts.

VI as Substitute for I: The Deceptive Cadence

vi may be used in both major and minor keys as a substitute for the ending tonic. In this progression V resolves to vi instead of I. Substituting vi for I in an authentic cadence results in a cadence called a *deceptive cadence*.

Figure 14.4 (b) illustrates some special considerations in the voice leading when writing this cadence. Generally the leading tone should resolve upwards to $\hat{1}$. The other two voices move in contrary motion (down) to the bass. The 3rd is doubled in chord vi.

When vi is approached by V^7 in this cadence as in 14.4 (c) and (d), the leading tone rises to $\hat{1}$, and the 7th of V^7 falls a step. The 3rd is doubled in vi.

Figure 14.4

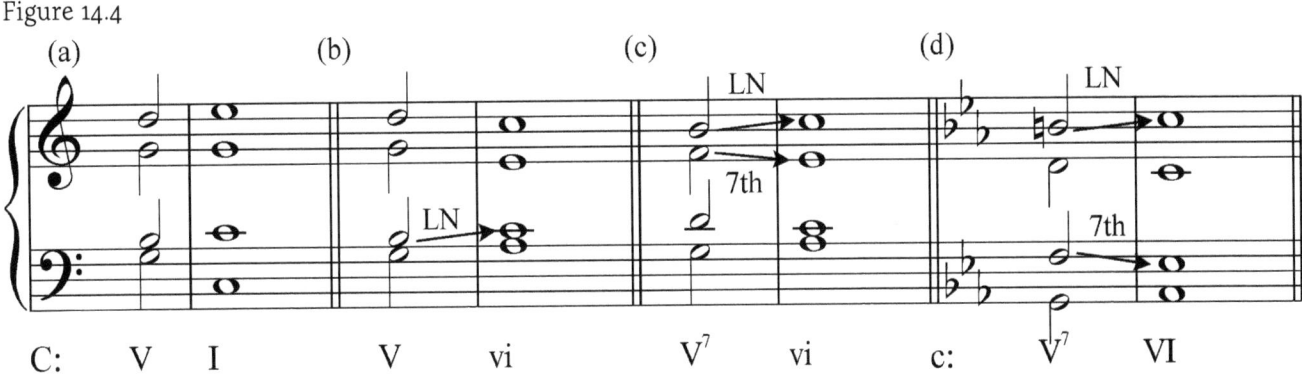

3. Name the keys and complete the following in four parts.

4. Complete the following in four parts.

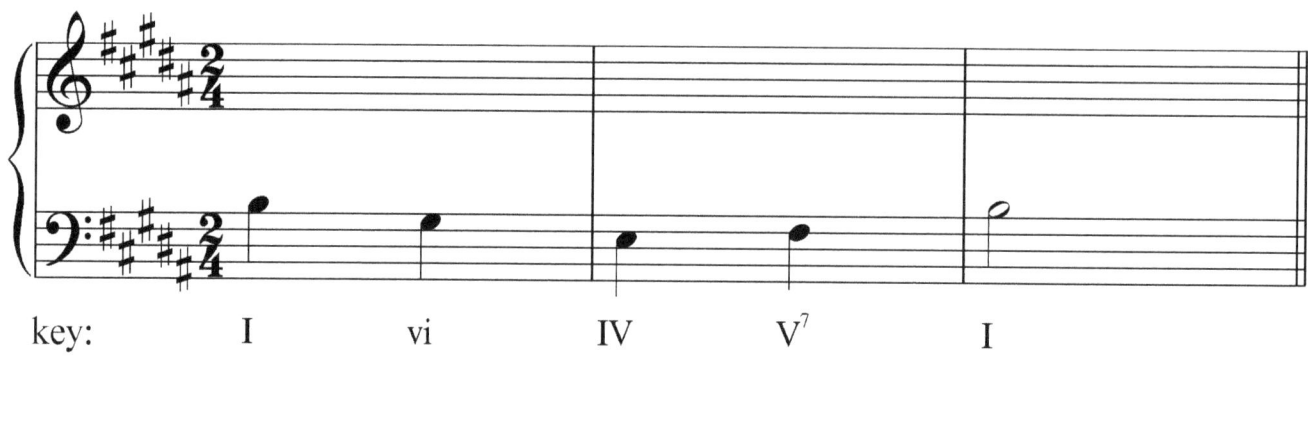

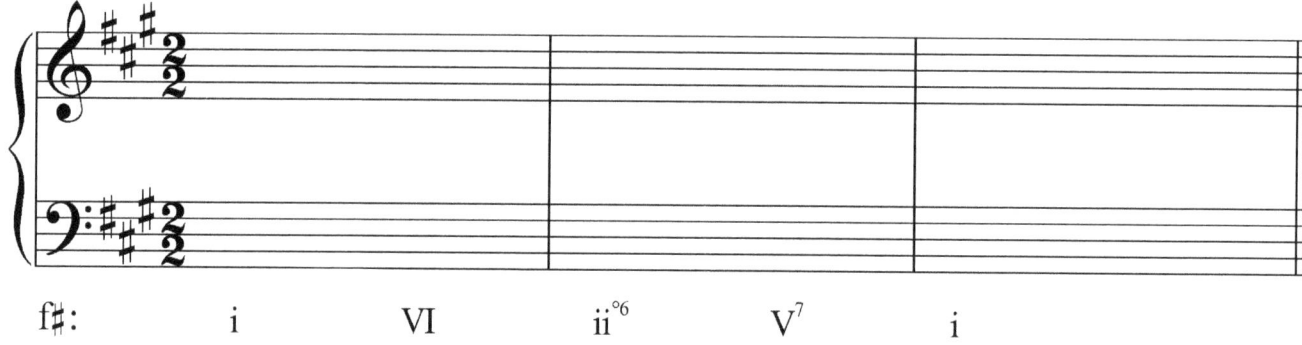

The Mediant Chord

The mediant triad, built on $\hat{3}$, consists of scale degrees $\hat{3}$-$\hat{5}$-$\hat{7}$. In major keys it is a minor triad (iii), and in minor keys it is most commonly used as a major triad (III) without raised $\hat{7}$. Note that the fifth of III in a minor key, scale degree $\hat{7}$, is not the leading tone. When $\hat{7}$ is not raised in a minor key it is called the *subtonic*.

Figure 14.6

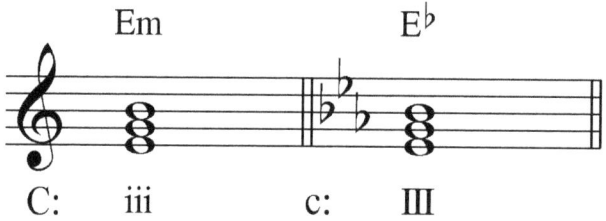

The mediant chord has two notes in common with the tonic chord. The roots of iii and I are a third apart and iii, like I⁶, often prolongs the tonic with arpeggiation. Figure 14.7 contains examples of I being prolonged with I⁶ (a) and with iii (b). A relationship can be seen with the bass arpeggiation in both progressions (C-E). There is a difference of only tone tone between I⁶ and iii.

Figure 14.7

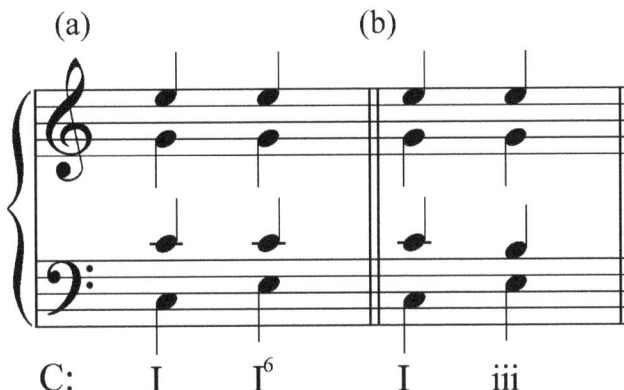

5. Name the keys and complete the following in four parts.

The mediant chord may occur between I and IV supporting a descending melody consisting of $\hat{1}$-$\hat{7}$-$\hat{6}$-$\hat{5}$. To this point, we have followed the rule that when the leading tone is in an outer voice it must rise to the tonic. However, if $\hat{7}$ is part of a descending melodic line it does not resolve to $\hat{1}$. When $\hat{7}$ in the soprano ascends to $\hat{1}$ it is usually harmonized with dominant harmony like V or vii°⁶. When $\hat{7}$ is part of a descending melody it is often harmonized with iii. In Figure 14.8 (a) iii prolongs the beginning tonic. It is followed by the predominant IV and an authentic cadence. In 14.8 (b) iii prolongs the tonic and divides the space between I and V.

In our previous four part writing, chords containing $\hat{7}$ used the leading tone, with an accidental raising $\hat{7}$. There are some cases in minor keys where $\hat{7}$ is not raised. In Figure 148 (c), scale degree $\hat{7}$ is not raised. Here, the melodic form of the minor scale is used. This avoids an augmented 2nd between raised $\hat{7}$ and $\hat{6}$ and results in a major III chord.

Figure 14.8

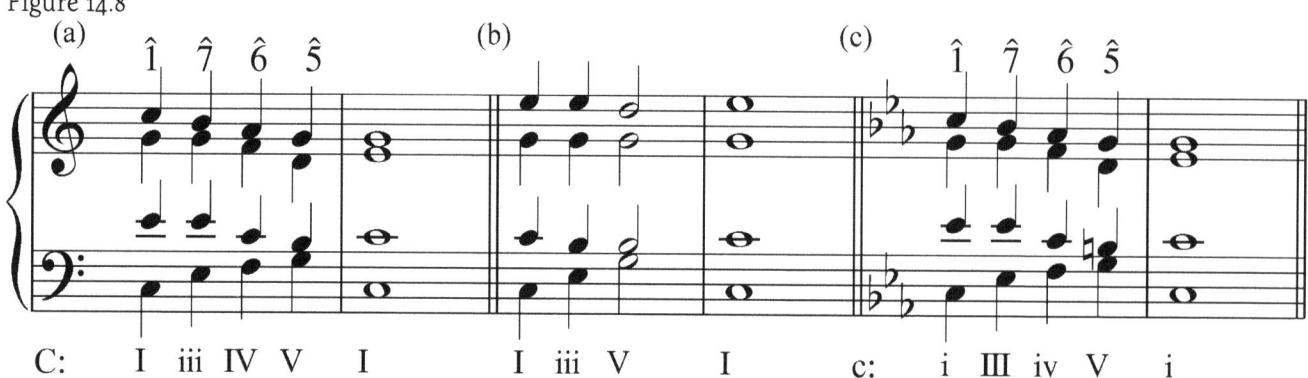

6. Complete the following progression in in four parts.

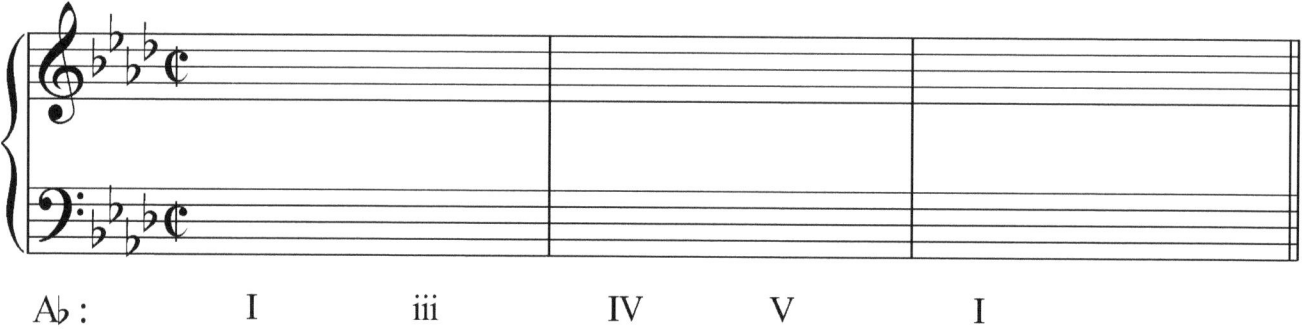

A♭:   I   iii   IV   V   I

7. Harmonize the following melody in four parts. Use III in tonic prolongation.

b:

123   Chapter 14: The Submediant and Mediant

Harmonic Analysis

8. Provide a harmonic analysis of the following using functional chord symbols. Circle and identify all nonchord tones.

Joseph Haydn
Sonata Hob.XVI: 35, I

key:

Johannes Brahms
Symphony IV, Op. 98

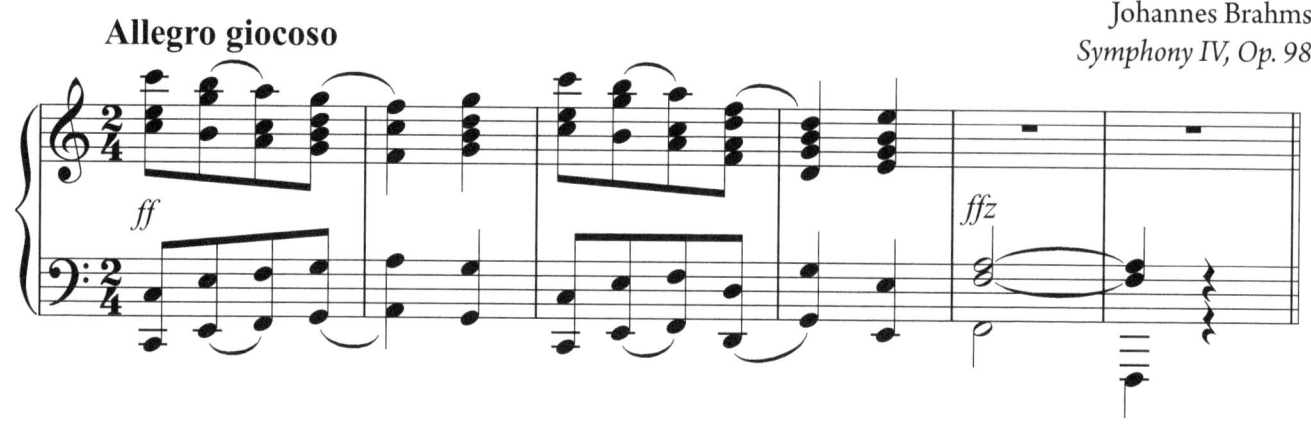

Pyotr Ilyich Tchaikovsky
Symphony IV, Op. 36

key:

Pyotr Ilyich Tchaikovsky
Symphony IV, Op. 36

key:

Chapter 14: The Submediant and Mediant

15

The Subtonic Chord and The Harmonic Sequence

The Subtonic Chord

When scale degree $\hat{7}$ is not raised in the minor key it is not a leading tone and is considered the *subtonic*. In order to be a leading tone, $\hat{7}$ must be a semitone away from the tonic. When $\hat{7}$ is not raised in minor keys, it is a whole tone away, and does not have a leading tone function. The chord built on $\flat\hat{7}$ (the subtonic) in a minor key is called the *subtonic chord*. This chord is made up of $\flat\hat{7}$-$\hat{2}$-$\hat{4}$. It is a major chord and is given the functional chord symbol VII.

In minor keys VII often precedes III in a progression. When this happens it sounds like VII is a temporary dominant of III. It is like a temporary authentic cadence with III as the tonic and VII as its dominant. Figure 15.1 contains this progression. Chord III is an E♭ major chord. Chord VII is a B♭ major chord. The dominant of E♭ is B♭, so this sounds like an authentic cadence in E♭ major. These two chords have a common tone. The easiest voice leading is to repeat the common tone in the same voice and move the remaining voices up a step.

Figure 15.1

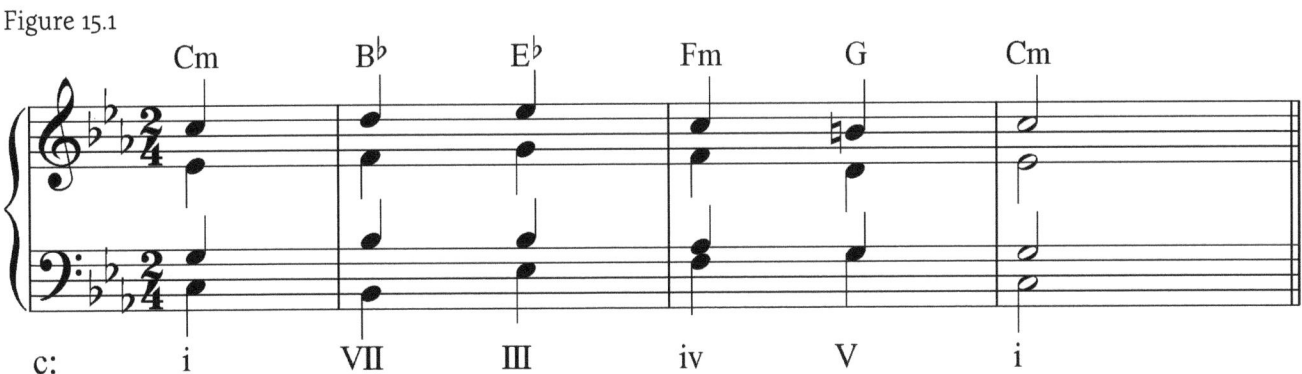

1. Name the keys and complete the following progressions in four parts.

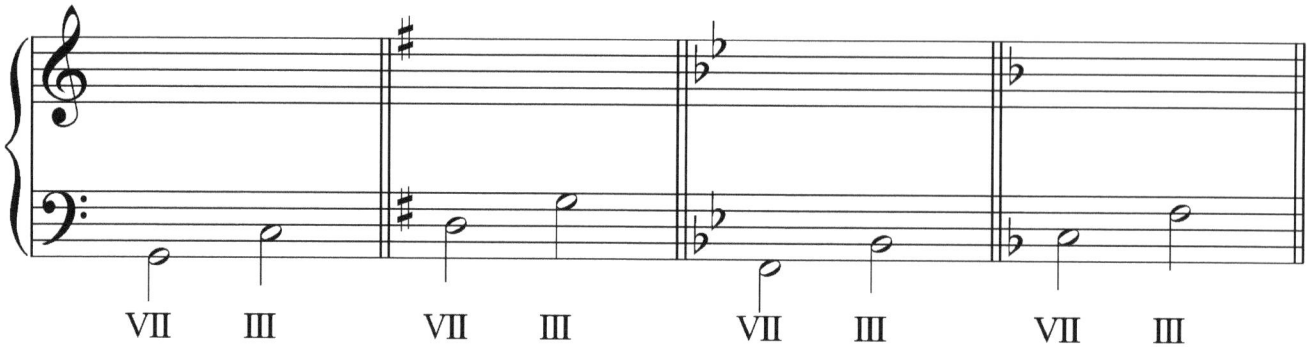

The Descending Fifths Sequence

An *harmonic sequence* is the repitition of a series of chords at a higher or lower pitch. A common use of the progression VII - III is in a sequence of chords that descend in 5ths. This is known as the *descending 5ths sequence*. Even though we say the roots move in descending 5ths, the bass actually alternates descending 5ths with ascending 4ths.

Figure 15.2 contains a descending 5ths sequence in G minor. The root is doubled in each chord. In this sequence in minor keys, $\hat{7}$ is not raised in VII and III making both of these chords major. It is raised in V at the end of the sequence for the authentic cadence. In minor keys we use the leading tone when we want to return to the tonic. It should be noted that ii is a diminished triad and is not normally used in root position. However, it can be used in a sequence. Here, we don't mind the sound of the diminished chord because it fits into the overall predictable pattern. In the sequence the movement of the voices is very important. Every voice must move in sequential motion. For example, the soprano steps up, skips down, steps up skips down, etc. The alto repeats, steps down, repeats, steps down, etc. Each voice maintains the same pattern. This is the essence of a sequence and this repetitive motion is essential.

Figure 15.2

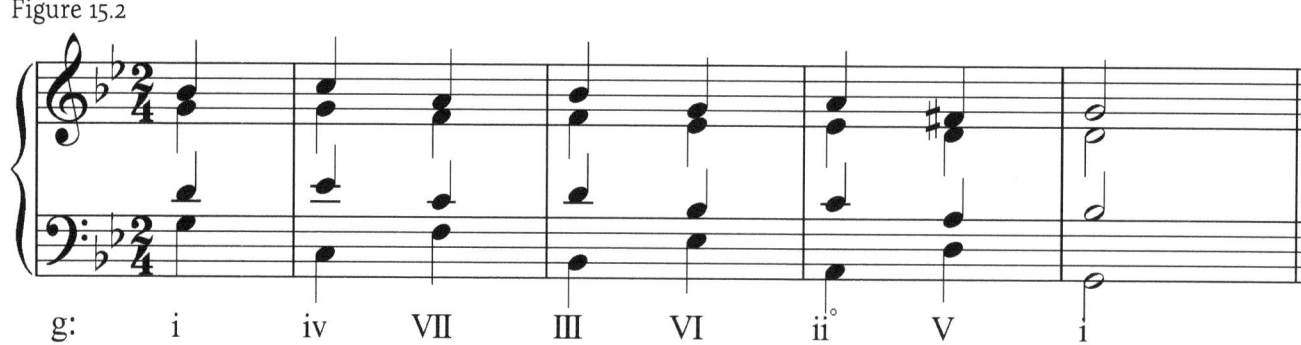

The descending 5ths sequence is effective in major keys (Figure 15.3). The chord qualities are different in this sequence. There are a number of rules that we have covered to this point that do not apply here. vii° is a diminished triad and not usually used in root position. However, it can be used in this sequence. The leading tone is doubled in vii°. Normally we do not double the leading tone but in order to maintain the sequential motion it is allowed. vii° moves to iii and not to I and $\hat{7}$ does not resolve to $\hat{1}$. It is not treated as a leading tone. A melodic augmented 4th occurs in the bass between IV and vii°. This interval does not stand out because we actually expect it as part of the sequential pattern.

Figure 15.3

G: I   IV   vii°   iii   vi   ii   V   I

2. Complete the following descending 5th sequence in four parts. Double the root in each chord.

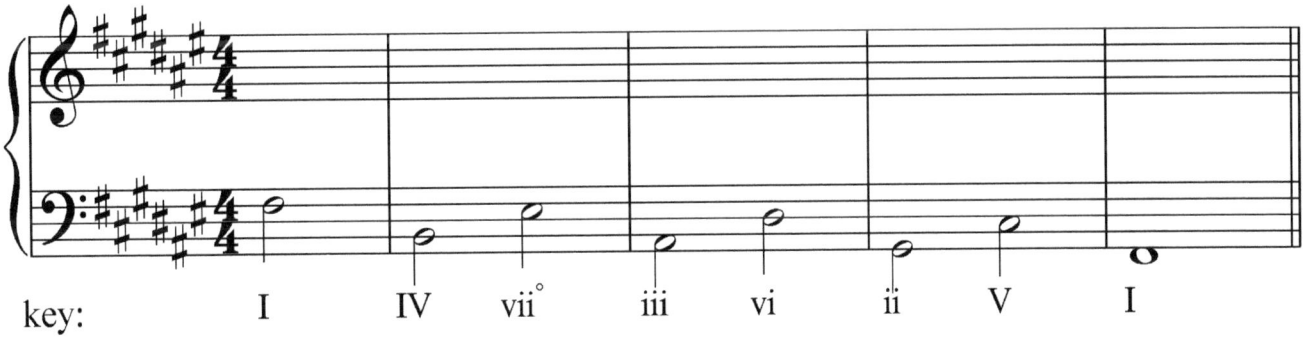

key: I   IV   vii°   iii   vi   ii   V   I

3. Harmonize the following melody in four parts using a series of descending 5ths.

f:

The descending 5ths sequence can often be seen in compositions in a shorter form. This shortened version is: I - iii - vi - ii - V - I (Figure 15.4). In this sequence, since the chord built on $\hat{7}$ is not used, all the chords keep their normal harmonic function.

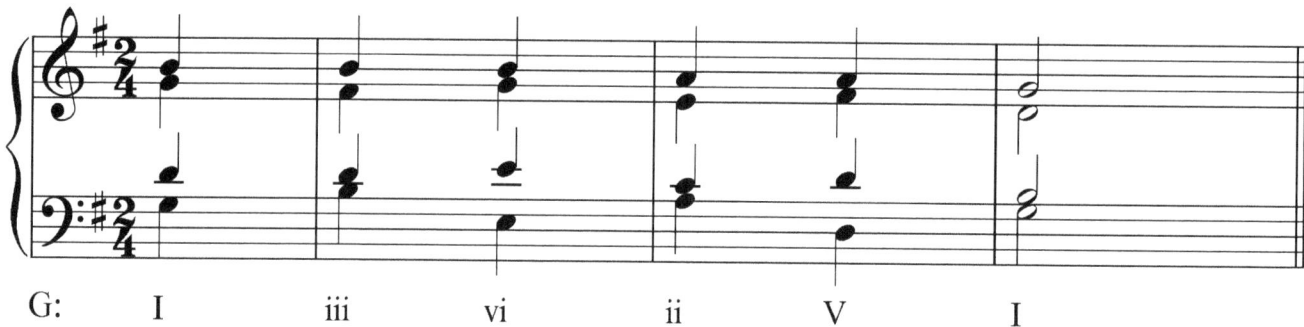

G: I   iii   vi   ii   V   I

The descending 5ths sequence may appear with alternating root position and first inversion chords. Figure 15.4 (a) illustrates this sequence with every second chord in first inversion. The sequential motion is maintained throughout. 15.4 (b) in the minor key, contains this sequence with alternating first inversion and root position chords. These sequences work in both major and minor keys. In minor keys $\hat{7}$ is not raised in VII and III because it is not functioning as the leading tone. It is raised in V at the end where a leading tone is needed for the authentic cadence.

Figure 15.4

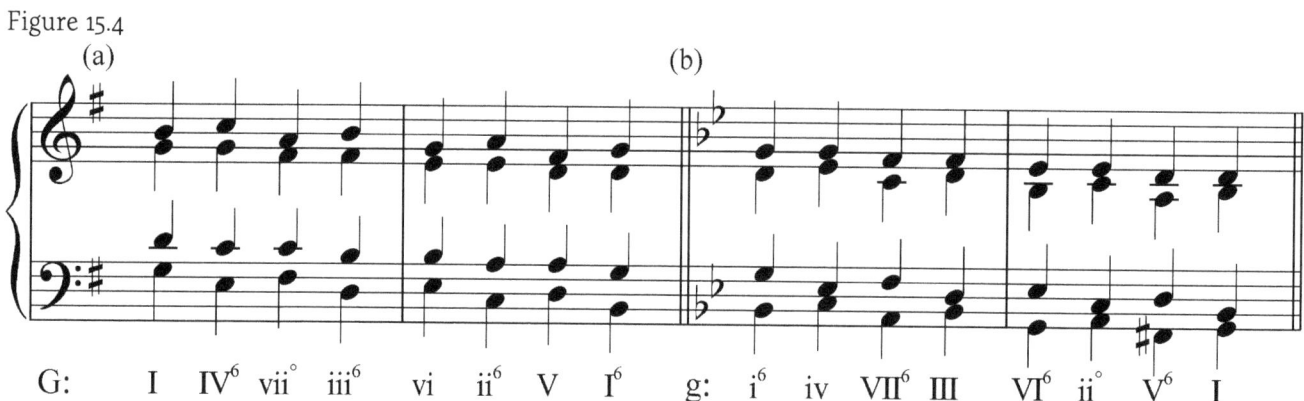

G: I IV^6 vii$^\circ$ iii^6 vi ii^6 V I^6 g: i^6 iv VII^6 III VI^6 ii$^\circ$ V^6 I

4. Complete the following sequences in four parts.

The Descending Thirds Sequence

If we build a sequence based on descending 3rds using root position chords, faulty parallel octaves and 5ths result as seen in Figure 15.5 (a). A common way to avoid this is to insert another root position chord between the 3rds as shown in 15.5 (b). When we do this we have a sequence where the bass moves by descending 4th and ascending 2nd. In this sequence the descending 3rds occur in every second chord.

Figure 15.5

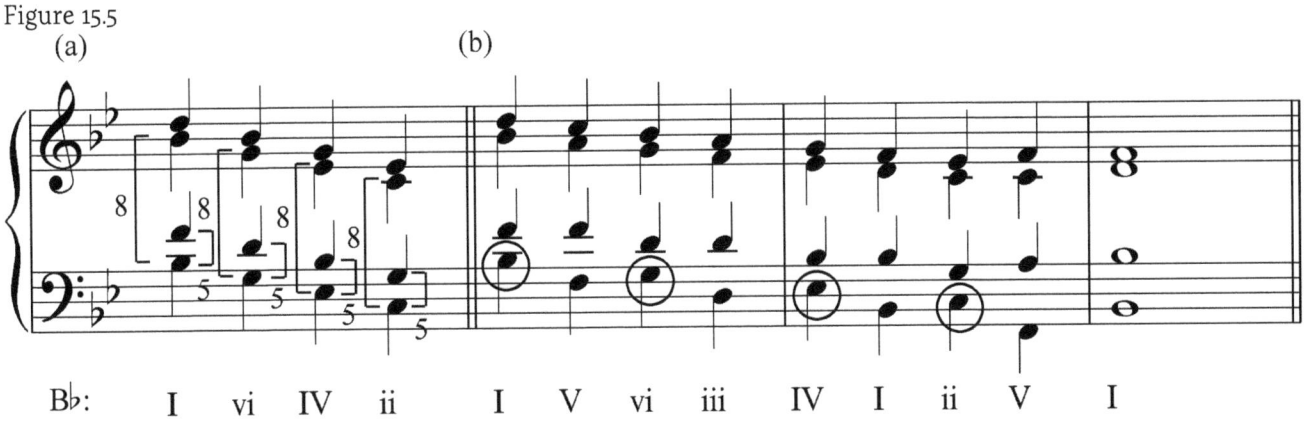

Many composers used this sequence in their work. Perhaps the most famous example of this is the famous Canon in D by Pachelbel. This piece consists of variations based on this sequence.

Johann Pachelbel
Canon in D major

Figure 15.6

This sequence is effective in minor keys. Here, v is a minor chord written without raised $\hat{7}$ in order to avoid a melodic augmented 2nd between $\hat{7}$ and $\hat{6}$ (Figure 15.7).

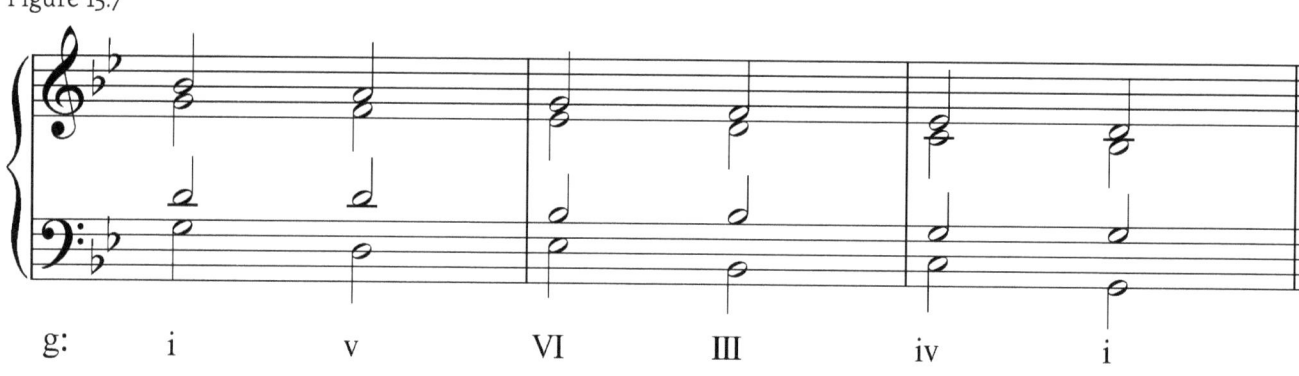

Figure 15.7

The sequence may also use first inversion chords. It is effecive when harmonizing a descending scale in the bass. The sequence is I - V⁶ - vi - iii⁶ - IV - I⁶. This can be completed with an authentic cadence using vii⁶ - I or V_3^4 - I as shown in Figure 15.8.

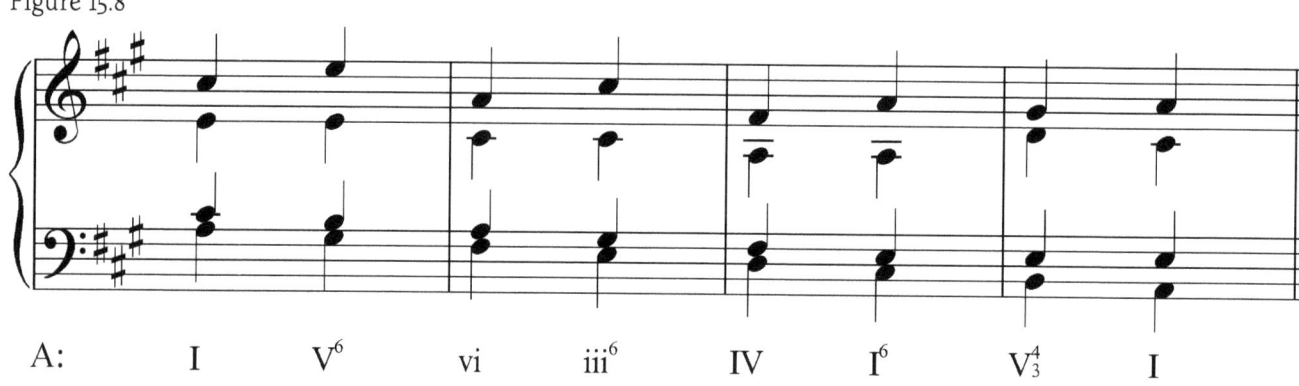

Figure 15.8

5. Write the following sequences in four parts.

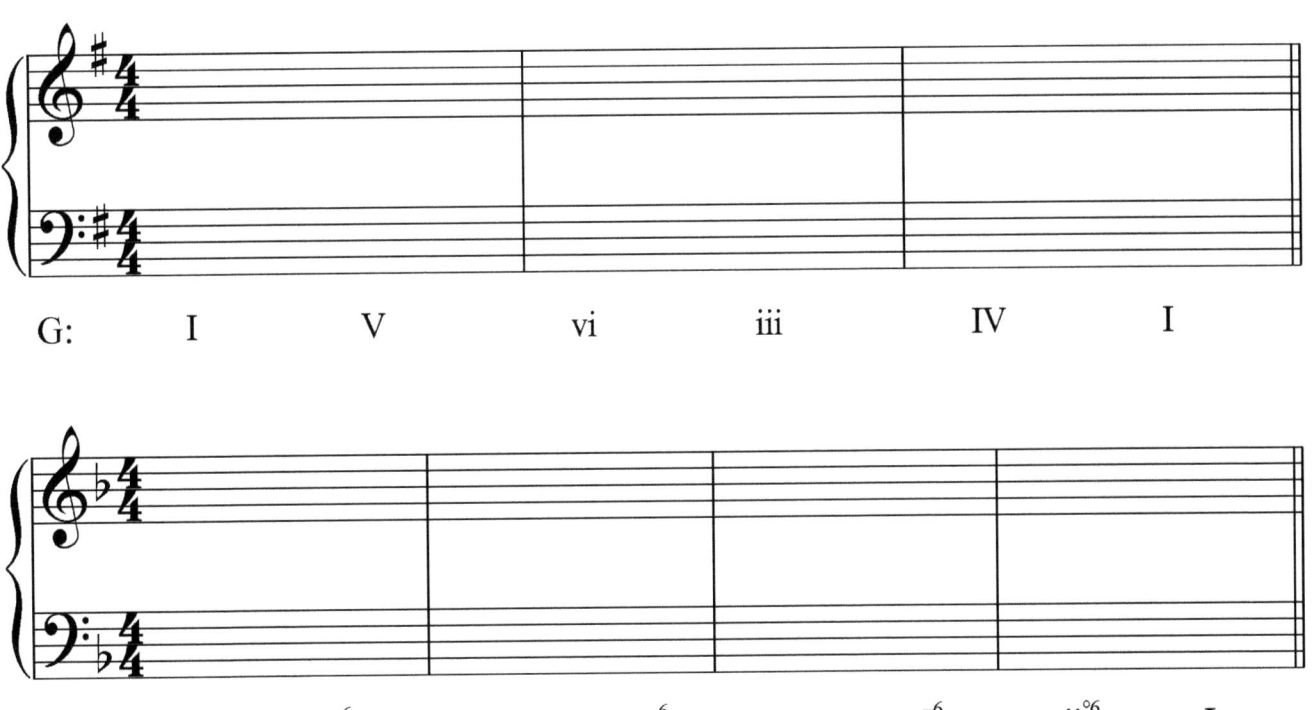

Chapter 15: The Subtonic

Harmonic Analysis

6. Provide chord symbols in the places indicated. State the type of sequence.

Wolfgang Amadeus Mozart
Piano Sonata, K. 545, I

G:

7. Provide a harmonic analysis of the following. State the type of sequence.

Vivace, ma non troppo

Ludwig van Beethoven
Piano Sonata, Op. 109, I

key:

16
Harmonic Rhythm

The rate of chord change or how often one chord progresses to another is known as *harmonic rhythm*. The rate at which the chords change may be slower than the rate of the actual notes heard. The opening of the Kuhlau Sonatina in Figure 16.1 gives the impression of a lot of activity with a lot of movement in the bass clef. However, the underlying harmonies are changing much more slowly. There is only one chord (I) for measures 1 to 4 and then one chord per measure for the next four measures. This pattern of chord changes forms the harmonic rhythm for the passage. Figure 16.2 is a representation of the harmonic rhythm of this passage. The harmonies are changing relatively slowly here so this is considered a slow harmonic rhythm. Often the harmonic rhythm is slower than any of the rhythms that are being played. Harmonic rhythm is very important in shaping the music. When the chords change, can be as important as the chords themselves. The harmonic rhythm reinforces the natural rhythm of the melody, in which an alternating pattern of strong and weak beats is created by using longer notes at the beginning of each measure.

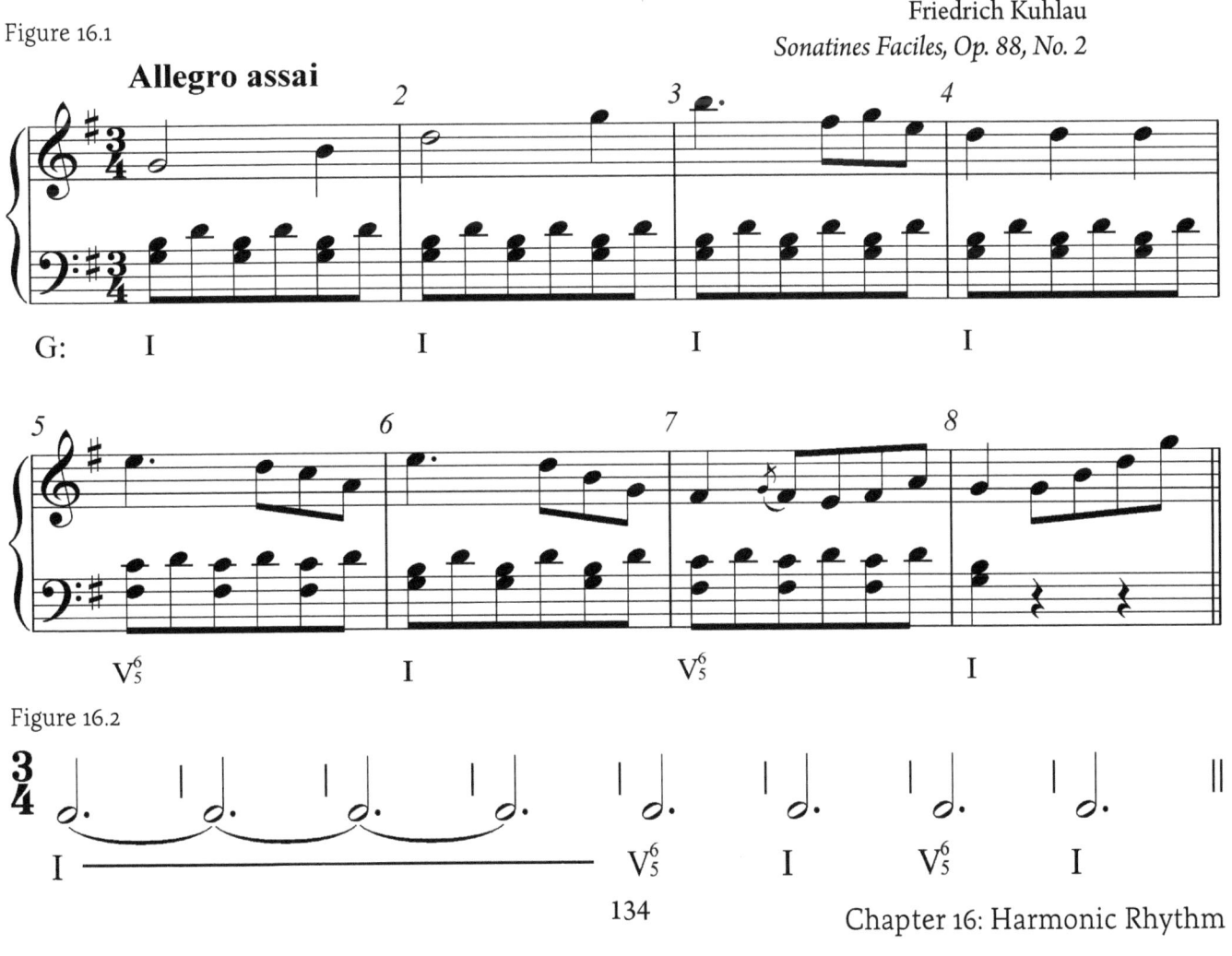

The harmonic rhythm in Figure 16.3 is much different than the previous example. This is a fast harmonic rhythm. This is a common feature of Chorale harmonizations where the chords often change on every beat. Figure 16.4 is a representation of the harmonic changes in this passage. The terms *slow* and *fast* in reference to harmonic rhythm have nothing to do with the tempo or speed of the piece. They refer to how fast the chords change. If the chords change frequently the harmonic rhythm is *fast*. If they change less often, the harmonic rhythm is *slow*. A piece where the chords change once per measure or less has a slow harmonic rhythm. A piece where the chords change on every beat or more has a fast harmonic rhythm.

Figure 16.3

Johann Sebasian Bach
Chorale: O Herre Gott, dein göttlich Wort

G: I vi iii IV V⁷ vi V I

Figure 16.4

I vi iii IV V⁷ vi V I

1. Provide a harmonic analysis of the following excerpts. State the harmonic rhythm on the blank staff provided below each example.

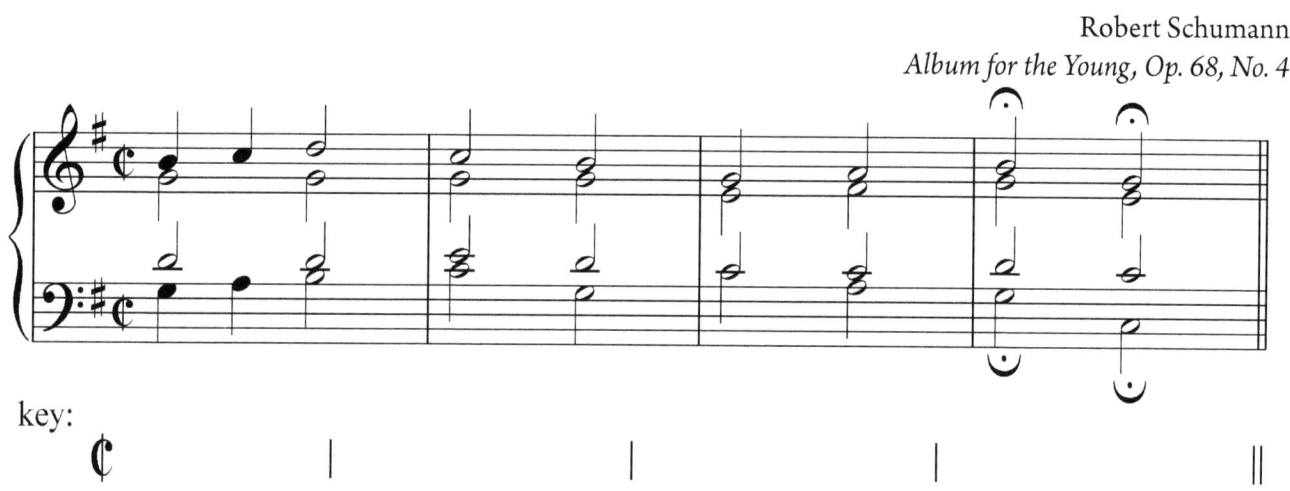

Robert Schumann
Album for the Young, Op. 68, No. 4

key:

Chapter 16: Harmonic Rhythm

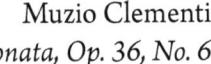

Allegro con spirito

key:

Wolfgang Amadeus Mozart
Sonatina No. 6

Allegro

key:

Rhythmic Placement

It is important that chord changes support the meter. There are a few things to watch out for when repeating chords. A repeated chord sounds like an extention or prolongation and creates very little rhythmic activity. Changing a chord sounds rhythmically stronger than repeating a chord. Avoid repeating a chord from a weak beat to a strong beat as in Figure 16.5 (a). The exception to this is when the opening tonic is repeated at the beginning of a piece 16.5 (d). In this case it emphasizes and enhances tonic harmony. A chord repeated from a strong beat to a weak beat is fine as in 16.5 (b). It is okay to hold a chord from a strong beat through a weak beat to a repetition on another strong beat as in 16.5 (c).

Repeating a bass note from a weak beat to strong beat while changing the chord can affect the meter and should be avoided as illustrated in Figure 16.6 (a). This neutralizes the natural accent in the music and results in a weak progression.

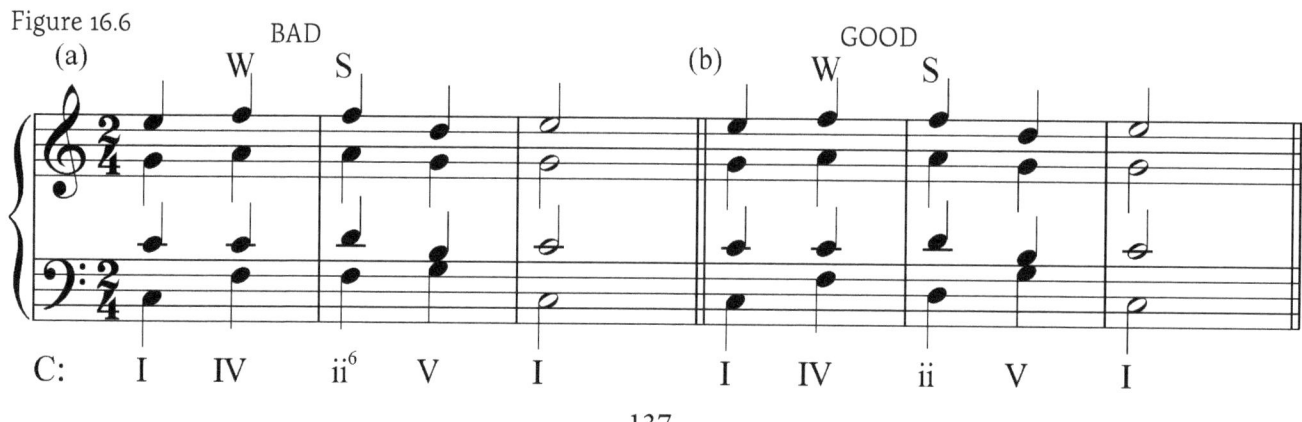

Chapter 16: Harmonic Rhythm

17

The Supertonic Seventh

We have studied the dominant seventh extensively. In Chapter 3 we learned that we can built a seventh chord on any degree of the scale. This chapter deals with the seventh chord built on the supertonic ($\hat{2}$). The function of the *supertonic seventh* is the same as the function of the supertonic chord: It is a predominant chord that precedes dominant harmony.

Figure 17.1 illustrates the two types of structural supertonic sevenths. In major keys ii^7 is a minor triad with a minor 7th above the root and is considered a *minor 7th chord*. In minor keys ii$^{\varnothing 7}$ is a diminished triad with a minor 7th above the root and is considered a *half diminished 7th chord*. The supertonic is built on scale degrees $\hat{2}$, $\hat{4}$, $\hat{6}$, and $\hat{1}$. The dissonant note in this chord is $\hat{1}$, which is the 7th of the chord.

Figure 17.1

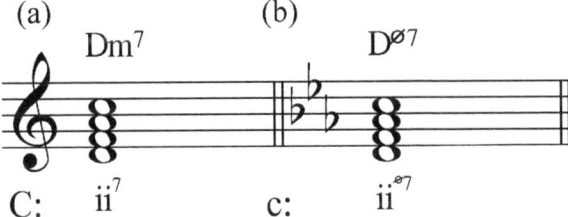

After the dominant seventh, the supertonic seventh is the most commonly used diatonic seventh chord. The inversions of ii^7 are labeled in the same way as the inversions of V^7. Figure 17.2 shows ii^7 and its inversions. Make note of both the functional and the root/quality chord symbols.

Figure 17.2

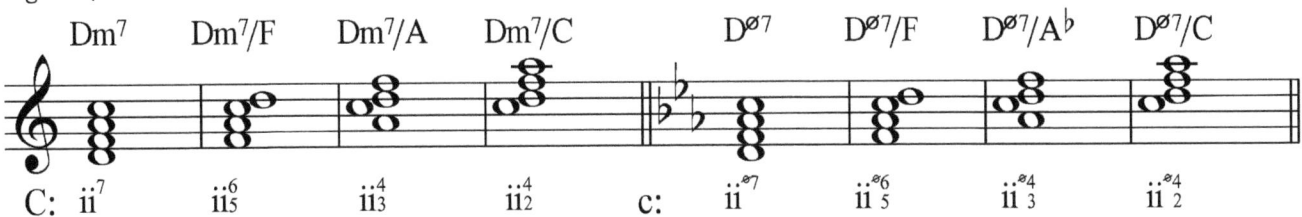

Figure 17.3 (a) contains the supertonic seventh written for four voices. Figure 17.3 (b) is a progression using ii⁷ as a predominant before V⁷. In this example, ii⁷ comes after IV as an extension of the predominant area. There are three common tones between IV and ii⁷ (C, A, and F) and they are all repeated as common tones. This includes the 7th (C) which is prepared in the tenor with common tone motion. It then resolves downward by step to the third of V⁷. Like V⁷, the 7th of ii⁷ must always resolve downward by step in its resolution to dominant harmony. Note in this example the 7th of V⁷ (F) is prepared in the soprano and resolves downward by step to the third of I. A couple of important points to consider when using ii⁷ are:

- *Prepare the 7th of ii⁷ with common tone motion from the previous chord.*
- *Always resolve the 7th of the supertonic seventh down by step.*

Figure 17.3

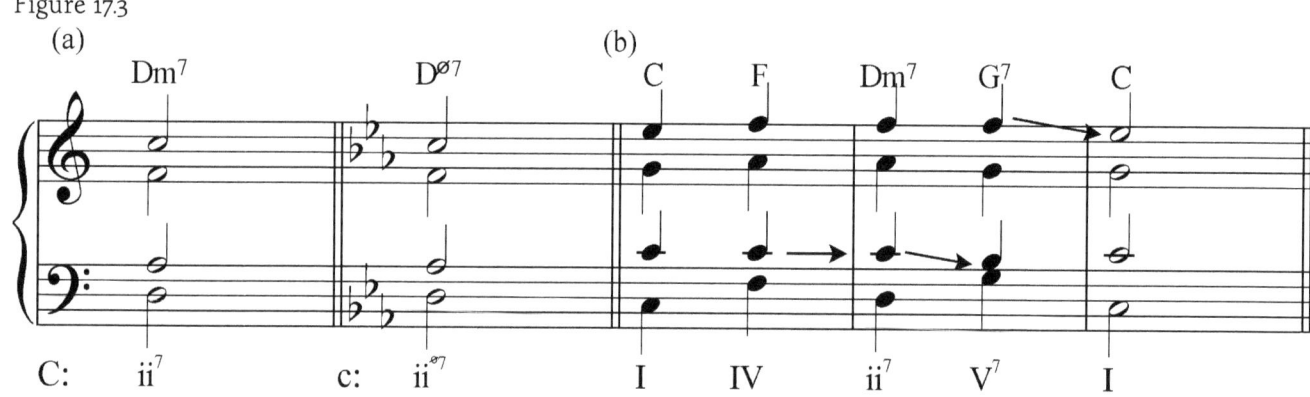

1. Write ii⁷ chords in four parts in the following keys.

2. Name the keys. Complete the following progressions in four parts.

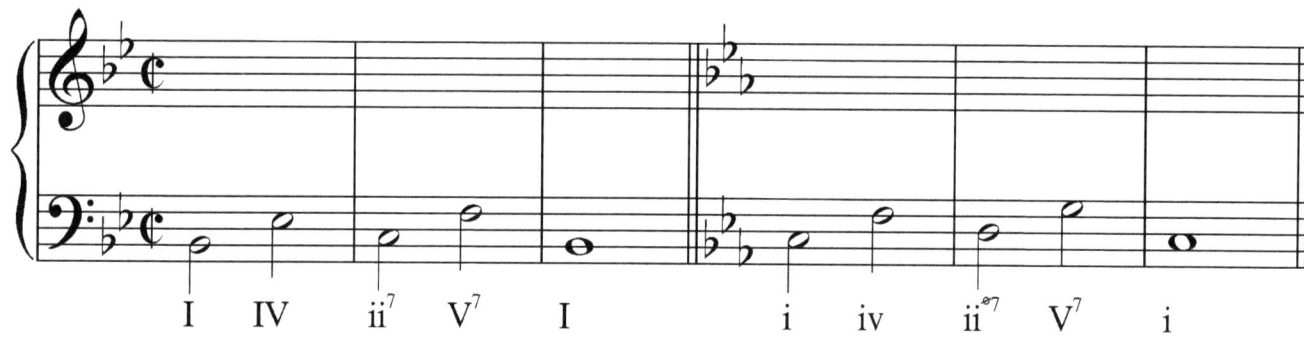

Unlike the root position ii triad which is often avoided in minor keys, ii^7 is used in root position in both major and minor keys. It typically occurs in the progression I - ii^7 - V^7 - I. ii^7 may be used as a complete chord containing the root, 3rd, 5th and 7th as shown in Figure 17.4 (b) or as an incomplete chord with the 5th omitted and the root or 3rd doubled. Figure 17.4 (a) contains a ii^7 with a doubled root, 3rd and 7th.

Figure 17.4

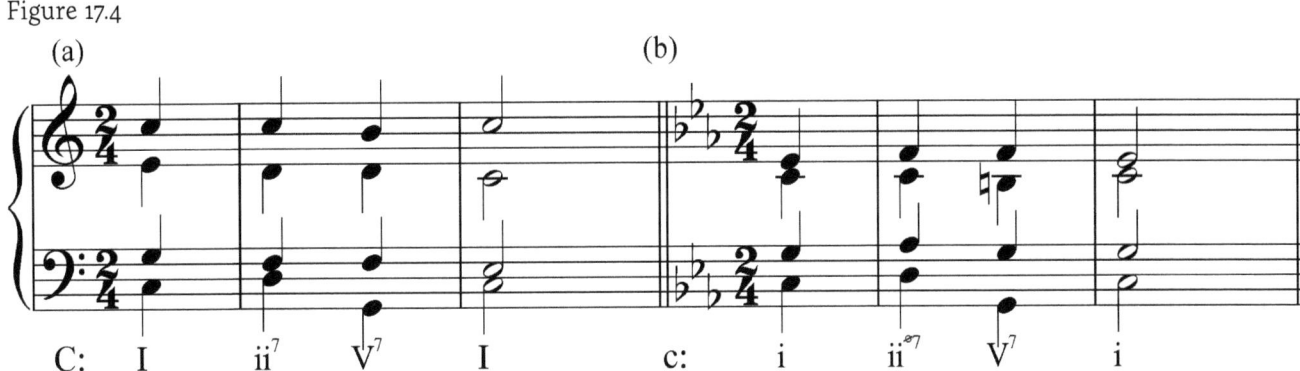

In the progression I - ii^7 faulty parallel motion can result as shown in Figure 17.5 (a). 17.5 (b) avoids this error by omitting the 5th and doubling the 3rd in ii^7. 17.5 (c) corrects the issue with a doubled root, 3rd, and 7th in ii^7.

ii^7 leads well to both V and V^7. Figure 17.5 (d) and (e) illustrates this progression using a complete and an incomplete ii^7 chord. In each case the 7th of ii^7 resolves downward by step.

Figure 17.5

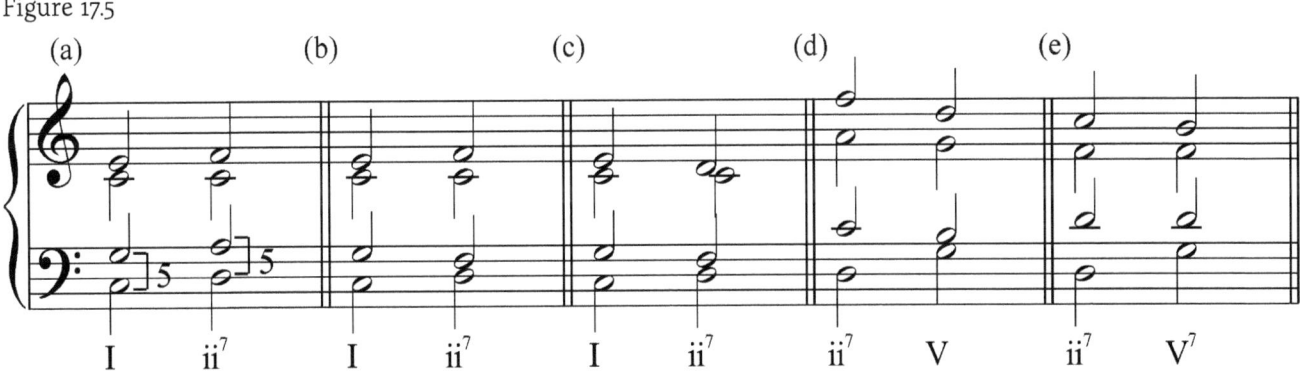

3. Name the keys. Complete the following progressions in four parts.

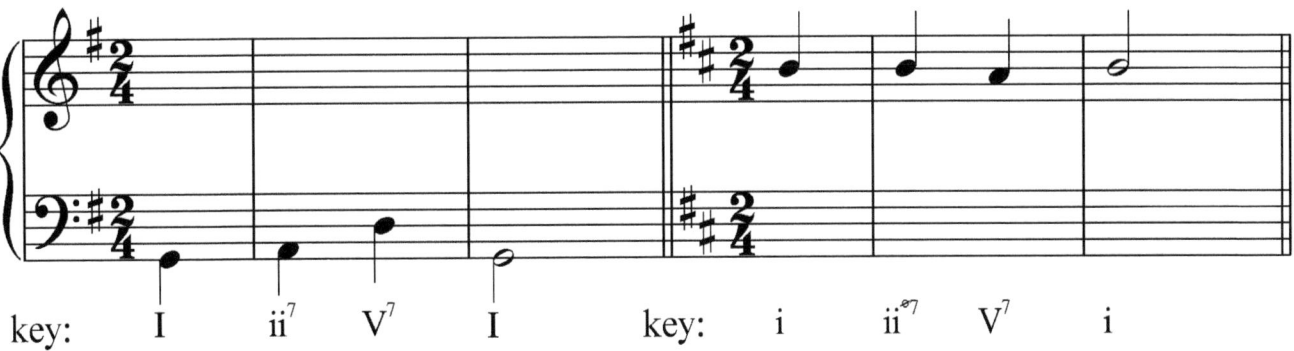

Chapter 17: The Supertonic 7th

The Supertonic Seventh in First Inversion

The supertonic seventh in first inversion (ii^6_5) is a very effective and commonly used chord. The strong melodic motion from $\hat{4}$ to $\hat{5}$ in the bass makes this a very powerful predominant chord.

ii^6_5 usually moves to V and not to V^7. Figure 17.6 (a) illustrates this progression. Here the 7th of ii^7 is prepared with common tone motion in the tenor and resolves downward by step to $\hat{7}$ which is the 3rd of chord V.

Figure 17.6(b) is another common progression using ii^6_5, ii^6_5 and V^4_2 have the same bass, $\hat{4}$, and this allows for a very smooth progression over the stationary bass. Since the 7th of V^4_2 is in the bass and must resolve down by step, it moves to I^6. The supertonic 7th in first inversion must be a complete chord containing the root, 3rd, 5th and 7th.

Figure 17.6

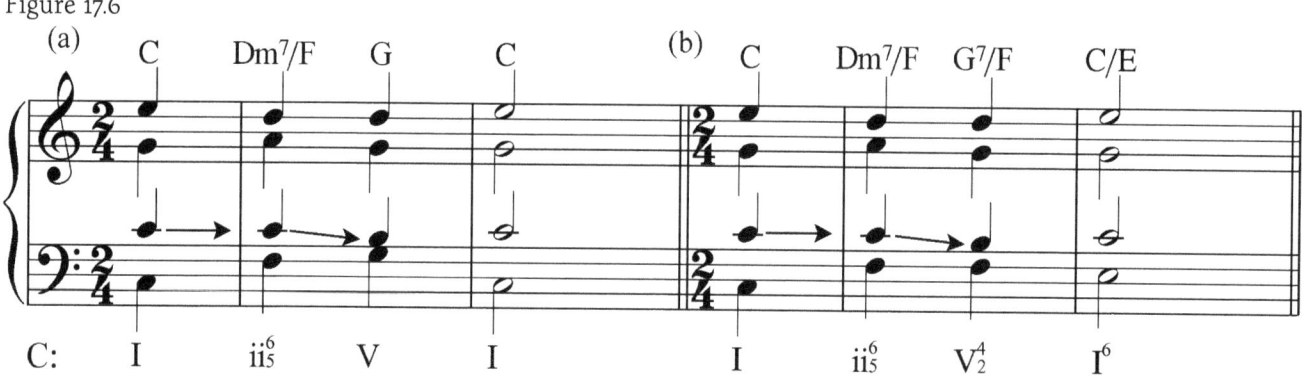

4. Complete the following progressions in four parts.

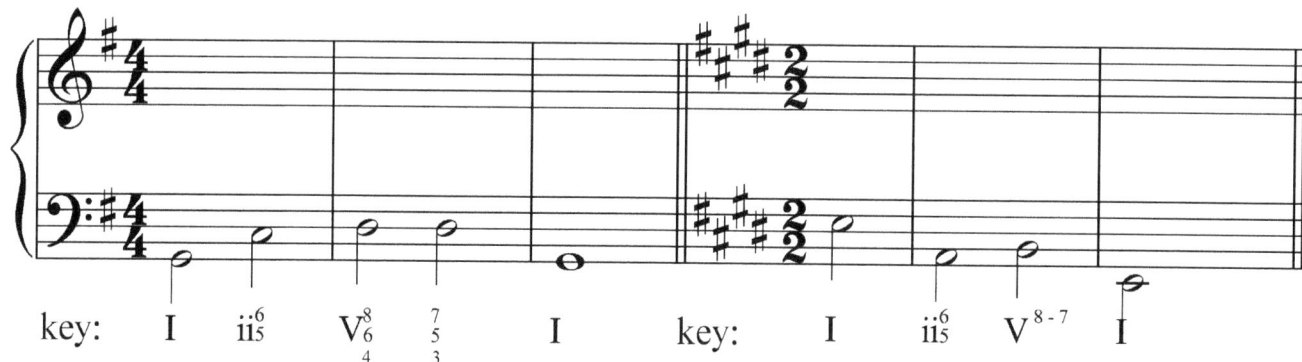

ii$^6_5$ often follows I^6 which may occur as a prolongation of the opening tonic. To avoid faulty parallels when writing this progression it is best to double the 5th in I^6 as shown in Figure 17.7 (a) or leap in one of the voices as is 17.7 (b).

In Chapter 14 we studied chord vi followed by ii^6 in a bass line descending in thirds. ii$^6_5$ may replace ii^6 in the progression I - vi - ii $^6_5$ V - I as shown in 17.7 (c). In this progresson there are two common tones between vi and ii$^6_5$. It is best to repeat these common tones in the same voices. This also prepares the 7th of ii$^6_5$.

Figure 17.7

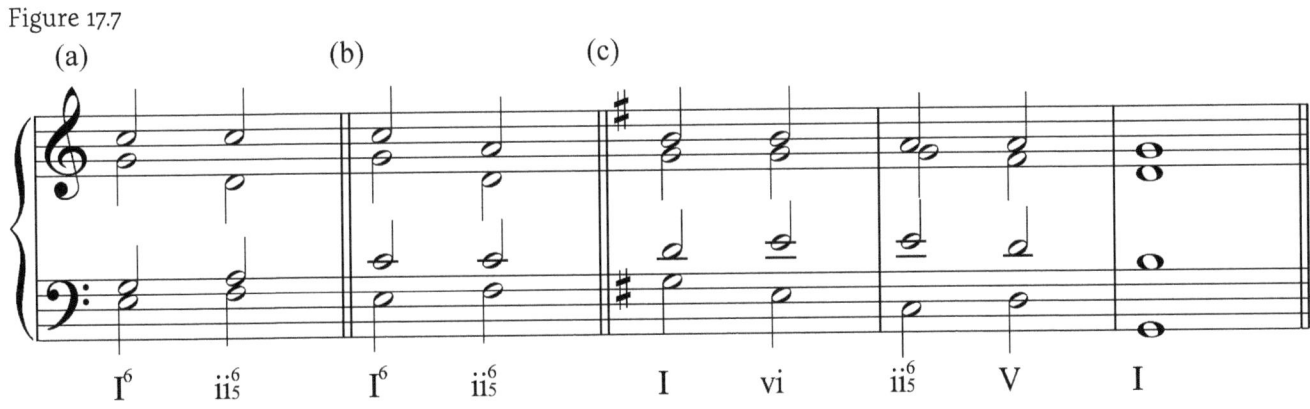

5. Complete the following progressions in four parts.

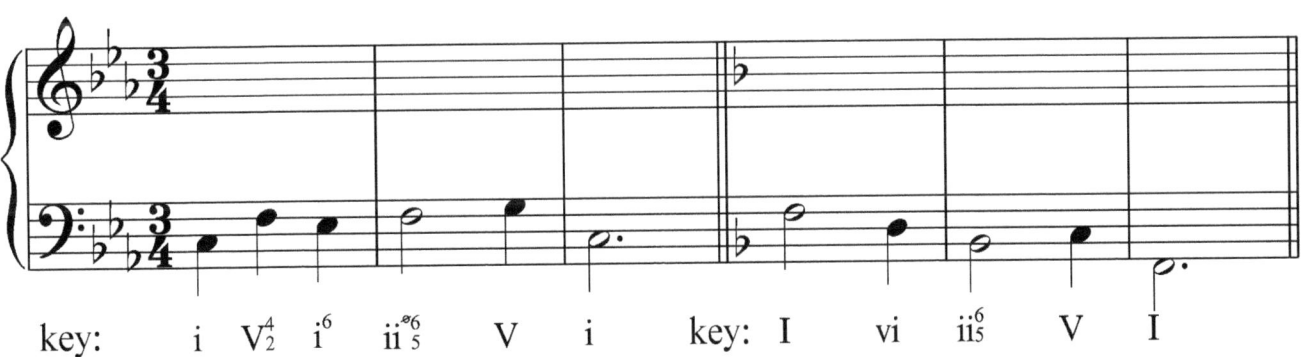

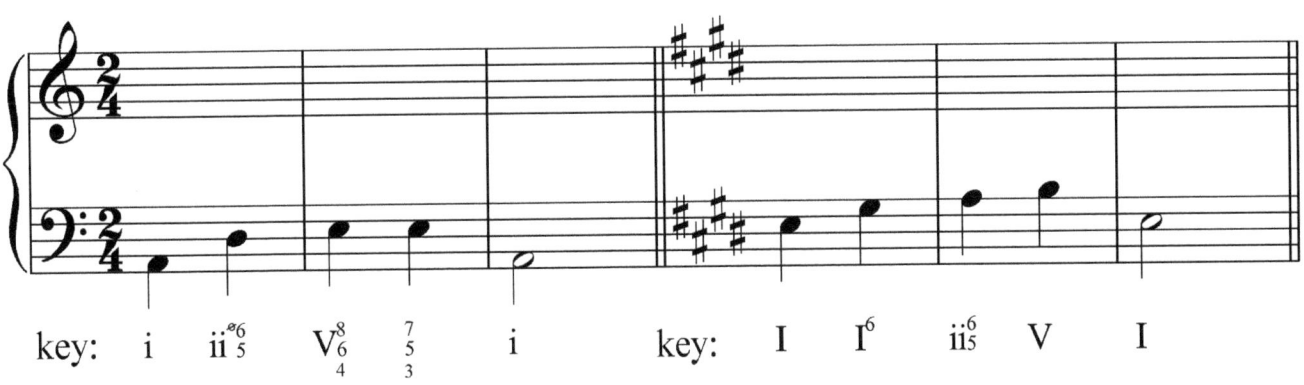

Other Inversions of ii⁷

The least commonly used supertonic 7th chord is ii$^4_3$. It can be used in the progression shown in Figure 17.8 (a). As with all supertonic 7th chords, the 7th is prepared with common tone motion and resolves downward by step.

ii$^4_2$ has the 7th in the bass and since it must resolve down, it never precedes to a root position dominant. It is frequently used as shown in 17.8 (b) in a prolongation of the opening tonic. The 7th is prepared with common tone motion in the bass and resolves downward by step to the first inversion of the dominant 7th.

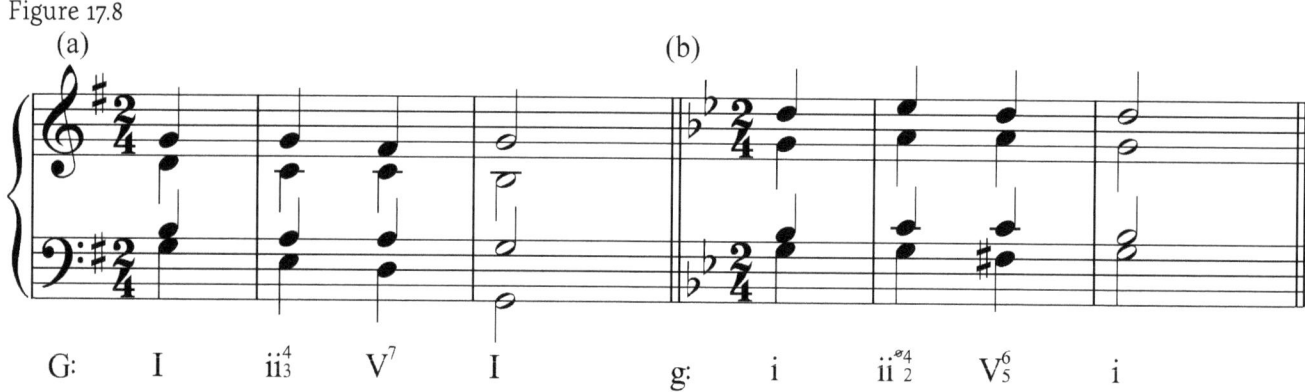

Figure 17.8

6. Complete the following figured basses in four parts.

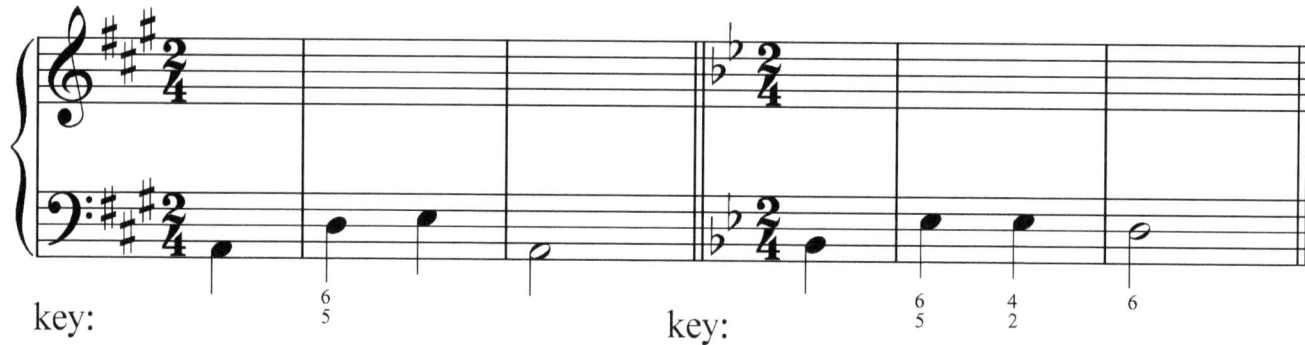

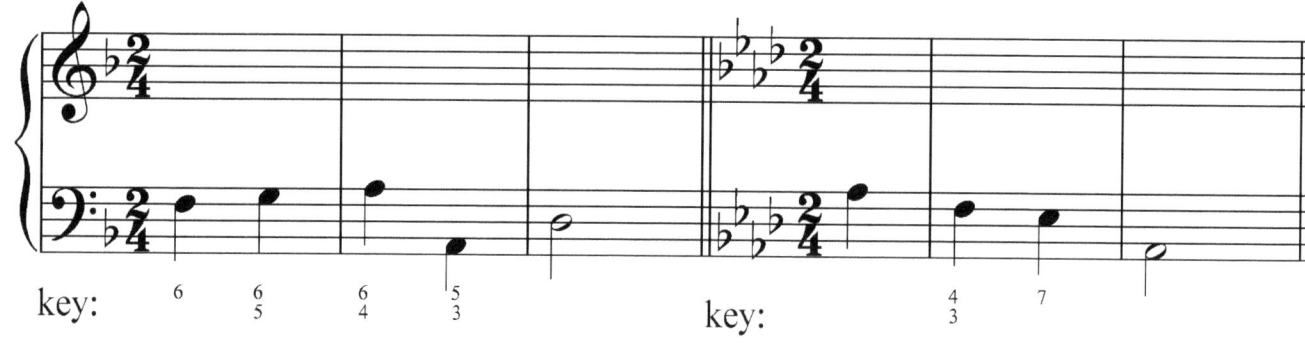

Harmonic Analysis

7. Provide a harmonic analysis of the following examples.

Johann Sebastian Bach
WTC I, Prelude in C major, BWV 846

key:

Robert Schumann
Papillons, Op. 2

key:

Wolfgang Amadeus Mozart
Quartet, K. 465

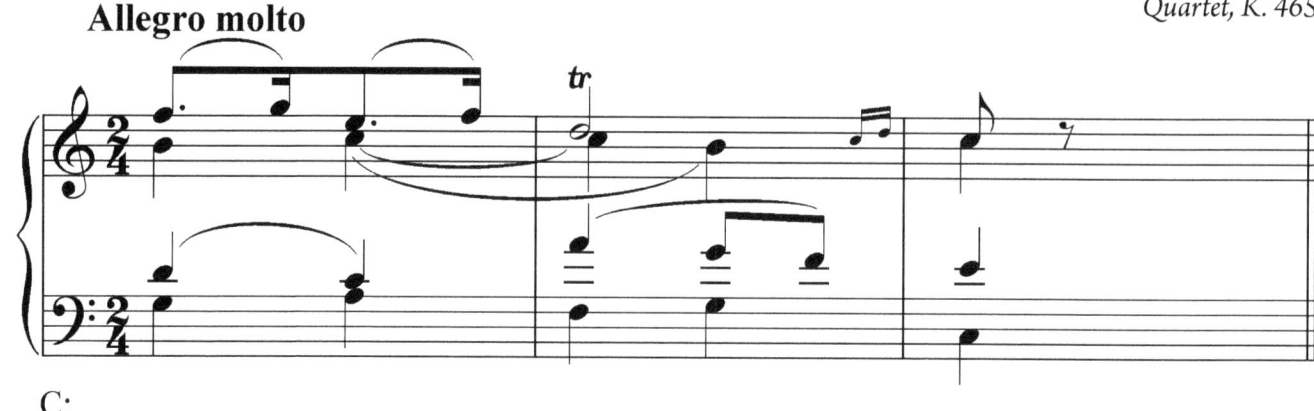

C:

Johann Sebastian Bach
Chorale: Herr Christ, der ein'ge Gott's-Sohn

B♭:

Frederic Chopin
Prelude, Op. 28, No. 22

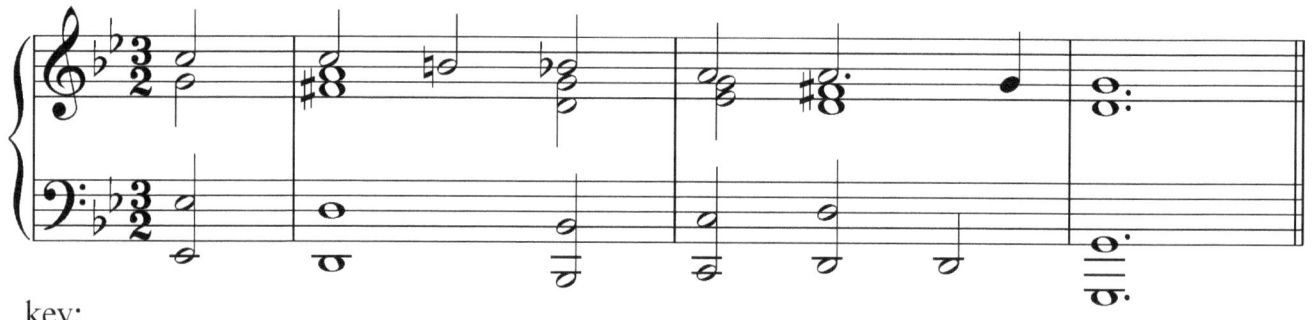

g:

Henry Purcell
When I am Laid in Earth, Dido and Aeneas, Act III

key:

Franz Schubert
"Ständchen" from Schwanengesang

key:

George Frideric Handel
"He was Despised" from Messiah

key:

Wolfgang Amadeus Mozart
Symphony, No. 41, K. 551. IV

key:

18
Secondary Dominants

The term *tonicization* is used to refer to a concept in which one of the chords in a key becomes a temporary tonic. Any major or minor chord can become a temporary tonic when it is preceded by its dominant. In Figure 18.1 the V in m. 3 becomes a temporary tonic because it is preceded by its dominant, V^6_5 of G major. This piece is in C major. The F# is not a note of C major and reflects the key of the temporary tonic (G major). We still hear the G chord as V of C major, but it is made a temporary tonic because of the D^7 chord that precedes it. D^7 is not a chord in C major and this example moves to G major for an instant. It then continues with an authentic cadence in C major. The D^7 chord is considered a *secondary dominant*.

Figure 18.1 — Johann Sebastian Bach, Chorale: Ach Gott, wie manches Herzeleid

V^7 of V

$\hat{5}$ is the most frequently tonicized scale degree. The dominant 7th of the dominant is symbolized V^7/V. The verbal expression for this is "five seven of five." V^7/V is built on scale degree $\hat{2}$ and contains a raised $\hat{4}$. This raised note functions as a temporary leading tone of $\hat{5}$ and should not be doubled. The secondary dominant 7th resolves exactly as the regular dominant 7th. The 7th falls and the leading note (#$\hat{4}$) rises to $\hat{5}$, resulting in a V chord with a tripled root and 3rd. V^7/V is a major-minor 7th chord and in minor keys we need to raise $\hat{6}$ as well as $\hat{4}$ in order to achieve this sonority. Figure 18.2 illustrates this progression in the major and minor key. 18.2 (c) contains the melodic gesture $\hat{4}$ - #$\hat{4}$ - $\hat{5}$ which is commonly harmonized using V^7/V. It is best to keep the chromatic semitone $\hat{4}$ - #$\hat{4}$ (here, G - G#) in the same voice to avoid a *cross relation*. A cross relation occurs when chromatically related pitches occur in two different adjacent voices. Cross relations create a dissonance between two voices, and the smoothest voice leading is achieved by keeping the chromatic semitone in the same voice.

Figure 18.2

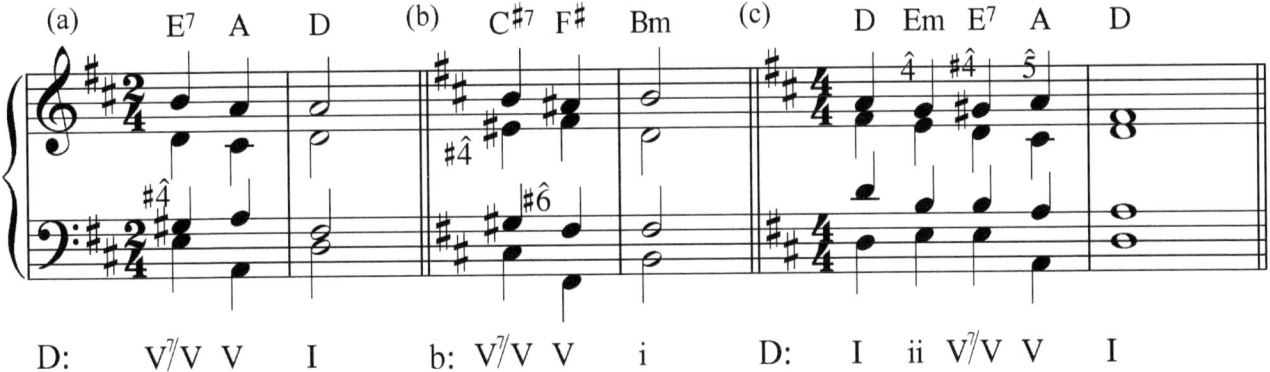

1. Write the following chords in four parts.

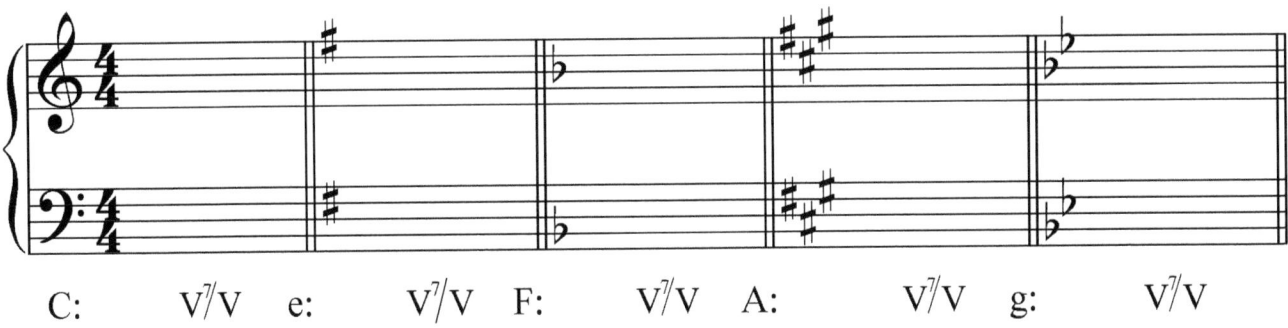

2. Name the keys and write the following progressions in four parts.

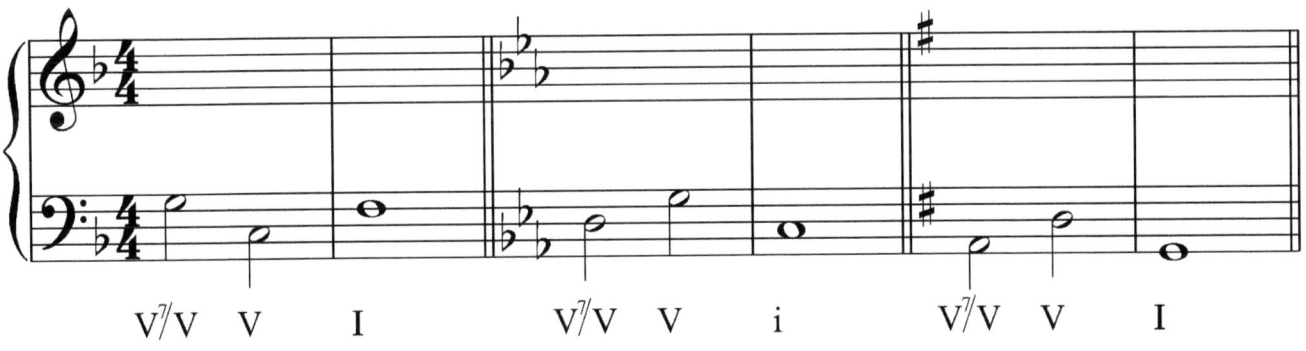

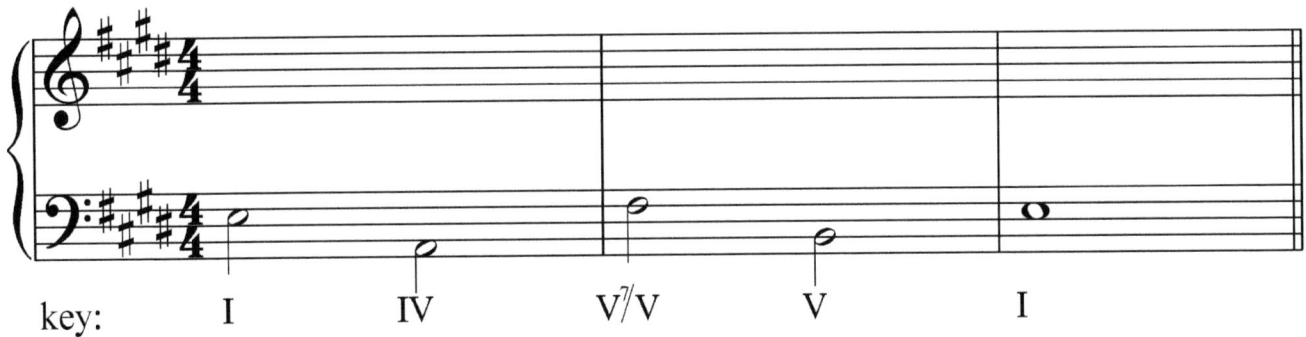

It is possible to use V^7/V in inversion as illustrated in Figure 18.3. All of these progressions are effective. V^4_2/V resolves to V^6 since the 7th is in the bass and must resolve downward by step as seen in 18.3 (c).

Figure 18.3

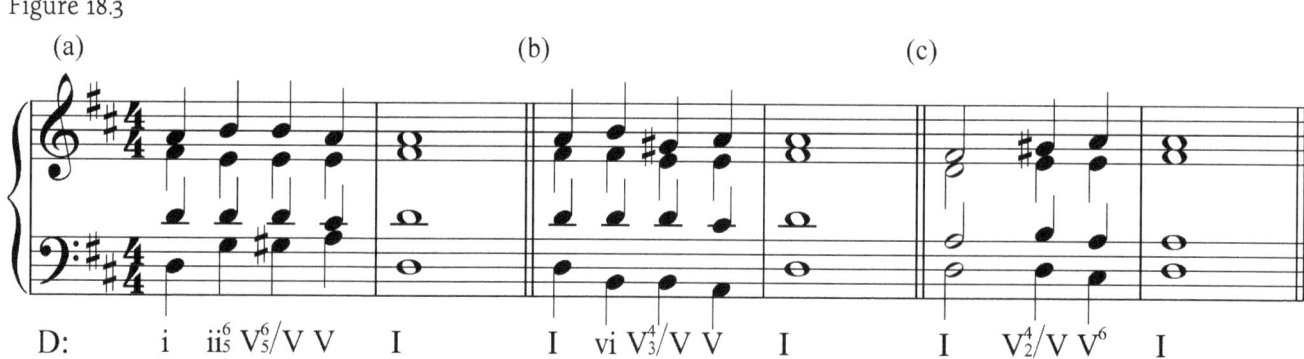

3. Write the following chords in four parts.

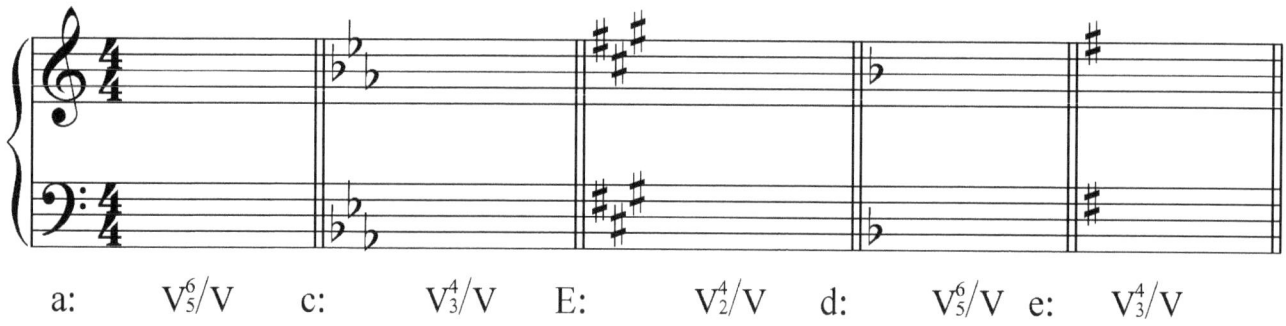

a: V^6_5/V c: V^4_3/V E: V^4_2/V d: V^6_5/V e: V^4_3/V

4. Write the following progressions in four parts.

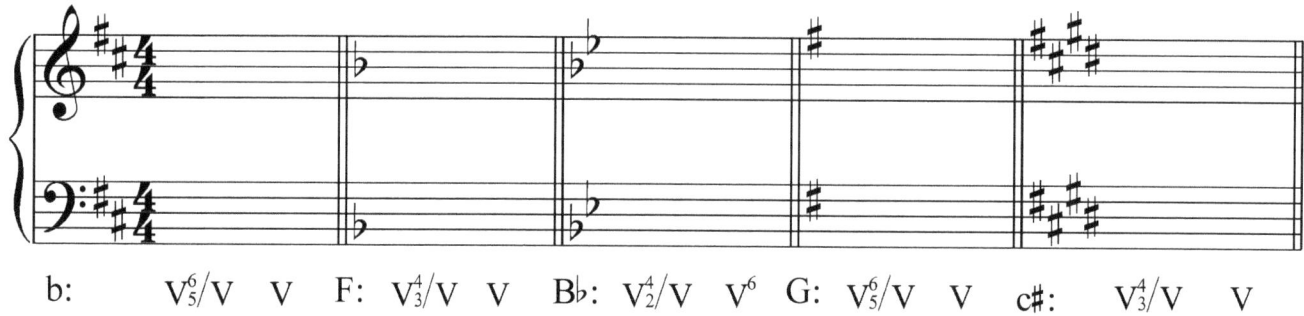

b: V^6_5/V V   F: V^4_3/V V   B♭: V^4_2/V V^6 G: V^6_5/V V   c♯: V^4_3/V V

5. Name the keys and write the following progressions in four parts.

The Secondary Leading Tone Chord - vii°6/V

Although V⁷ and its inversions are used commonly for secondary dominants, V/V or V⁶/V may also be used to tonicize the dominant as shown in Figure 18.4 (a) and (b).

Another common dominant function chord used as a secondary dominant is vii°⁶/V. 18.4 (c) illustrates this chord. In this example F♯ is not part of C major and its pull to G creates a tonicization of V. Since vii° is a diminished chord it is used in first inversion. The temporary leading tone (F♯) is not doubled. The 3rd of vii°⁶, which is the bass note, is doubled.

It is important to note that the temporary leading tone in all secondary dominant progressions is never doubled.

Figure 18.4

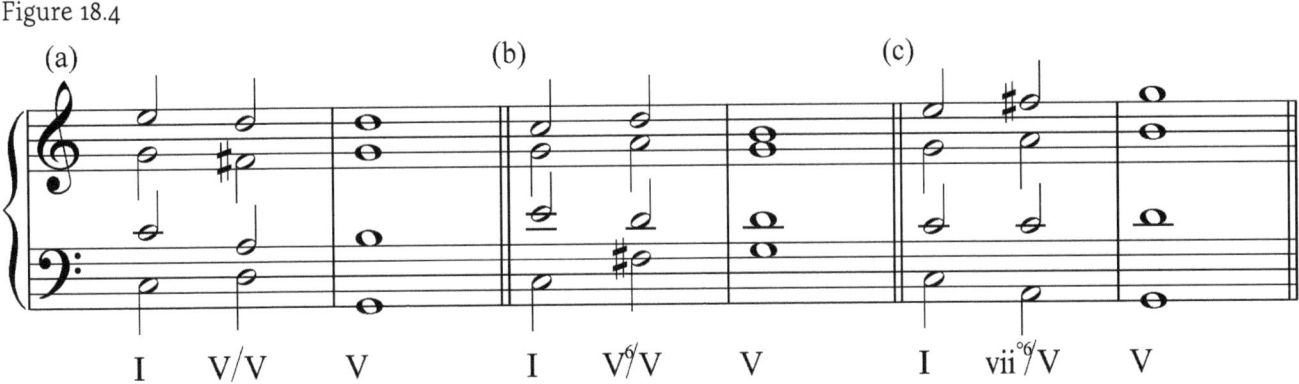

Chapter 18: Secondary Dominants

6. Complete the following progressions in four parts.

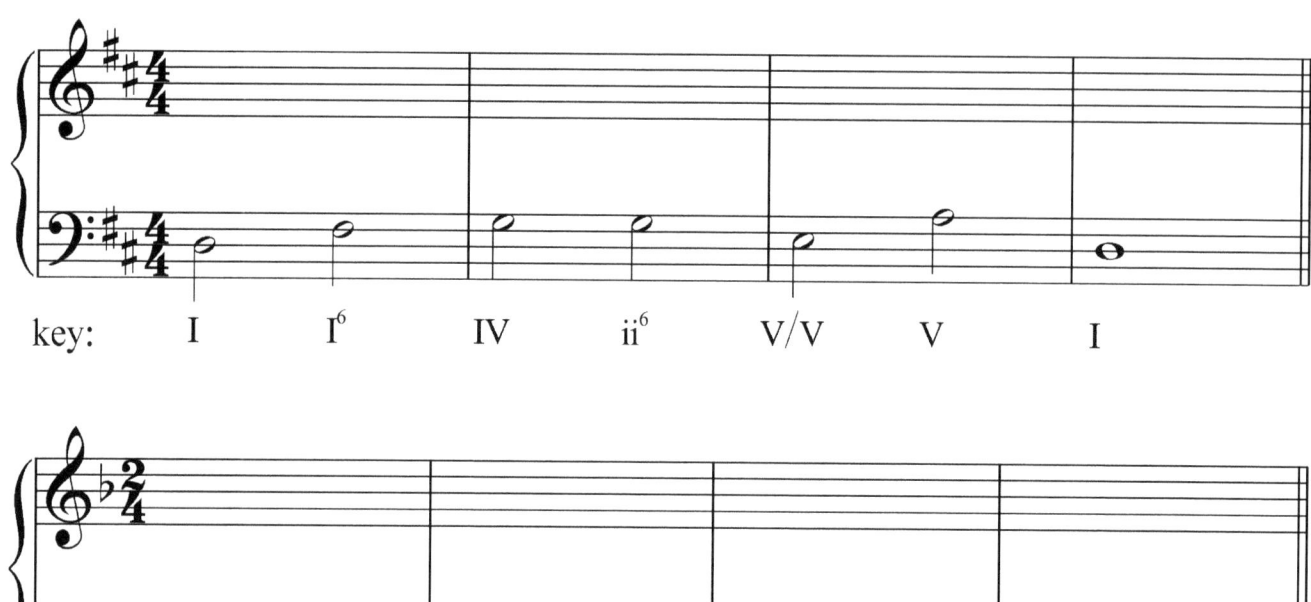

7. Harmonize the following melodies which contain secondary dominants.

Harmonic Analysis

8. Provide a harmonic analysis of the following using functional chord symbols.

Robert Schumann
Album for the Young, Op. 68, No. 4

key:

Johann Sebastian Bach
Chorale 69: Komm, heiliger Geist, Herre Gott

key:

152 Chapter 18: Secondary Dominants

Joseph Haydn
Symphony No. 94, II

Andante

key:

Johann Sebastian Bach
Chorale 106: Jesu Leiden, Pein un Tod

key:

Chapter 18: Secondary Dominants

Joseph Haydn
String Quartet, Op. 76, No. 4, III

key:

Johann Sebastian Bach
Chorale 102: Ermuntre dich, mein schwacher Geist

key:

Chapter 18: Secondary Dominants

19
Modulation

All of the music we have studied thus far stays in the same key. Secondary dominants provide some tonal variation but are too short to reflect an actual change of key. Most compositions change keys. Changing key in piece of music provides tonal variety and often affects the form and structure of the music. The process of establishing a new key or tonality using a chord progression is called *modulation*. Unlike tonicization, modulation involves several chords in the new key and causes the tonal center of a piece of music to change.

Figure 19.1 contains a tonicization of V. The dominant, E major, assumes a tonic role for a brief instant and the music immediately returns to A major. After the tonicization, the phrase ends with a perfect authentic cadence in the original key of A major. It does not stay in E major.

Figure 19.1

Johann Sebastian Bach
Chorale 106: Jesu Leiden, Pein und Tod

A: V^6_5/V $V^{8\ 7}$ I

Figure 19.2 contains a modulation. Measure 2 contains the dominant of V (a B major chord) moving to V (E major), and the music stays in E major. It does not return to the original key of A major and the second phrase is entirely in the new key, E major. This is too long to be considered a tonicization and is a modulation to the dominant key.

Figure 19.2

Johann Sebastian Bach
Chorale 156: Ach Gott, wie manches Herzeleid

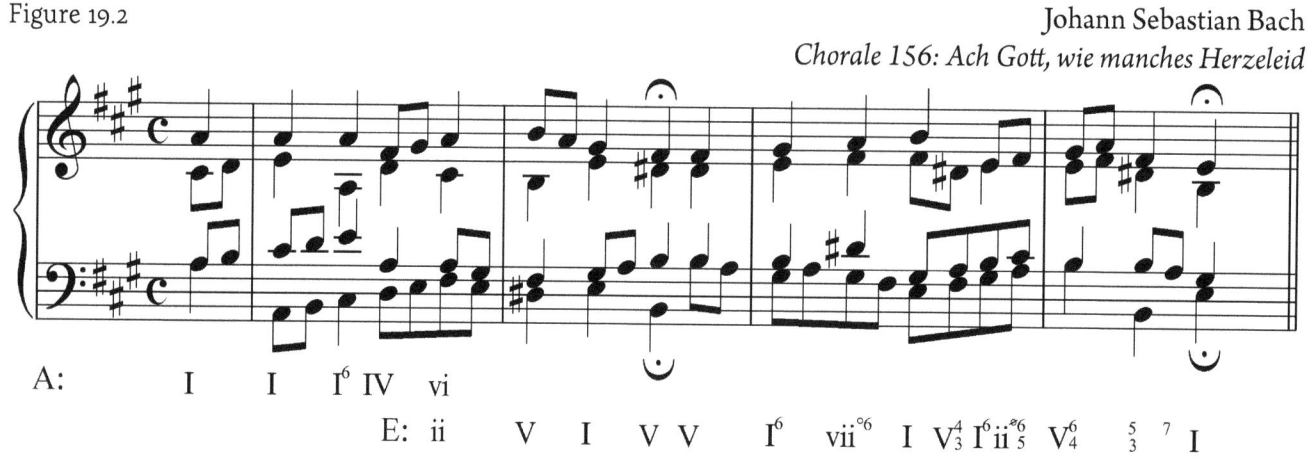

A: I I I^6 IV vi

E: ii V I V V I^6 vii^{o6} I V^4_3 $I^6 ii^{o6}_5$ V^6_4 $^{5\ 7}_3$ I

Closely Related Keys

In modulation, key relationships are very important. Some keys are farther away from a tonal center than others. In this chapter we will learn to modulate to *closely related keys*. Closely related keys have key signatures that differ from one another by not more than one sharp or flat. The five keys that are closely related to any key are:

- The relative major or minor of the original key.
- The relative major or minor keys with one less sharp or flat in the key signature.
- The relative major or minor keys with one more sharp or flat in the key signature.

The box over the circle of 5ths in Figure 19.3 shows all the closely related keys to C major. The relative minor of C major is a minor (no sharps or flats). The key with one less sharp is F major and and its relative minor, d minor (one flat). The key with one more sharp is G major and its relative minor, e minor (one sharp).

The keys that are closely related to f♯ minor are:

Its relative major, A major.
The keys with one less sharp (2 sharps), D major and b minor.
The keys with one more sharp (4 sharps), E major and c♯ minor.

Figure 19.3

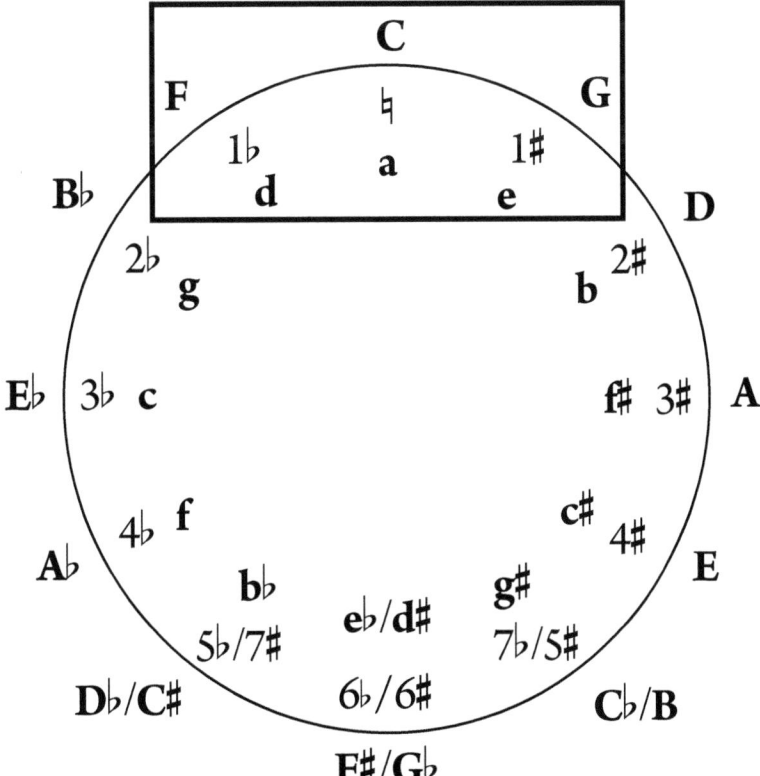

1. List the closely related keys to the following given examples.

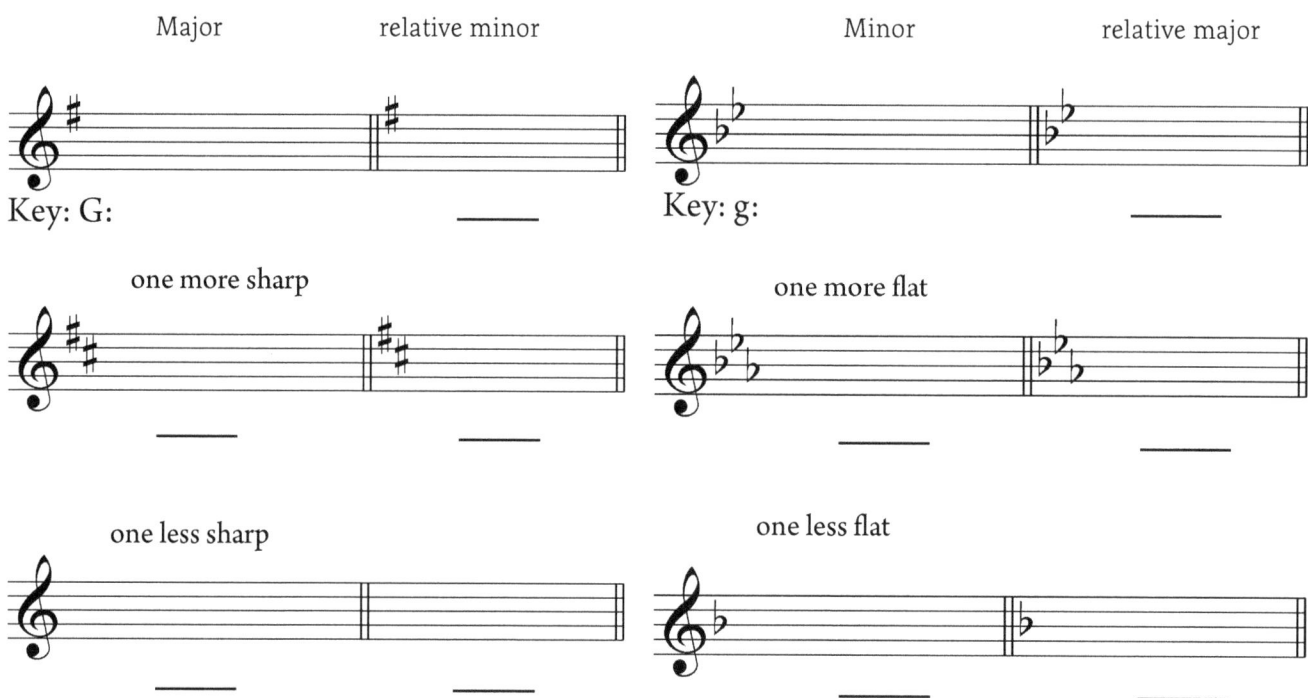

2. Add key signatures and list the closely related keys to the following given examples.

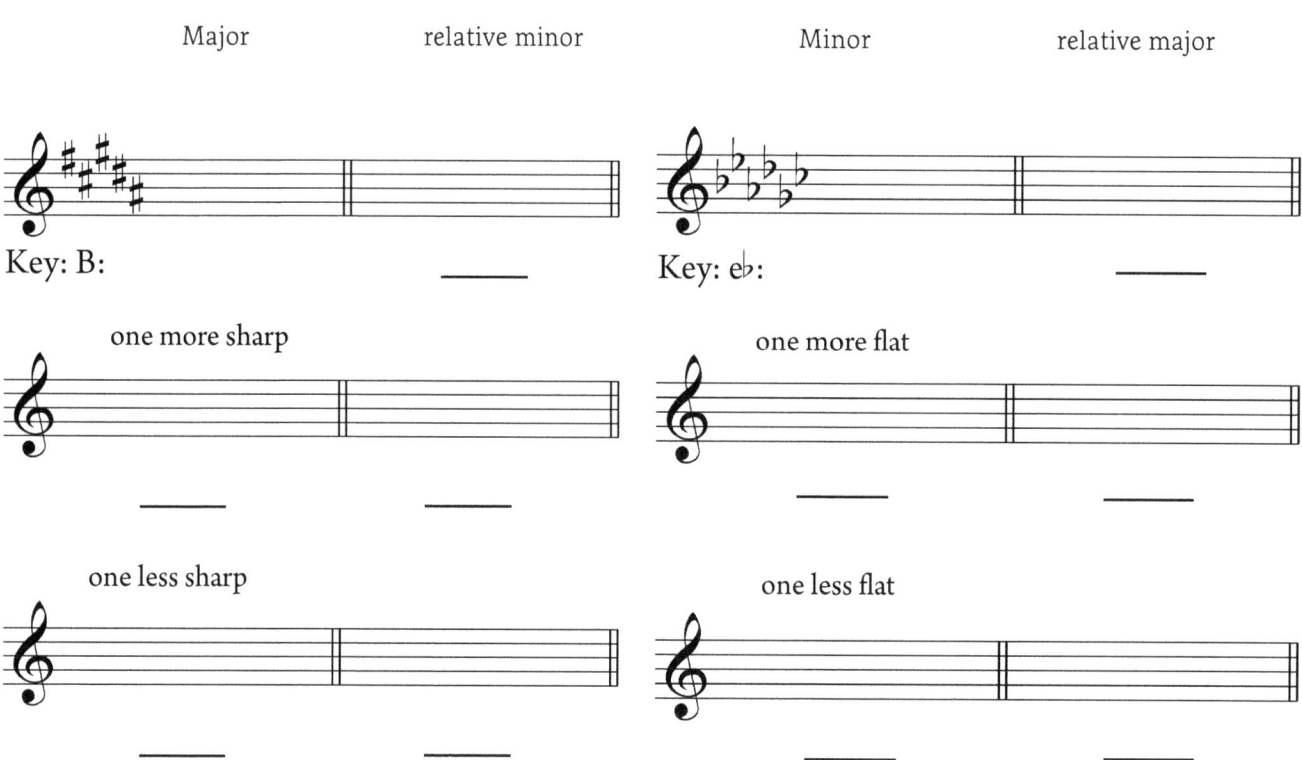

Chapter 19: Modulation

Another way to determine closely related keys is to find the subdominant and dominant of the original key and the relative keys of all of them. For example:

	Major	Minor
Original key:	G	e
Subdominant:	C	a
Dominant:	D	b

It should be noted that two keys with the same tonic like C major and C minor are not closely related. Movement from C major to C minor, or any tonic major and minor, is not a modulation since the tonal center remains the same. It is considered a change of mode. Parallel major and minor keys are not closely related because their key signatures differ by more than one sharp or flat.

3. Circle the keys that are not closely related f minor.

1) E♭ major   2) d minor   3) A♭ major   4) c minor   5) B♭ major   6) D♭ major   7) b♭ minor

4. Circle the keys that are not closely related E major.

1) D major   2) c♯ minor   3) B major   4) f♯ minor   5) A major   6) g♯ minor   7) b minor

5. Circle the keys that are not closely related c minor.

1) E♭ major   2) d minor   3) A♭ major   4) g minor   5) D♭ major   6) F major   7) e♭ minor

6. Circle the keys that are not closely related D major.

1) E major   2) b minor   3) B major   4) e minor   5) A major   6) G major   7) c♯ minor

Pivot Chord Modulation

The use of diatonic chords to change key is called *diatonic modulation*. Diatonic chords are chords that belong to a particular key. These chords are derived from the major scale for major keys and the minor scale for minor keys.

Closely related keys may have one or more diatonic chords in common. For example, the key of F major and the key of C major each contain the F major triad. The F major triad could be analyzed as I in F major or as IV in C major as shown in Figure 19.4. When a chord is analyzed in more than one key it is written as shown below.

Figure 19.4

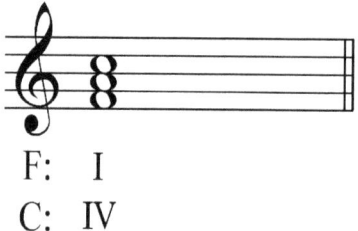

F: I
C: IV

When you are modulating to a new key it helps to know which chords the original and the new key have in common. These common chords are called *pivot chords*. These chords are easy and effective to use in a modulation. Figure 19.5 shows the diatonic chords that are common between C and F major. Pivot chords are effective in modulation. For example if we are modulating from F major to C major a good chord to use might be D minor. This chord belongs to both keys and works well as a pivot from one key to the next. D minor is chord vi in F major and chord ii in C major. So when we write this chord we could effectively be in F major or already in C major. Of course we need other chords to complete the modulation, like V - I in C major, but this chord creates a smooth transition between the two keys. It acts like a pivot, shifting us seamlessly from one key to the next.

Figure 19.5

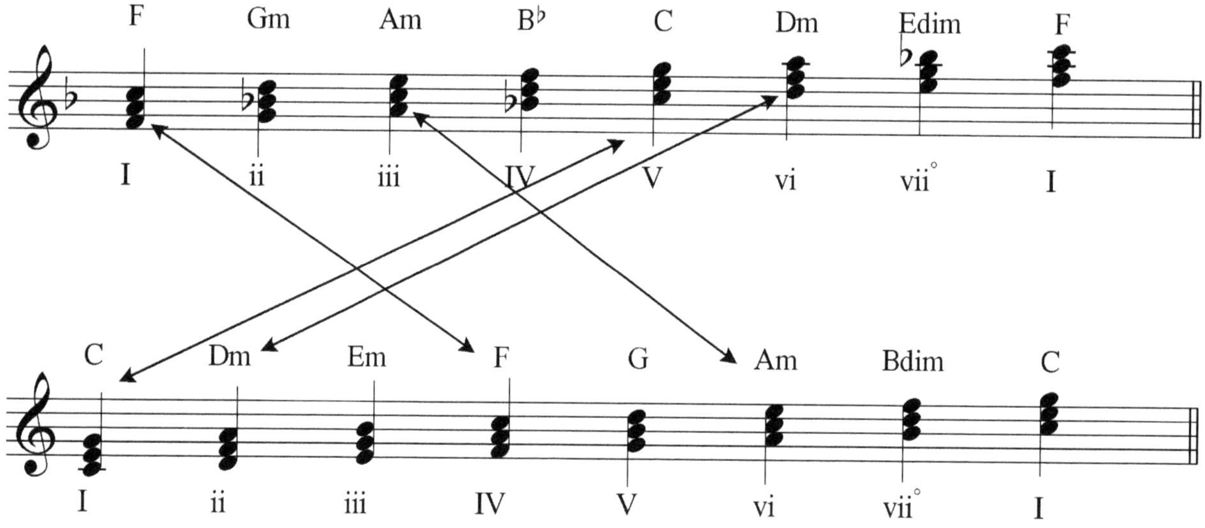

7. Provide a harmonic analysis for the following chords in the two indicated keys.

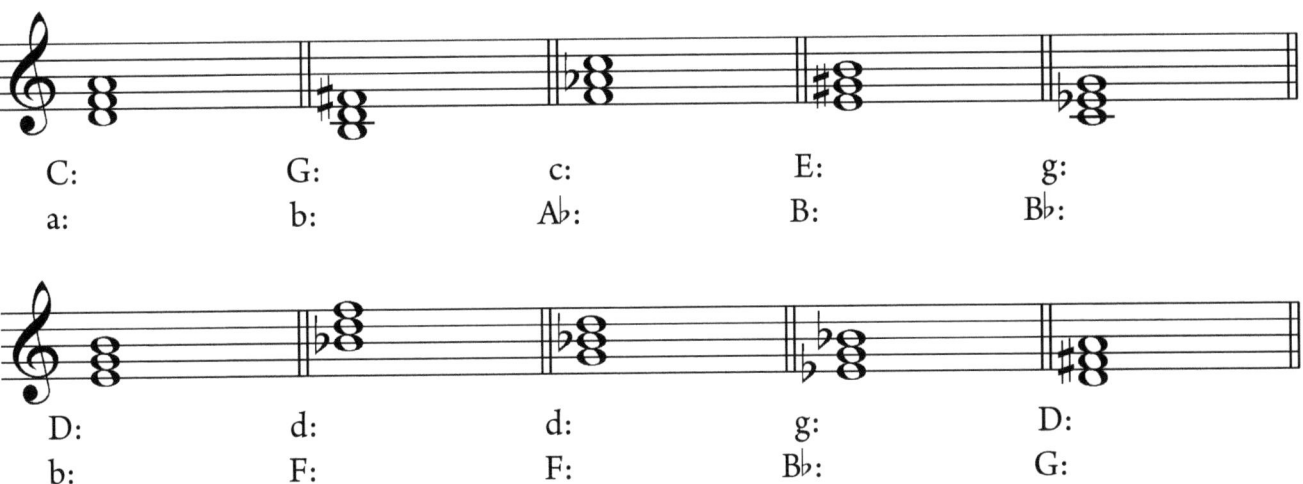

C: G: c: E: g:
a: b: A♭:   B: B♭:

D: d: d: g: D:
b: F: F: B♭:   G:

Before a modulation can occur the original key must be established. This should include a progression with V - I. It is preferable to have an authentic cadence in the original key. This defines the first key completely. In Figure 19.6 the original key of C major is established with a progression ending in an imperfect authentic cadence (V - I^6).

Once the original key is established, modulation can take place. The first step in diatonic modulation is the pivot chord. Remember that a pivot chord is a diatonic chord which is common to the original key and the new key, the key to which we are modulating. Diatonic 7th chords are also useful as pivot chords. In 19.6 the pivot chord is I^6 in the original key, C major, and IV^6 in the new key, G major. Any common chord can function as a pivot but the best pivot chords are predominant chords in the new key because they can be followed by the new dominant. Notice that this chord is analyzed twice, once in the original key and once in the new key.

Right after the pivot chord we have a chord which is not diatonic in C major since it contains an F♯. After examining the chords that follow we can see that this example is modulating to the closely related key of G major. Bach writes a complete progression in the new key beginning with V^6 - I in G major and ending with a half cadence (I - V), firmly establishing the new key. It is not necessary to write a new key signature when modulating. The new key is reflected with accidentals.

Johann Sebastian Bach
Chorale 217: Ach Gott, wie manches Herzeleid

Figure 19.6

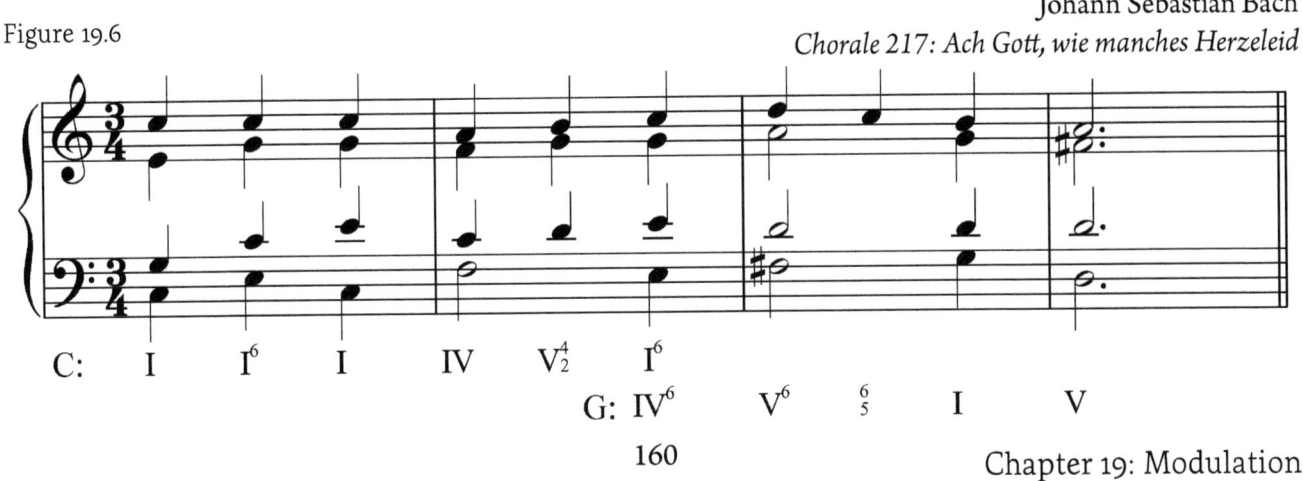

Chapter 19: Modulation

Finding the Pivot Chord

The steps for finding a pivot chord are:

1. Find the first chord that indicates movement to a new key. This is a chord that will contain a accidental.
2. Look at the chord that immediately precedes this chord. Analyze it in both the original and the new key. Sometimes there may be more than one chord acting as a pivot.
3. In Figure 19.6 the first chord indicating the new key is on the first beat of measure 3. This chord contains an F♯ which is not part of the original key C major. The chord that immediately preceds this chord is I⁶ in the original key of C major and IV⁶ in the new key, G major. This chord functions in both keys. It has a tonic function in the original key and a predominant function in the new key. It is followed by dominant harmony (V⁶) in the new key of G major.

8. Provide a harmonic analysis of the following examples using functional chord symbols.

Johann Sebastian Bach
Chorale 148: Uns ist ein Kindlein heut' gebor'n

key: ___ ___ ___ ___ ___

new key: ___ ___ ___

Johann Sebastian Bach
Chorale 222: Nun preiset alle

key: ___ ___ ___ ___

new key: ___ ___ ___ ___ ___ ___

Chapter 19: Modulation

Modulating to the Dominant (V)

The most common modulation from a major key is to the dominant. Figure 19.5 illustrated the possible pivot chords when moving from F major (I) to C major (V). For a modulation from F major to its dominant C major the chords that are common to both keys are:

Chord:	F	Am	C	Dm
Key: F:	I	iii	V	vi
Key: C:	IV	vi	I	ii

The chords that contain a B♭ in F major are not found in C major and will not function as pivot chords since they cannot be common chords. The best chords to use as pivot chords are those that function as predominant chords in the new key. In this case, I/IV, iii/vi and vi/ii. V/I is not the best choice for pivot chord since it is the dominant in the original key and wants to resolve to I. Study Figure 19.7 which contains a modulation from F major to C major. The original key is established with a progression ending in an authentic cadence. The pivot chord is vi⁶/ii⁶ and occurs just before V⁷ of the new key. ii⁶ in C major acts as a predominant before the dominant 7th of C. The example finishes with a progression in the new key of C major.

Figure 19.7

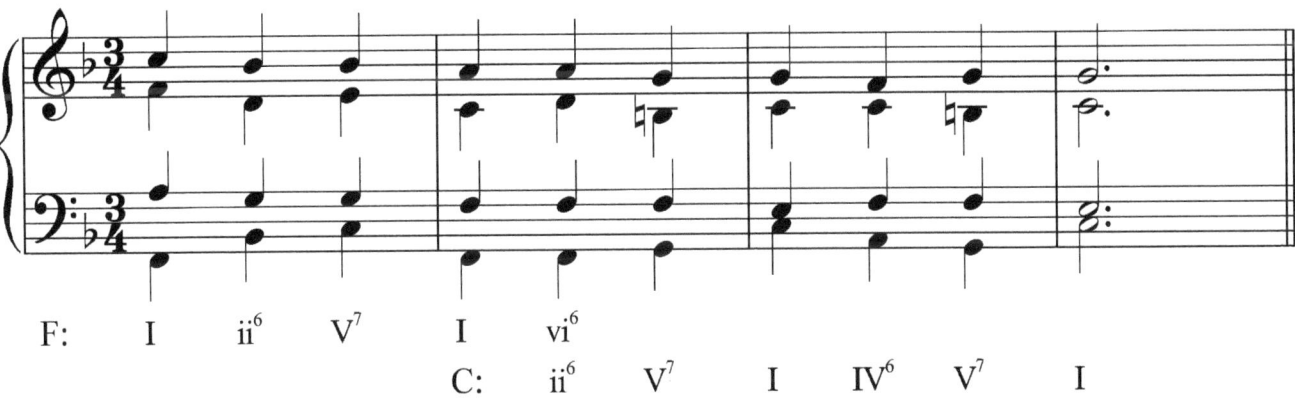

9. Complete the following progression in four parts.

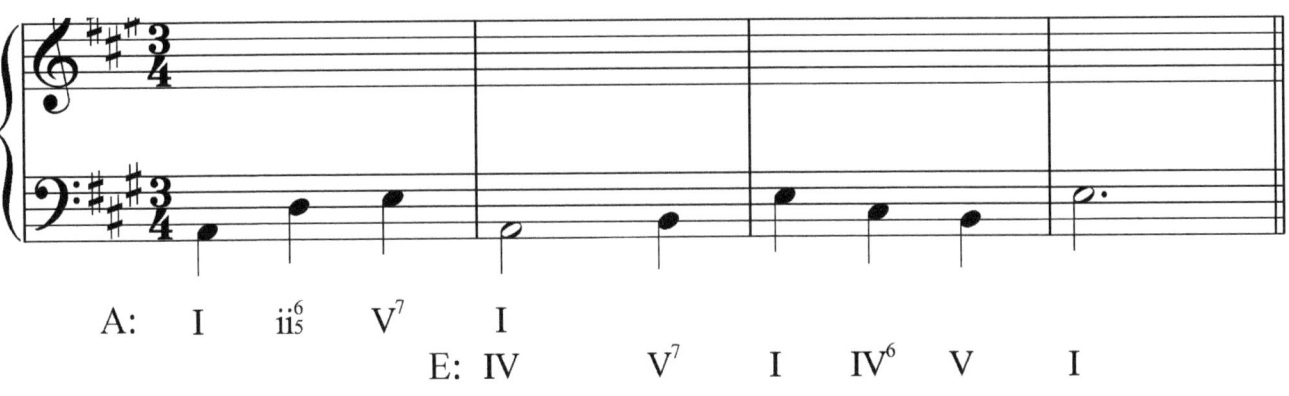

Modulating to the Relative Major

Compositions in minor keys can modulate to the dominant minor (v). For example, C minor might modulate to G minor. However, the most common modulation for a minor key composition is to its relative major. These two keys share the same key signature with the exception of the raised $\hat{7}$ in the minor key. For a modulation from A minor to its relative major, C major, the chords that are common to both keys are:

Chord:	C	Dm	F	Am	Bdim
Key: a:	III	iv	VI	i	ii°
Key: C:	I	ii	IV	vi	vii°

The only chords that are not common between these two keys are the two chords in A minor containing G♯ (V and vii°). Figure 19.8 contains a modulation from A minor to C major. The original key is established with a progression ending in an authentic cadence. The pivot chord is iv/ii and acts as a predominant in the new key of C major. An authentic cadence follows the pivot chord and the new key is established with a short progression.

Figure 19.8

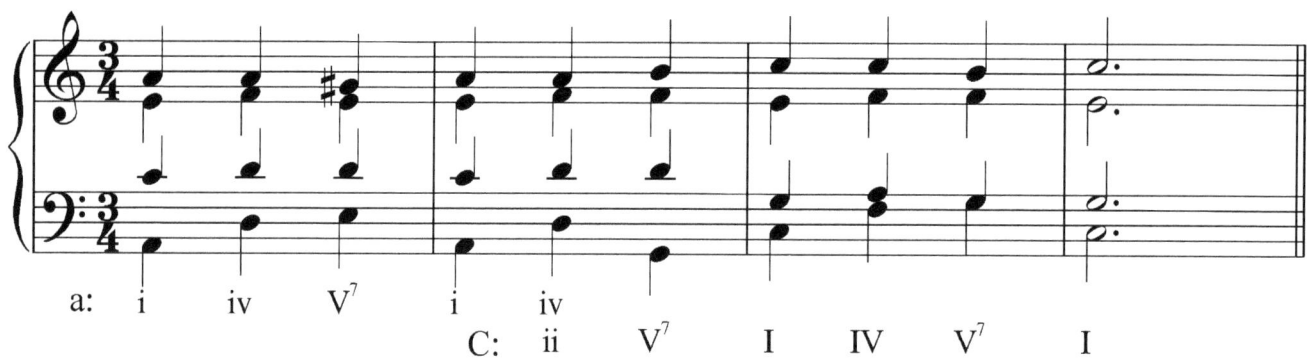

10. Complete the following progression in four parts.

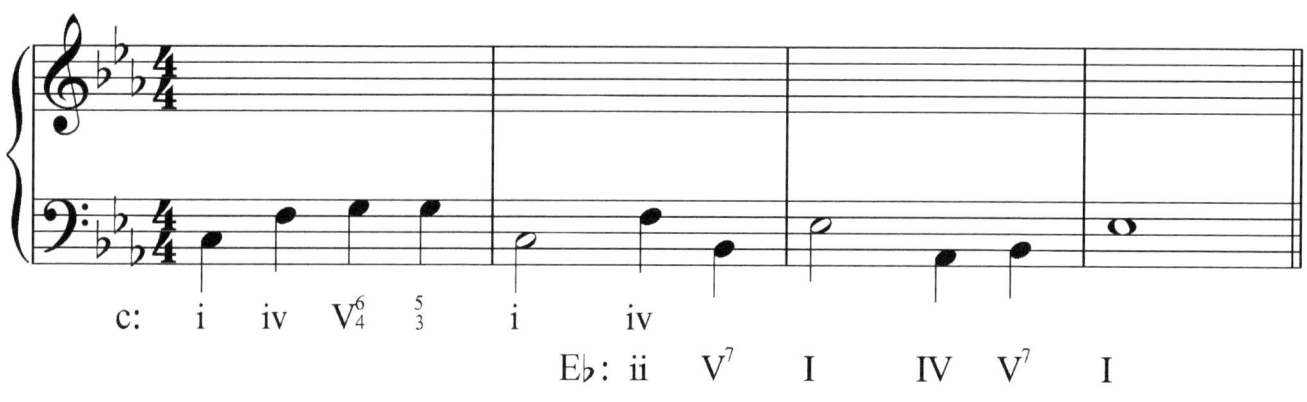

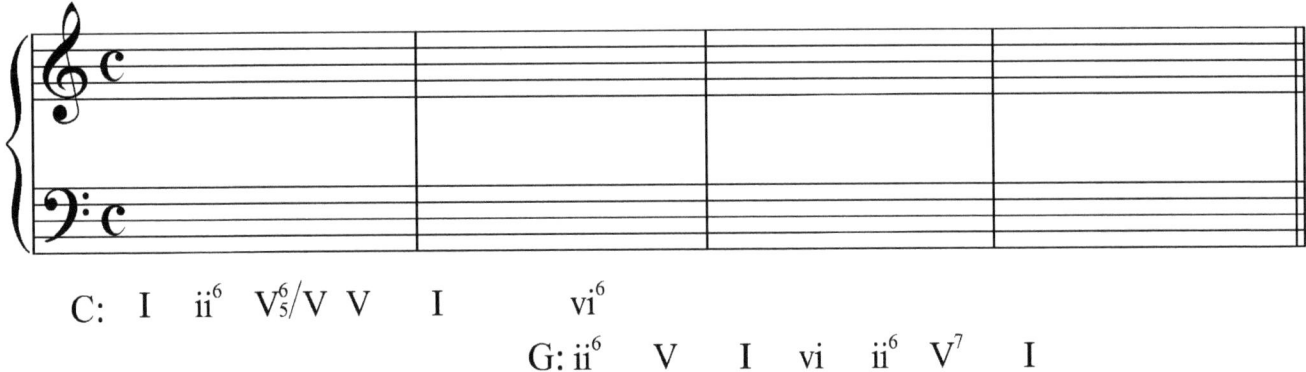

C: I   ii⁶ V⁶₅/V V   I   vi⁶
              G: ii⁶   V   I   vi   ii⁶ V⁷   I

Harmonizing a Melody with a Modulation

A melody that contains a modulation often has enough information to provide a clear harmonization. The steps for harmonizing a melody that contains a modulation are:

1. Go through the entire melody and determine the beginning and ending keys. Check to see if there might be an inner passage that is in a different key. Remember that these melodies will only be modulating to closely related keys. The melody in Figure 19.9 has a key signature of one sharp indicating G major or E minor. The opening measures start on G and will support a chord progression in G major. The phrase ends G-F♯- E. The only cadence in G major that will support this ending is a deceptive cadence (V - vi). This is a possibility, but this ending will also support an authentic cadence in E minor, the relative minor.

Figure 19.9

G: e:

2. Look for places in the melody that may indicate a cadence and identify the melodic area that clearly indicates the new key. Sketch them in in the original and the new key and write in the bass line. Figure 19.10 contains a place for an authentic cadence in G major. The modulation to E minor is sketched in with a cadential six-four and and authentic cadence in E minor.

Figure 19.10

3. Complete the opening chord progression establishing the original key. Just before the chords indicating the modulation to the new key find a place for a pivot chord and sketch it in. Label it in both keys. Figure 19.11 contains the pivot chord ii/iv just before the authentic cadence in the new key.

Figure 19.11

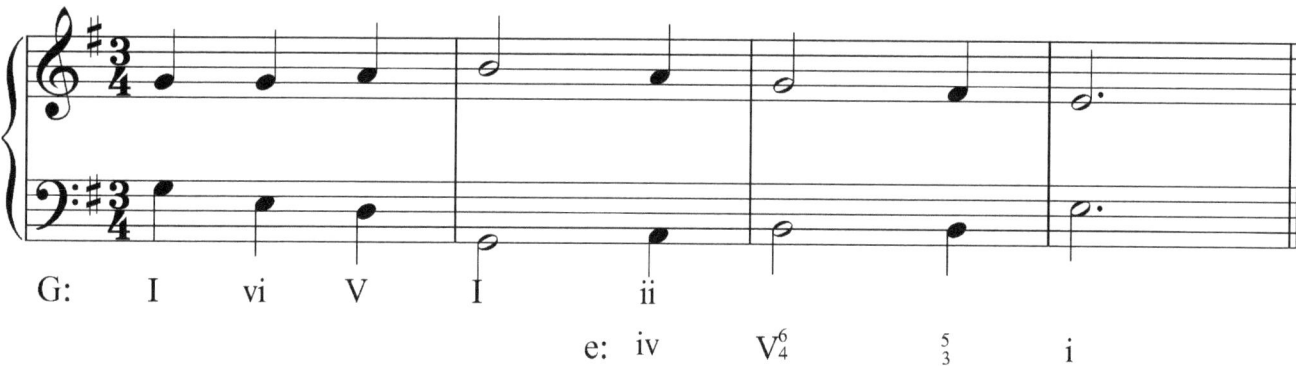

4. Complete the harmonization by adding the alto and tenor. Here a D♯ is required to reflect the leading tone of the new key, E minor.

Figure 19.12

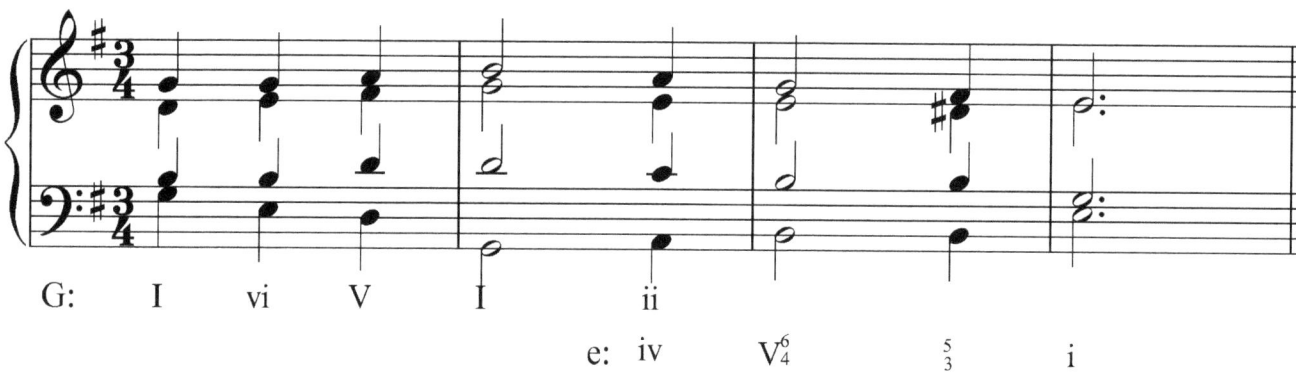

Chapter 19: Modulation

11. The following melody contains a modulation from E minor to C major. Choose the chords and harmonize it in four parts.

12. The following melody contains a modulation. Complete it in four parts.

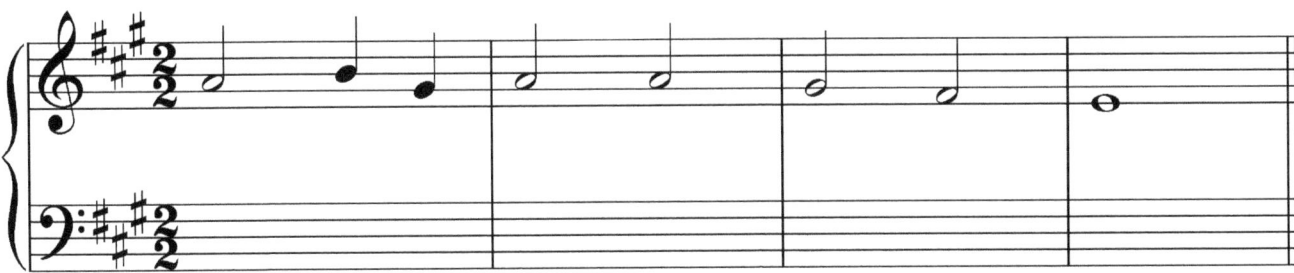

Harmonic Analysis

13. The following musical examples contain modulations. Provide a harmonic analysis of each.

Johann Sebastian Bach
Chorale 74: O Haupt voll Blut und Wunden

Franz Schubert
Heidenröslein, Op. 3, No. 3

Sah ein Knab' ein Röslein stehn Röslein auf der hei den war so jung und
mor gen schon lief er schnell, es nah' zu sehn, sah's mit vie len Freu den.

Ludwig van Beethoven
Sonata, Op.2, No. 3

F:

Chapter 19: Modulation

Johannes Brahms
Waltz, Op. 39, No. 15

Robert Schumann
Symphonic Études, Op. 13

Presto possibile

20
Chorale Harmonization

Johann Sebastian Bach
Chorale 13: Allein zu dir, Herr Jesu Christ

Chorale is the English spelling of the German word Choral which means hymn-tune. These hymn-tunes or melodies were sung in the German protestant church. The earliest examples of chorales date from the year 1524. Some chorales were original works and some were based on existing music such as the Latin hymns from the Catholic Church, popular German hymns, and even folk songs. The early chorales had a free rhythm but by the 18th century they consisted of stricter rhythmic patterns and symmetrical phrase structures.

By the end of the 16th century many composers wrote four part harmonizations of the chorale melodies. These chorale settings were written to encourage congregational singing in church. The greatest harmonizations of the chorales were done by J.S. Bach. These were written for four part choir (SATB). In the church service, the voice parts were doubled by instruments and supported by an organ.

Some of the characteristics of Bach's harmonizations are:

- The melody is always in the soprano.
- There is usually a change of chord for each note of the melody, and sometimes a single melody note is harmonized by more than one chord.
- The majority are in common time (4/4) with a few in triple (3/4) time.
- There is a clear cadence at the end of each phrase.
- The fermata (⌒) is used to indicate the end of a phrase and does not necessarily indicate that a note should be held longer.
- Bach uses suspensions and other nonchord tones to create movement and expression.
- The melodic shape of each individual part is important and occasionally the alto and tenor parts cross each other.

The most commonly used nonchord tones in Bach's harmonizations are unaccented passing tones. These add to the shape of a melody and create motion in a line. In the chorale in Figure 20.2 Bach writes six passing tones in the alto, tenor and bass parts. These added passing notes compliment and reflect the character of the stepwise melody which also contains two passing tones.

Unaccented passing tones are often used in two parts at once as seen in m.1 of 20.2. Here the bass and tenor move together in thirds on beat three.

Figure 20.2

Johann Sebastian Bach
Chorale 54: Lobt Gott, ihr Christen, allzugleich

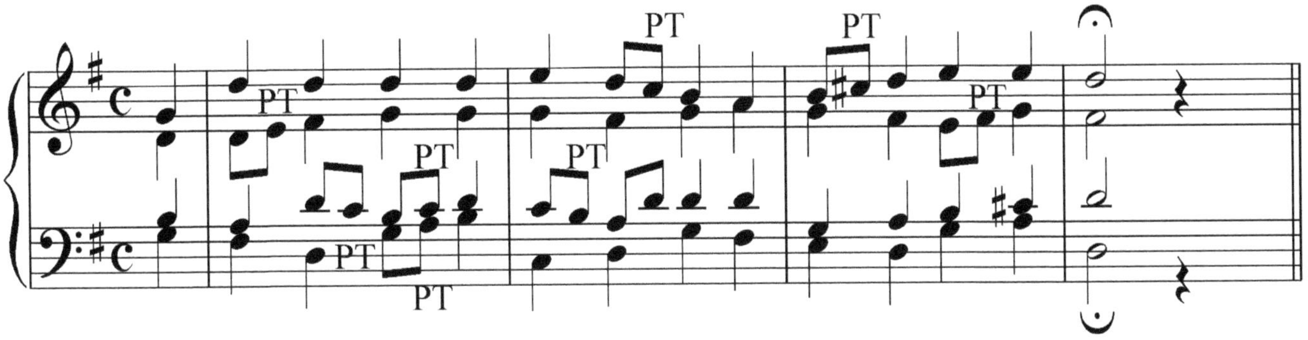

Generally, harmonic tones that are a third apart may be joined by a passing tone. However, at authentic cadences the leading tone sometimes falls to the fifth of the tonic chord in order to have a complete I chord containing the doubled root, third and fifth. This is shown in the alto in Figure 20.3 (a) When this happens, Bach never inserts a passing tone like the example in 20.3 (b). The reason for this is that it would draw attention to the fact that the leading tone is not rising to the tonic. Bach often adds a passing tone at cadences creating V^{8-7} as shown in the tenor of 20.3 (c). Note that the alto does not move with the tenor in this progression.

Figure 20.3

Johann Sebastian Bach
Chorale 54: Lobt Gott, ihr Christen, allzugleich

G: V   I   V   I V^8 ^{7} I

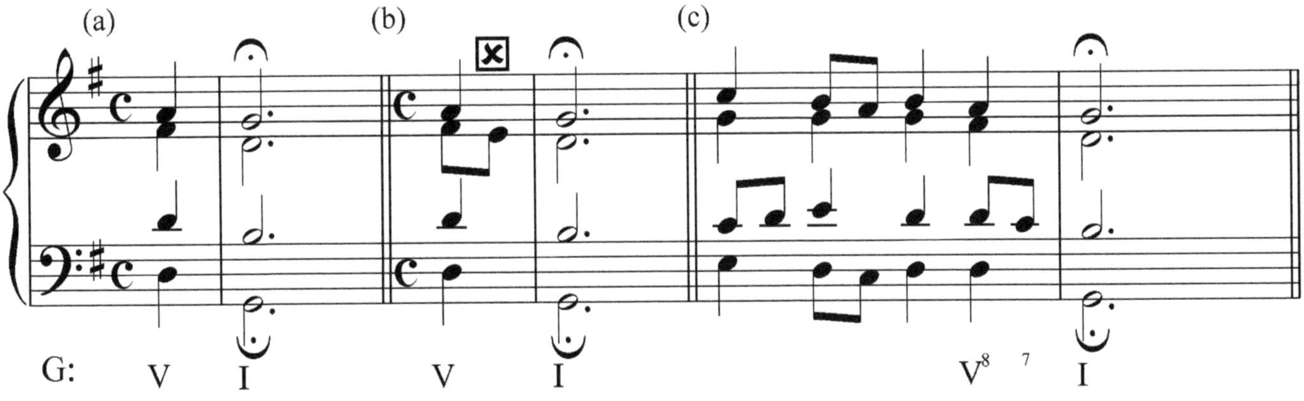

Bach uses neighbor notes fairly regularly, especially in the bass. Figure 20.4 contains a lower neighbor in m.2. A lower neighbor is usually followed by a rising melodic line while an upper neighbor is often followed by a descending melodic line.

Figure 20.4

Johann Sebastian Bach
Chorale 75: Das walt' mein Gott

Bach uses accented nonchord tones for their expressive nature. The most commonly used are accented passing tones and suspensions. Accented passing tones are used in the first measure of Figure 20.5. Bach uses the picardy third and ends this chorale in A minor on the A major chord.

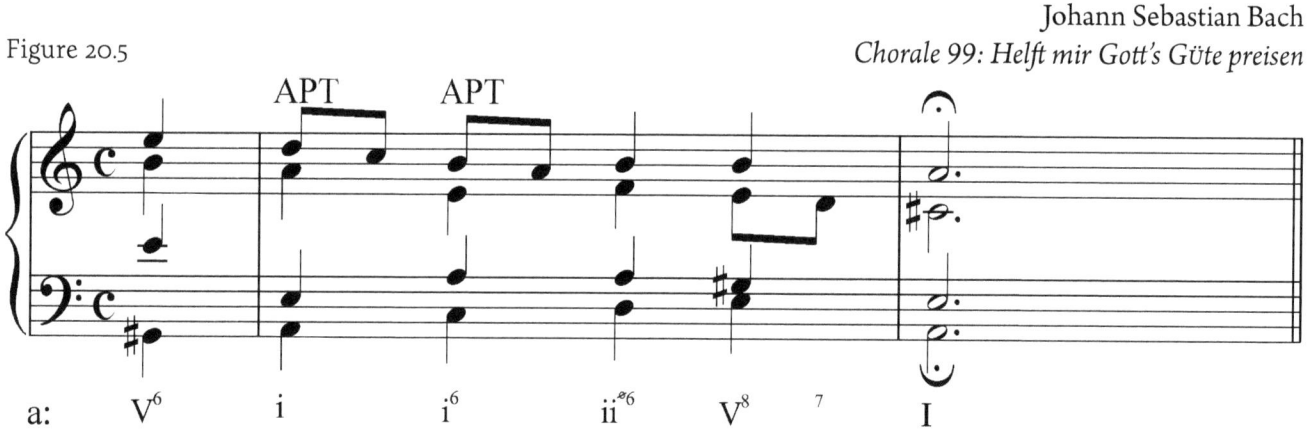

Figure 20.5

Johann Sebastian Bach
Chorale 99: Helft mir Gott's Güte preisen

Suspensions are often used at cadences but can also be found in the middle of a phrase. The two suspensions in Figure 20.6 are easy to see because they are tied. Many times Bach writes suspensions without ties. The reason for this is that sometimes a word being sung in a chorale may have a syllable that must be stressed and sung by all four voices at the same time on a strong beat.

Figure 20.6

Johann Sebastian Bach
Chorale 243: Jesu, du mein liebstes Leben

Chapter 20: Chorale Harmonization

It is important to remember that the texture of the chorale is vocal in nature, not instrumental. You should keep within the voice ranges and try to maintain a good melodic shape in each voice. The addition of passing tones and neighbor notes will create stepwise motion, but the occasional leap of an interval smaller than a octave can make a melody interesting.

1. Under the bracketed area in section B, rewrite the alto, tenor and bass from section A. Include nonchord tones such as passing tones, neighbor notes and suspensions. Begin each exercise as shown. Provide a harmonic analysis using functional chord symbols.

172 Chapter 20: Chorale Harmonization

A

B

173 Chapter 20: Chorale Harmonization

Harmonizing a Chorale

You may be asked to harmonize a chorale melody. Chorale melodies were sung by a congregation in Lutheran churches in parts of Germany. The text of the chorale is important and every voice sings the text. Each of the words are sung by the four parts at the same time. You must not omit syllables when there are held notes. The melodies are recognisable, and are divided into phrases, which are identified by fermatas. These marks indicate where you should put your cadences.

Look at any accidentals, if they occur. Find the key of the piece and places that indicate a possible modulation. This modulation will always be to a closely related key.

Start by harmonizing the final cadence. This will normally be a perfect authentic cadence (V-I with both chords in root position), though one shouldn't rule out the possibility of plagal (IV-I) cadences, although this is extremely rare. Figure 20.7 is in G major. There is a perfect authentic cadence at the end of every phrase. In m.6 it is a perfect authentic cadence in the dominant, D major. The C♯ in the melody clearly indicates a secondary dominant. Here, we have sketched in the bass part at the cadences.

Figure 20.7

Chapter 20: Chorale Harmonization

After sketching in the cadences look through the rest of the part you have to harmonise, and pencil in the bass line. Remember that this is only a sketch and you may have to alter it as you go along. These chords should fit into the chorale melody, and have logical chord progressions. Most chorales have similar cadential progressions.

Chapter 20: Chorale Harmonization

Complete the chorale by adding the alto and tenor. You may have to alter the bass you chose in order to avoid faulty parallels, space issues, etc.

Go through and try and put in any suspensions (the most common are 4-3 in the alto at a cadence and a 7-6 in the tenor in the middle) and dissonances such as 7ths. Remember that these should be prepared and resolved. Also add in any passing notes, anticipation notes and neighbour notes that you can. These add more interest and movement to the chorale.

Go through and check all voices for faulty parallel perfect fifths, octaves, or unisons. Bach occasionally used parallel 5ths or octaves, but they are rare and hidden with the skill of an expert. Check for correct spacing and voice crossing errors.

2. **Complete the following for four voices (SATB). Symbolize the harmony throughout using functonal chord symbols.**

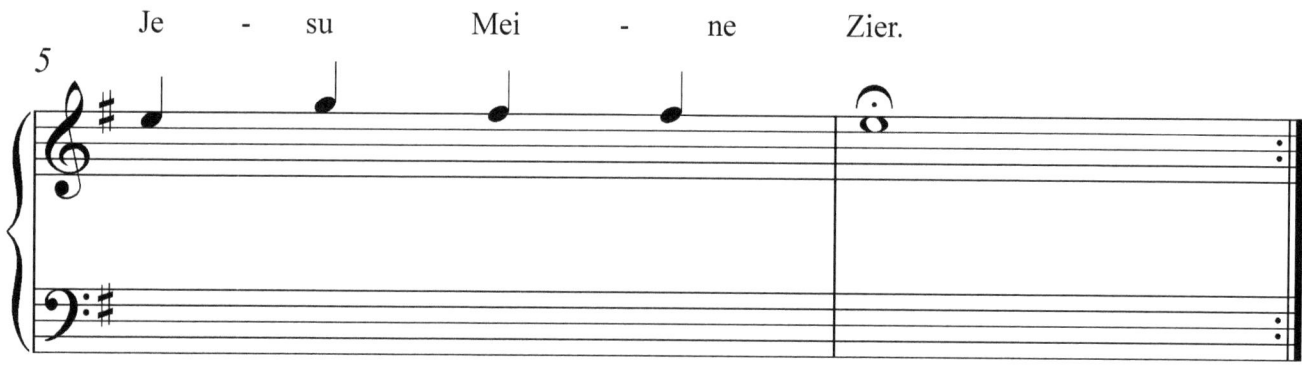

Chapter 20: Chorale Harmonization

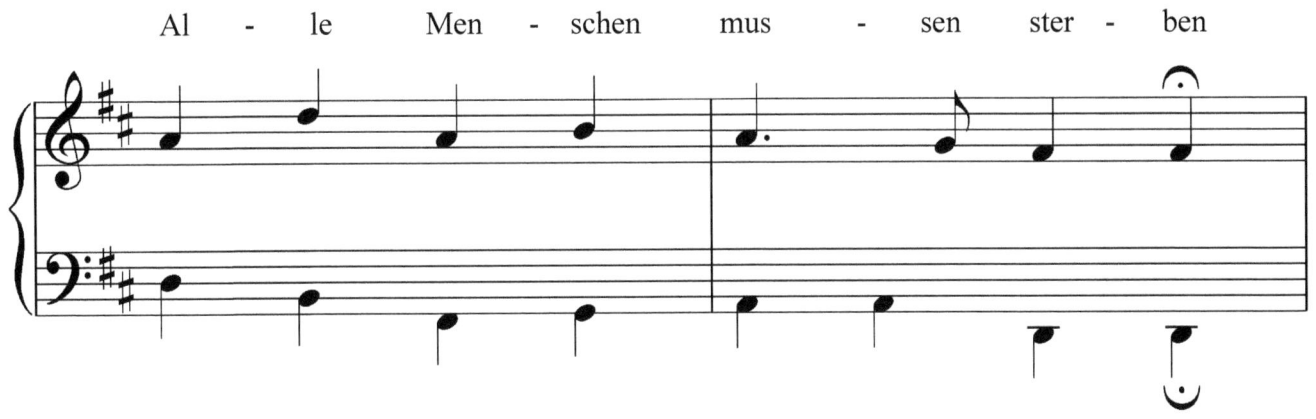

21
Form

Most music has an overall plan or structure, which is the "big picture." This is called the *form* of the music.

Musical forms differ in size and complexity. It's easy to understand a simple piece of music that is constructed of a number of repetitions. The average person can listen to a popular song and be able to identify the verses and the chorus, but will have trouble figuring out what's going on in a Brahms Symphony. Many traditional classical music forms are much longer and more complex. They are difficult to understand without hearing them numerous times or studying them carefully.

Music can still be appreciated without understanding its form, but anyone studying music theory or playing an instrument will benefit from having an understanding of form. Seeing the "big picture" helps one to become a better musician and enjoy the music even more.

The 18th Century Dance Suite

An important form in the 18th century was the dance suite. This form is also referred to as the Baroque dance suite. These suites consisted of groups of stylized dances that were intended for listening rather than dancing. They were written for small ensembles and for solo instruments including the harpsichord, lute, guitar and cello.

The main dances from this period are:
>Allemande
>Courante
>Minuet
>Sarabande
>Bourrée
>Gavotte
>Gigue

Each of these dances has distinct characteristics. They can be distinguished by tempo, rhythm, meter, musical characteristics and country of origin. They were most often written in binary or ternary form.

Study the following examples of each of these dances.

Allemande

Country of origin:	Germany
Meter:	4/4 or 2/2
Tempo:	Allegretto, Moderato, Allegro moderato
Characteristics:	A one note upbeat, usually a 16th note, and often a flow of continuous running sixteenth notes throughout. Stately and dignified character.

Johann Sebastian Bach
Partita No. 1, Allemande

Courante

Country of origin:	France
Meter:	3/4, 3/2, 3/8, or 6/4
Tempo:	Moderato (Italian version *Corrente* in Allegro, or Vivace)
Characteristics:	Often begins with an upbeat. Light texture and rapid figures. (Name means "running.") Italian corrente is in quick triple time (usually 3/4) with running passages. French courante is in moderate tempo (3/2 or 6/4) with shifts from triple to duple time (hemiola).

Johann Sebastian Bach
French Suite No. 2 BWV 813, Courante

Minuet

Country of origin:	France
Meter:	3/4 or 3/8
Tempo:	Moderato grazioso, Andante
Characteristics:	Graceful French dance; unhurried tempo, balanced phrases usually four measures long.

Johann Sebastian Bach
Partita No. 1, Minuet II

Sarabande

Country of origin:	Spain and Latin America
Meter:	3/2 or 3/4
Tempo:	Adagio, Lento
Characteristics:	Emphasis on second beat with long or accented notes. Can be chordal in texture.

Archangelo Corelli
Sarabande

Bourrée

Country of origin:	France
Meter:	2/4, 4/4 or 2/2
Tempo:	Vivace, Allegro vivace
Characteristics:	Usually begins with an upbeat (quarter note or two eighth notes). Quick duple time, rhythmic and bright with steady quarter notes.

Johann Sebastian Bach
Partita BWV 831, Bourrée I

Gavotte

Country of origin:	France
Meter:	4/4 or 2/2
Tempo:	Allegro, Allegro moderato
Characteristics:	French dance; usually two quarter note upbeats, so the phrase begins and ends in the middle of the measure.

Johann Sebastian Bach
French Suite 5 BWV 816, Gavotte

Gigue

Country of origin: England
Meter: Compound time, often 6/8 or simple time in triplets
Tempo: Allegro, Vivace, Presto
Characteristics: Derived from the English word jig, but evolved differently in Italy and France: French gigue is in compound time (often 6/8). Italian giga is faster and has running notes.

Johann Sebastian Bach
French Suite V, BWV 816, Gigue

1. For the following examples: Name the key, name the dance type and add an appropriate tempo marking.

Tempo: _____   Dance type: _____

Key:

Tempo: _____   Dance type: _____

Key:

Tempo: _____   Dance type: _____

Key:

Chapter 21: Form

Tempo: _____ Dance type: _____

Key:

Tempo: _____ Dance type: _____

Key:

Tempo: _____ Dance type: _____

Key:

Tempo: _____ Dance type: _____

Key:

Labelling Formal Sections

Generally we use letters to label sections of a piece of music. Each major section receives a letter to identify it. (A, B, C). If you label the first section A, and the next section or the sections after that are the same, they would be labelled A as well. The next major section that is different than A would be labelled B. Sections that are different than A or B would be labelled C, D, etc.

How do you recognize the sections in order to label them? With simple music, this is fairly easy. With unfamiliar types of music, it can be more of a challenge. The first step is to listen for repeated sections. Also, listen for changes, in the rhythm, melody and harmony. A new section that is not a repetition will usually have noticeable differences in more than one of these areas. One of the important factors in identifying form is to recognize when something new or different is being introduced.

The sections of the melody in Figure 21.1 have been labelled with capital letters. The beginning is labelled A. This section is repeated. The new section labelled B has a different rhythm and melodic shape. The A section returns with a different anacrusis. The rest is an exact repeat of the original A and is labelled A^2.

Figure 21.1

Scottish Air

Binary Form

Binary form was one of the most common forms used in the Baroque and Classical periods. Pieces in binary form consist of two parts. These two parts can be labelled A and B. Each of these sections is usually, but not always, repeated.

Section A:
- Begins in the tonic key and may end in the tonic. In this case it would be considered harmonically closed.
- It may also end in a half cadence in the tonic key or in another closely related key. This would be considered harmonically open.

Section B:
- May begin and end in the tonic or more often, it may begin in a closely related key (often the key A ended in) and end in the tonic.
- This is the final section so it must finish in the tonic key and end harmonically closed.

Figure 21.2

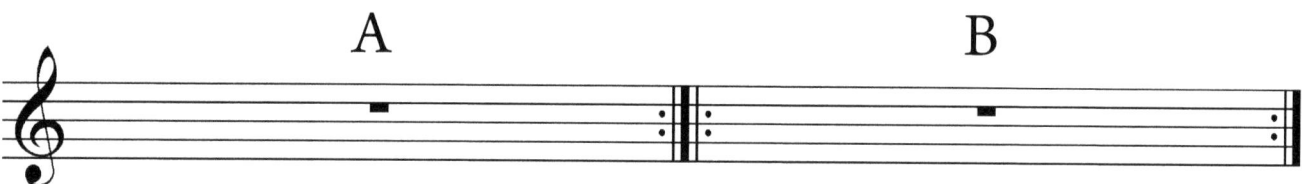

We will study three types of binary form.

Simple Binary
In simple binary the A and the B section are different and there is no reprise of material from section A in the B section. This form was popular in the Baroque period between 1600 and 1750.

Balanced Binary
In balanced binary, material from the end of the A section returns at the end of the B section, but it may be transposed.

Rounded Binary
This type of binary form became popular in the Classical Period between 1750 to 1820. It gained prominence in the late 18th century when composers developed and refined it into sonata form. In this form we see a reprise of Section A after Section B.

Simple Binary Form

The Sonata in Figure 21.3 is in simple binary form. In this piece, phrases are four measures long, which is common. Section A ends in a half cadence in the tonic, C major, making this section harmonically open. Section B is in C major, and stays there for the final authentic cadence, making this section harmonically closed. In binary form Section B must end with a closed cadence in the tonic. Pieces of this era begin and end in the tonic.

In *simple binary form*, there is no restatement of material from section A. Here, the phrases are marked with slurs and the sections are labelled with capital letters on the score. The cadences are given functional chord symbols and named at the end of each phrase.

Figure 21.3

Form: Simple Binary

George Frideric Handel
Sonata Op. 1 No. 7

Chapter 21: Form

2. For the following example:
- Name the principal key.
- Name the form.
- Verify the form with capital letters placed directly on the music.
- Mark the structural phrasing.

For each phrase ending:
- Name the key.
- Name the cadence as: authentic, half, plagal or deceptive.

Form: _____

George Phillip Telemann
Gigue

Balanced Binary Form

The Sonata movement in Figure 21.4 is in *balanced binary form*. Section A ends in an authentic cadence in the dominant, G major, making this section harmonically open. The beginning of section B is in the dominant, G major, but this section ends in an authentic cadence in C major making B harmonically closed. In balanced binary form, there is a brief return of a portion of section A at the end of the B section. This is often 2 to 4 measures. Here, a transposed version of mm. 7-8 return in mm. 15-16 of the B section.

Pieces in major keys often modulate to the dominant, and pieces in minor keys often modulate to the relative major. These are considered *traditonal or standard goal keys*.

Figure 21.4
Form: Balanced Binary

Wolfgang Amadeus Mozart
Sonata K 6, III

Chapter 21: Form

3. For the following example:
- Name the principal key.
- Name the form.
- Verify the form with capital letters placed directly onthe music.
- Mark the structural phrasing.

For each phrase ending:
- Name the key.
- Name the cadence as: authentic, half, plagal or deceptive.

Form: _____

Joseph Haydn
German Dance Hob IX: 22

Chapter 21: Form

Rounded Binary Form

In *rounded binary form* all or part of Section A returns after Section B. This form may occur in a few different ways.

Section A¹
The first A section (A¹) begins in the tonic and may end in a number of ways:

- It may end with an authentic cadence in the tonic.
- It may also end with a half cadence in the tonic.
- It may modulate to a closely related key. If it starts it a major key it often modulates to the dominant. If it starts in a minor key it often modulates to the relative major. Thus, Section A¹ may end in a cadence in another key.
- If Section A ends in an authentic cadence in the tonic, the piece must include repeat signs for it to be rounded binary.

Section B
The key feature of Section B is that it will differ from Section A. This difference may be melodic, rhythmic, tonal, or a combination of all of these elements. If Section A¹ modulated, B may begin in the key that concluded A¹. It may modulate on its own as well.

Section A²
The key elements of A² are:

- It may begin exactly like A¹ or it might be a slight variation of A¹.
- It will be in the same key as A¹. A transposed version is not considered A².
- There may be only part of the original A¹ stated.
- The restatement might occur in a different voice or clef.
- This section must end in an authentic cadence in the tonic.
- If there are repeats, B and A² will be repeated together as the second part of this form.

As a special note, sometimes this form does not include repeats. In order for this to be rounded binary form without the repeats, Section A¹ must end in an half cadence or any cadence in another key. If there are no repeats and A¹ ends in an authentic cadence in the tonic, it is not rounded binary form.

Figure 22.4

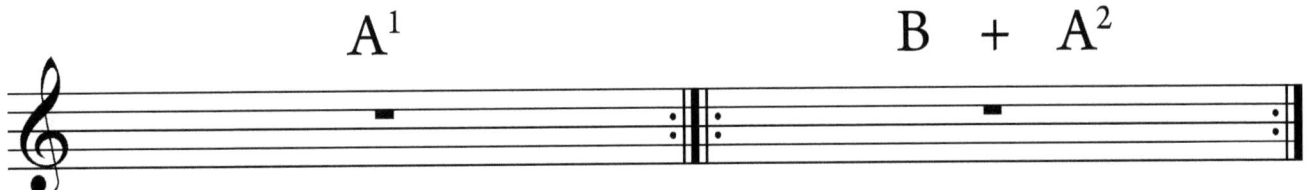

Figure 21.5 is in rounded binary form. Section A¹ begins in C major and ends with an authentic cadence in the dominant, G major. It is repeated.

Section B begins where A¹ left off, in G major, and modulates back to C major.

Section A² is a return of the original material, but the ending is altered to produce an authentic cadence in the tonic. B and A² are repeated together. This piece would be in rounded binary form even if there were no repeats. The cadence at the end of A¹ determines this. It is an authentic cadence in a key other than the tonic. If A¹ ends in a half cadence or a cadence in another key, even if there are no repeats, it is rounded binary form.

Figure 21.5

Form: Rounded Binary

Samuel Arnold
Gavotte

4. For the following example:
- Name the principal key.
- Name the form.
- Verify the form with capital letters placed directly on the music.
- Mark the structural phrasing.

For each phrase ending:
- Name the key.
- Name the cadence as: authentic, half, plagal or deceptive.

Form: _____

Johann Krebs
Menuet

Ternary Form

A piece in *ternary form* is made of of three independant sections. These parts may fall into a number of different configurations such as A-B-A, A-A-B, A-B-B, or A-C-C. In this chapter we will concentrate on the formal structure consisting of the design A-B-A. In this form, the original A section returns after the B section. The two A sections are closed tonally. The B section may be closed or open tonally and is often in a contrasting key like the dominant or the relative major.

Section A:

- Starts and ends in the tonic key.
- Usually ends with an authentic cadence in the tonic.
- May or may not be repeated

Section B:

- Contrasting in character to Section A
- Often in a standard goal key like the dominant or relative major.
- May be open or closed tonally and may end with a cadence in the new key or another cadence in the tonic key.
- May or may not be repeated

Section A:

- May be an exact or slightly varied repeat of the first section A.
- Is closed tonally. Ends in an authentic cadence in the tonic.
- The entire section may be written out or it may be repeated by using the term *D.C. al fine*.
- May or may not be repeated.

Figure 21.6

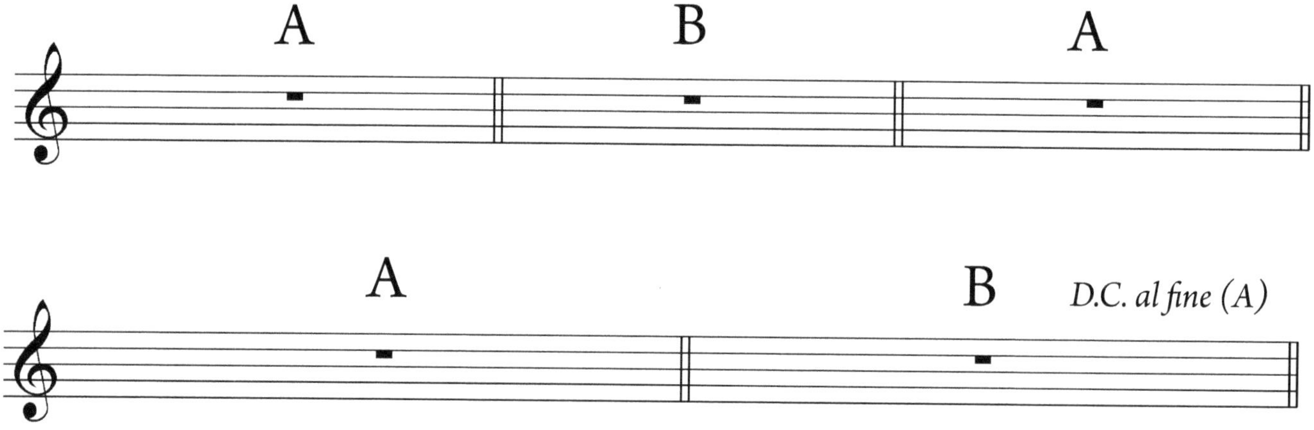

The piece in Figure 21.7 is in ternary form. Section A ends with an authentic cadence in the tonic and is closed tonally. Section B is four measures long, remains in the tonic key and ends with a half cadence in the tonic. Section A returns and is written out exactly as it appeared the first time, ending in an authentic cadence in the tonic.

Figure 21.7

Form: Ternary

5. For the following examples:
- Name the principal key.
- Name the form.
- Verify the form with capital letters placed directly on the music.
- Mark the structural phrasing.

For each phrase ending:
- Name the key.
- Name the cadence as: authentic, half, plagal or deceptive.

Form: _____

Leopold Mozart
Entree

Chapter 21: Form

Form:_____

George Frideric Handel
Gavotta

Form: _____

Johann Phillipp Kirnberger
Bourrée

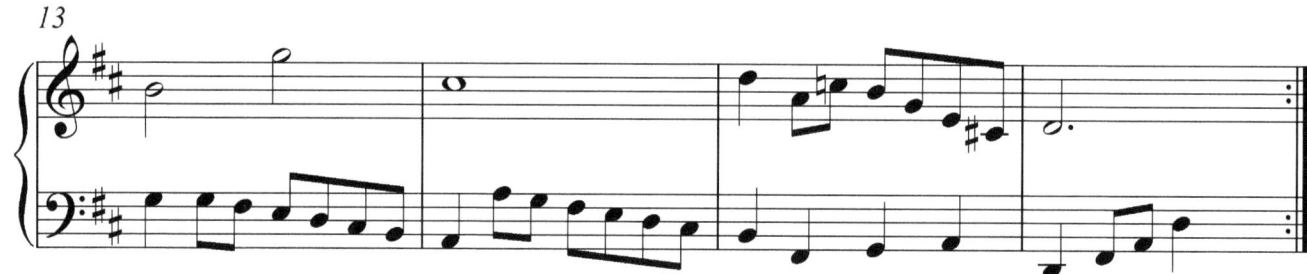

Form: _____

Henry Purcell
Borry

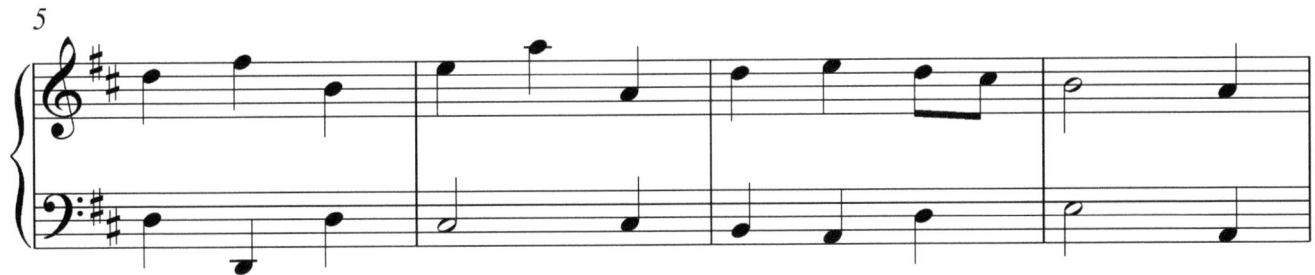

Form: _____

François Couperin
The Reapers

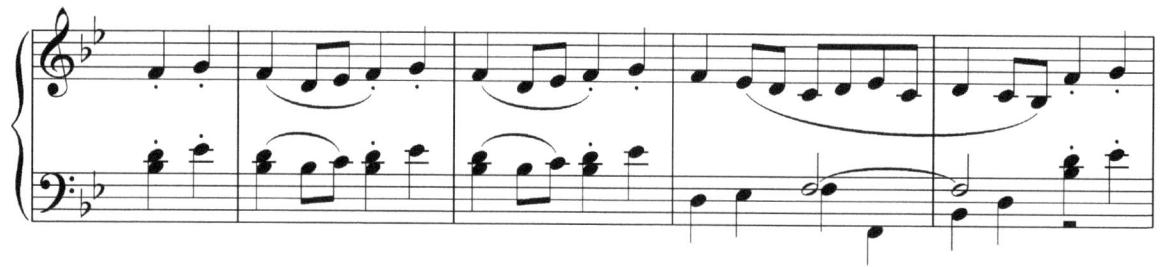

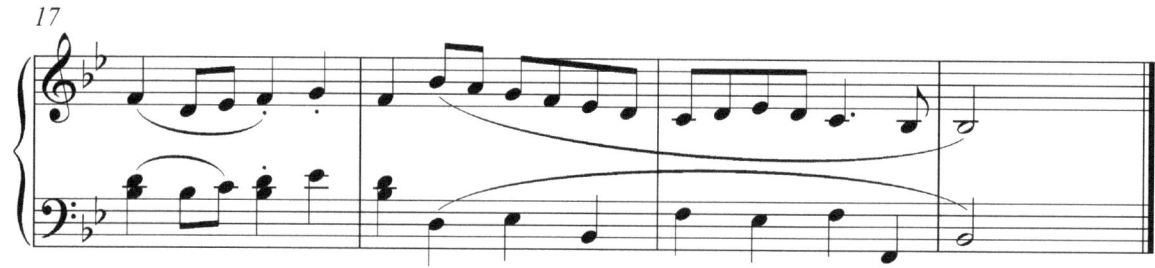

Form: _____

Christoph Graupner
Gavotte

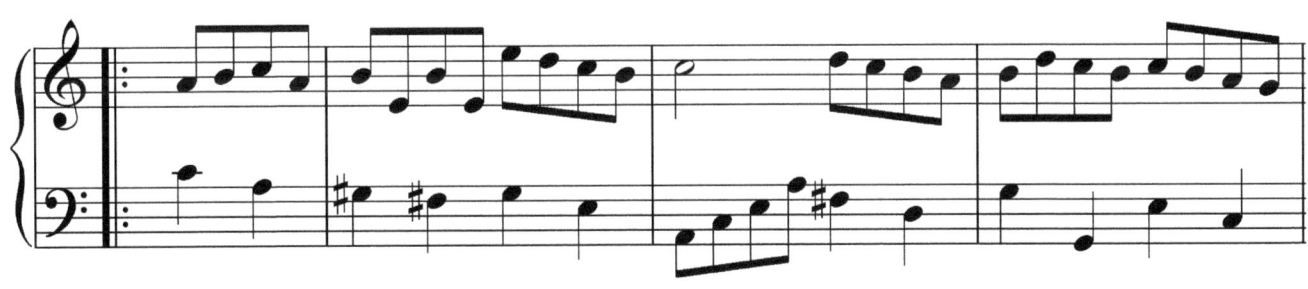

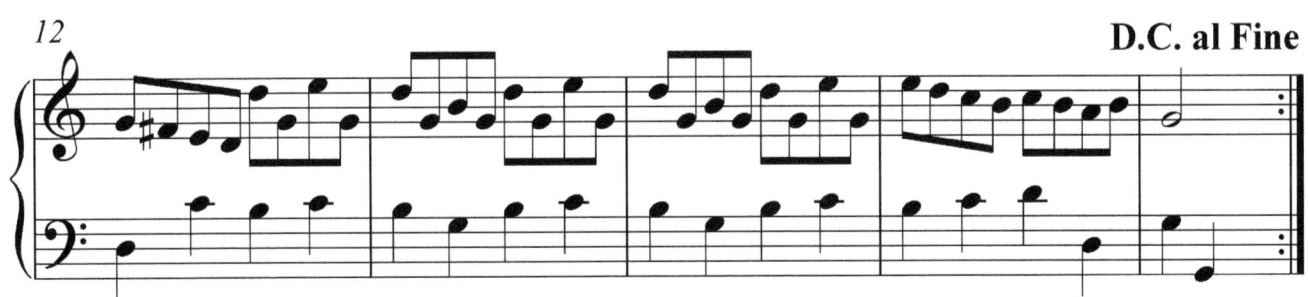

Form: _____

Johann Sebastian Bach
Menuet

22
Melody Writing

A *melody,* sometimes called a tune or a voice, is a line of musical notes that the listener hears as a single entity. Melody consists of both pitch and rhythm. In most cases melody is designed to go hand in hand with harmony, but melodies can also exist on their own. A lot of folk music was written before the concept of harmony was around.

The earliest melodies were sung. However, the voice has a certain range and certain capabilities. Notes may be too high or too low for the voice or too far apart in pitch to make them easy to sing. Usually the notes of a melody relate to a particular scale. Augmented intervals and some diminished intervals can be awkward to sing.

As harmony developed, we became accustomed to the sound of chords, and many melodies became based on the notes of these chords. It became easy to sing many of these melodies even if they consisted of numerous leaps, because they were based on chords.

Sometimes melodies that are difficult to sing are not difficult to play on an instrument. Many instruments have a much larger range than the human voice and are easily able to play wide leaps and odd intervals. Even so, many instrumental melodies are very "singable" because we have come to understand the singable melody as expressive and elegant (cantabile).

Melodies are divided into phrases. A phrase is comparable to a sentence in written language. Phrases can vary in length but are usually two to eight measures long. We will be looking at writing melodies in 18th century style which are commonly four measures long. Figure 22.1 illustrates a melody consisting of two four measure phrases.

Figure 22.1

Certain components make up a phrase. Within every phrase the rhythm and the shape of the melody combine to create a goal for the phrase. Every phrase concludes with a cadence which is a place of rest. A melodic phrase is usually shaped so that it is musically complete, and has a clear sense of design. The melody in Figure 22.2 consists of four measures in an arch shape with the climax being the highest note F, in measure 2. The phrase ends with a half cadence (I - V). This phrase also begins on the first beat of a measure.

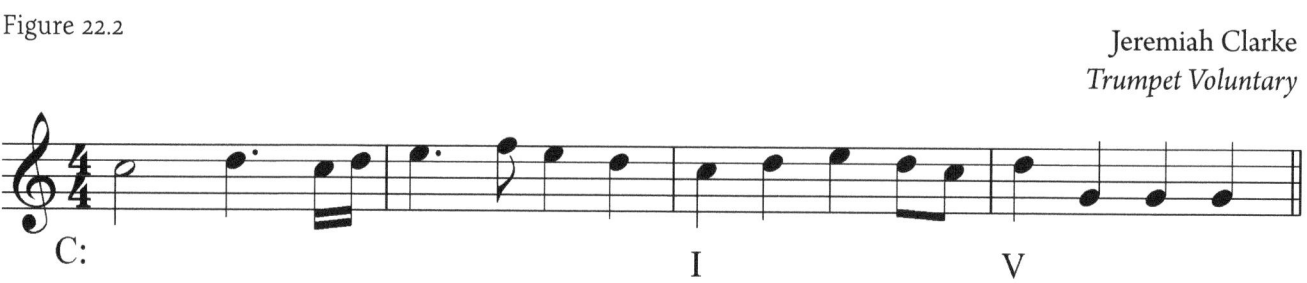

Figure 22.2

Jeremiah Clarke
Trumpet Voluntary

A phrase may begin with movement into the first beat of a measure. The note or notes that precede the first strong beat of the melody are called the *anacrusis*. Sometimes this is known as the *pick up* or *upbeat*. The anacrusis is not the first measure of a melody. The first measure is after the anacrusis, beginning with the first strong beat of the melody. If the first phrase of a melody begins with an anacrusis, often every subsequent phrase will also begin with an anacrusis. This is a unifying characteristic in the design of the melody. Each phrase in the melody in Figure 22.3 begins with an anacrusis. The first measure begins with the F on the first strong beat after the anacrusis.

Figure 22.3

The British Grenadiers
English Air

The anacrusis can appear in several different melodic patterns. The most common is seen in Figure 22.3 where the anacrusis is the dominant (C) and moves to the tonic (F) on the first beat of the measure. Another pattern for the anacrusis may be seen in Figure 22.4 with a two note anacrusis moving from the tonic to the third. The interval of the 3rd is filled in with a passing note. The opposite of this also occurs with the anacrusis starting on the third and moving down to the tonic with passing motion.

Figure 22.4

George Frideric Handel
Gavotte

Another common anacrusis using more than one note consists of the broken triad. Figure 22.5 begins with a two note anacrusis using the notes of the G major triad.

Figure 22.5

Ludwig van Beethoven
Symphony No. 5, II

Certain notes of a melody are strong tendency tones. These notes want to move or resolve in a certain predictable way. For example, the leading tone is a strong tendency tone because it has a strong need to move melodically to the tonic. The melody in Figure 22.6 ends on the tonic and is approached by the leading tone ($\hat{7}$-$\hat{1}$). When you play or sing this melody and stop on the leading tone, you can feel the strong urge to move to the tonic. This produces an effective melodic ending that supports a perfect authentic cadence (V - I).

Figure 22.6

All Through the Night
Welsh Air

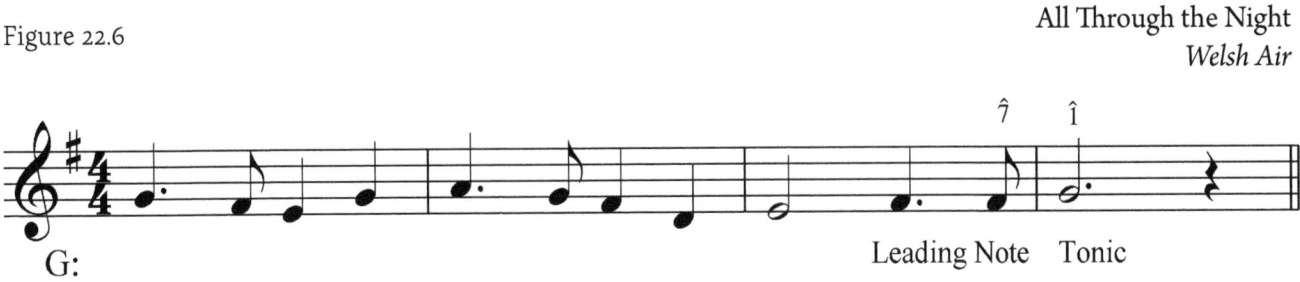

In Figure 22.7, the melody moves down to the tonic from the supertonic ($\hat{2}$-$\hat{1}$). This is another common melodic ending that supports a perfect authentic cadence. Melodies that end on the tonic and are approached from the supertonic ($\hat{2}$ -$\hat{1}$), or the leading tone ($\hat{7}$-$\hat{1}$), offer an exceptionally strong conclusion that reinforces the tonality. They also support a perfect authentic cadence.

Figure 22.7

George Frideric Handel
Impertinence

If a melody skips to the tonic at the cadence it usually moves from the dominant ($\hat{5}$ - $\hat{1}$) as seen in Figure 22.8. Here, the melody skips up a 4th from C to F. Another option for this cadence from $\hat{5}$ to $\hat{1}$ is to skip down a 5th.

Figure 22.8

Auld Lang Syne
Scottish Air

Melodies may be *conjunct* or *disjunct*. A conjunct melody moves primarily by step and a disjunct melody moves by leap. Good melodies are usually a combination of these two types of motion. Figure 22.9 is a disjunct melody that contains many leaps. In this example the leaps outline the E♭ major chord.

Figure 22.9

Ludwig van Beethoven
Symphony No. 3, Op. 55, I

The melody in Figure 22.10 consists primarily of stepwise or conjunct motion.

Figure 22.10

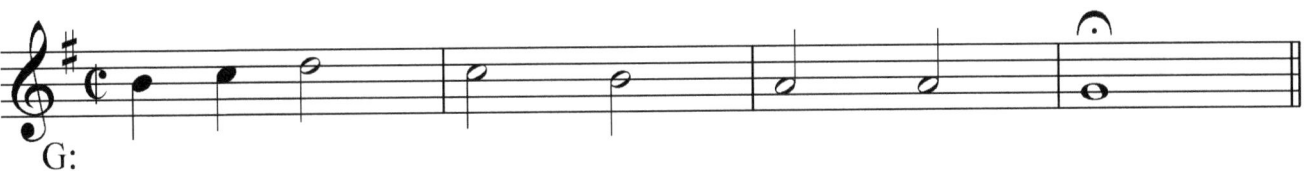

Melodic Motives, Repetition, and Sequence

A phrase may by built from smaller musical units called *motives*. A *rhythmic motive* is a short rhythmic pattern that may be repeated at different pitches. In Figure 22.11 a distinctive rhythmic pattern repeats but the pitches change. This is a rhythmic motive.

Figure 22.11

George Frideric Handel
Messiah, Hallelujah Chorus

A *melodic motive* is based on a rhythmic pattern and a specific pattern of pitches. Figure 22.12 is the famous four note motive from Beethoven's fifth symphony.

Figure 22.12

Motives may be altered slightly when they are repeated as long as they are not changed so much that they are not recognizable. Figure 22.13 illustrates a little of what Beethoven did with his four note motive.

Figure 22.13

Ludwig van Beethoven
Symphony No. 5, Op. 67, I

A motive may be repeated at different pitch levels. This repetition is called a *sequence*. Figure 22.14 contains a motive that is repeated sequentially a step lower than the original.

Figure 22.14

Johann Sebastian Bach
Invention No. 13, BWV 784

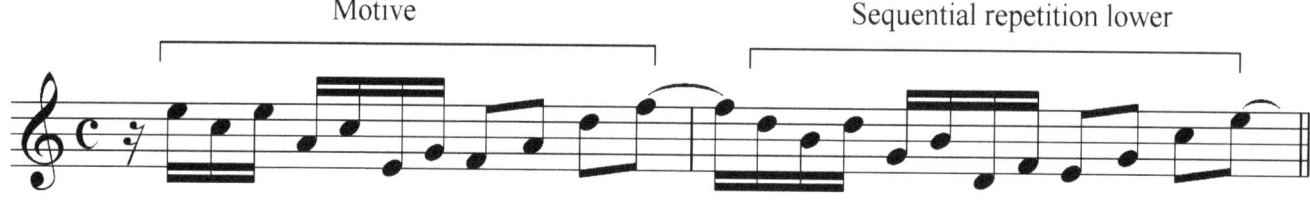

Antecedent and Consequent Phrases

Typical phrases are four measures long. Often two melodic phrases will compliment each other in a question answer type of format. These phrases are considered *antecedent* and *consequent*. Figure 22.15 contains two phrases. The first phrase, the question or antecedent phrase, ends in a half cadence. The second phrase, the answer or consequent phrase, repeats the opening idea and changes the ending to accomodate an authentic cadence. This is a common compositional technique used by composers over the centuries.

Figure 22.15

Johannes Brahms
Symphony No. 1, IV

The cadence at the end of the antecedent phrase often has less feeling of finality than the one at the end of the consequent phrase. Figure 22.16 uses the dominant note ($\hat{5}$) as the last note of the first phrase to create an half cadence. The second phase ends on the tonic ($\hat{1}$) allowing it to be harmonized with an authentic cadence.

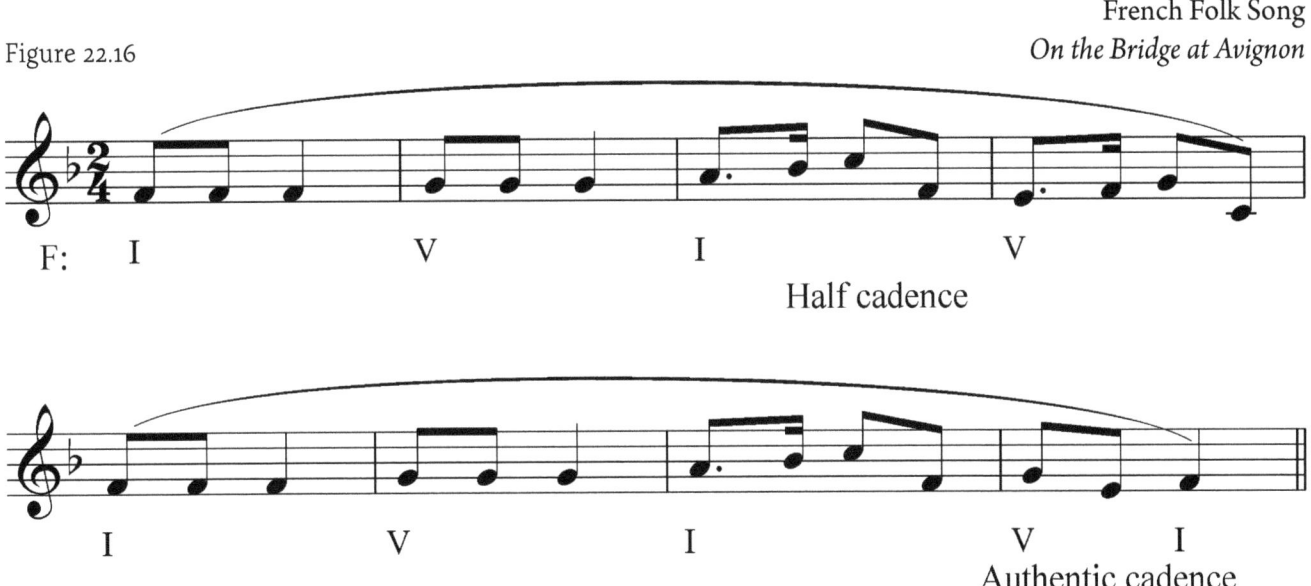

Figure 22.16

French Folk Song
On the Bridge at Avignon

The antecedent phrase often ends in an authentic cadence if it is rhythmically weak. The first phrase in Figure 22.17 ends in an imperfect authentic cadence in a rhythmically weak position. The consequent phrase ends in a perfect authentic cadence but it is rhythmically strong with the final chord on the strong beat. Here Mozart alters the melody in phrase two for the answer.

Figure 22.17

Wolfgang Amadeus Mozart
Piano Sonata, K.332

Sixteen Measure Melodic Form

Many melodies are composed in a 16 measure form. In this structure the music is made up of four phrases that are four measures each. Phrases one, two, and four are the same except for their endings. Phrase three is a contrasting phrase.

Figure 21.18 contains the famous "Ode to Joy" theme from Beethoven's ninth symphony. The four phrases are labelled A, A¹, B, and A¹. A¹ indicates that the phrase is the same as A but with a slightly different ending. B is a different phrase melodically. The first two phrases are antecedent and consequent. Phrase one, the question phrase, ends on an half cadence and phrase two, the answer phrase, ends on an authentic cadence. Phrase three (B) is different melodically and provides contrast to the "A" phrases. Phrase four completes the form with a return of A¹ and an authentic cadence.

Figure 21.18

Chapter 22: Melody Writing

You may be asked to compose a sixteen measure melody based upon a single phrase. Figure 22.19 is an example of this type of question.

1. Name the key.
2. Name the type of baroque dance the melody represents.
3. Complete the exercise to create a sixteen measure melody in rounded binary form.
4. Mark the phrasing.
5. Add a bass part at the cadence points.
6. Symbolize the cadences with functional chord symbols and name them.

Figure 22.19

Dance type: _____

The first steps in working through this question are shown in Figure 22.20.

The dance type indicated by the pick-up, the time signature, and the tempo marking, is a Bourrée. The key is D major. The half cadence in D major at the end of the given phrase is indicated. Repeat signs are added to the score in order to prepare it for rounded binary form.

Figure 22.20

Dance type: Bourrée

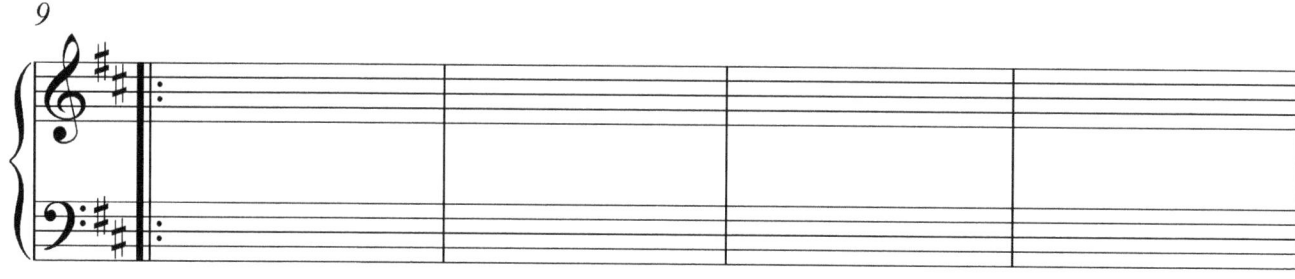

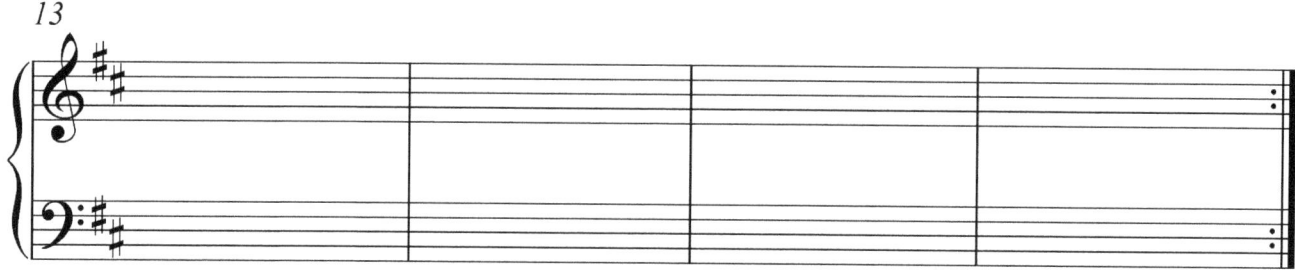

Chapter 22: Melody Writing

In Figure 22.21 the second phrase is added. Since the first phrase begins with a pick up, each subsequent phrase will begin with a pickup. This will become a unifying element in the piece. The second phrase is a repeat of the given phrase with a different ending. The new ending supports an authentic cadence in D major by ending the melody on $\hat{2}$ - $\hat{1}$. The bass line is added and follows the elements established in the given melody. Here, a downward moving arpeggio is placed in the bass part. This bass line keeps up the motion of the piece, and is much more effective than stopping on a dotted half note completely at the end of each phrase.

Figure 22.21

Dance type: Bourrée

In Figure 22.22 we copy the phrase we wrote in mm. 5 - 8 into mm. 13 - 16. This is an important step in creating rounded binary form. Section A must return at the end in this form. Phrase marks are added.

Figure 22.22

Dance type: Bourrée

The last step shown in figure 22.23 is to write the B section in mm. 9 - 12. This section must be contrasting to the A sections, but must still maintain the characteristics of a Bourrée. Keeping the same or close rhythmic ideas and writing new melodic material here creates a contrasting section. The bass part is added at the cadence and follows the same pattern as the other phrases. Make special note of the placement of the repeat signs and pickup in this section. The phrase is marked and the half cadence is indicated.

Figure 22.23

Dance type: Bourrée

1. For the following melodies:

   a. Name the key.
   b. Name the type of baroque dance the melody represents.
   c. Complete the exercise to create a sixteen measure melody in rounded binary form.
   d. Mark the phrasing.
   e. Add a bass part at the cadence points.
   f. Symbolize the cadences with functional chord symbols and name them.

Dance type: _____

key:

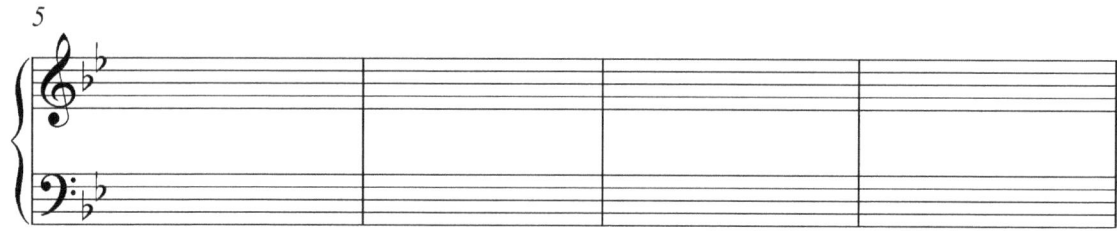

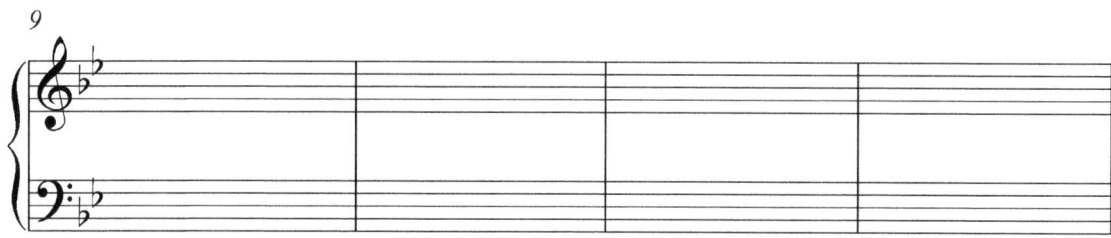

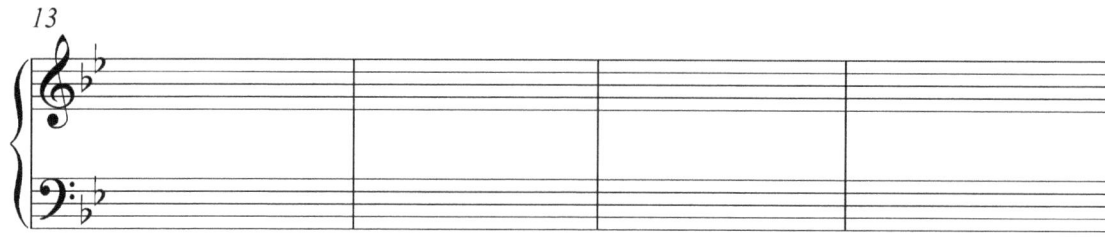

Chapter 22: Melody Writing

Dance type: _____

key:

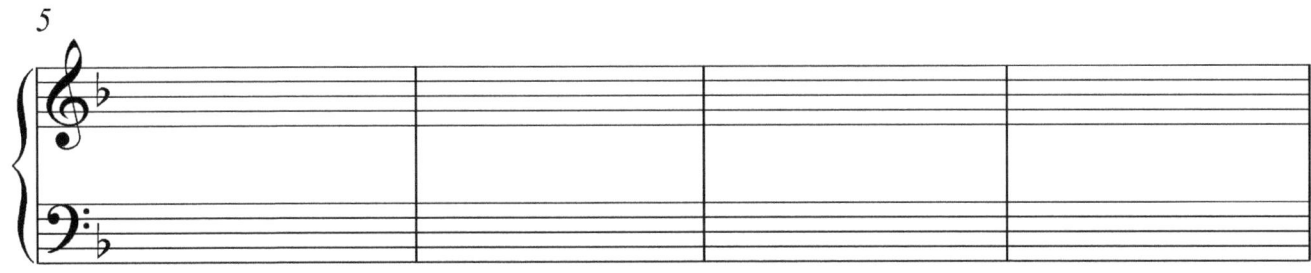

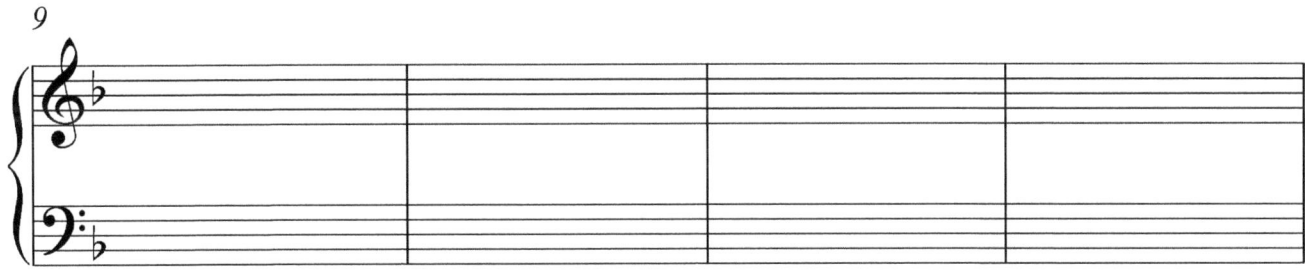

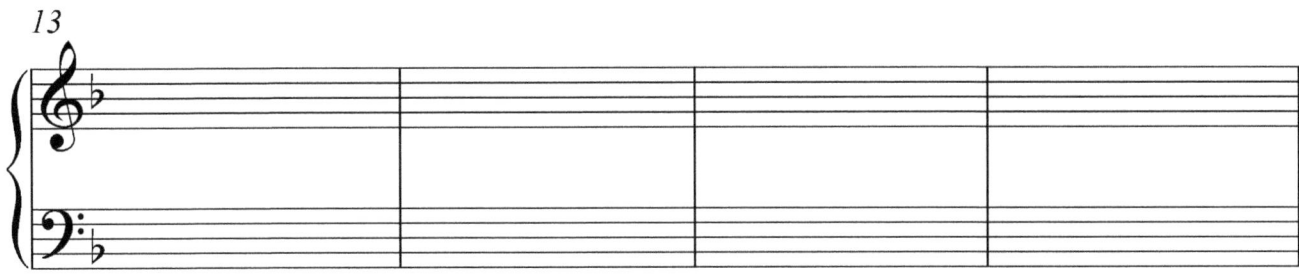

Dance type: _____

key:

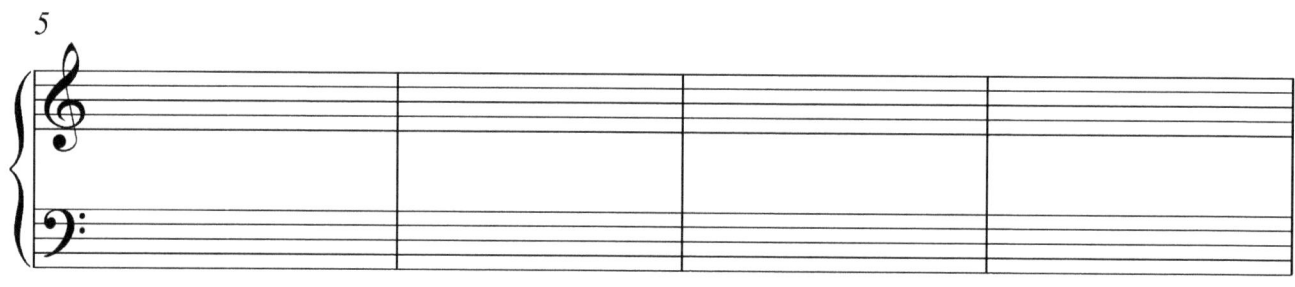

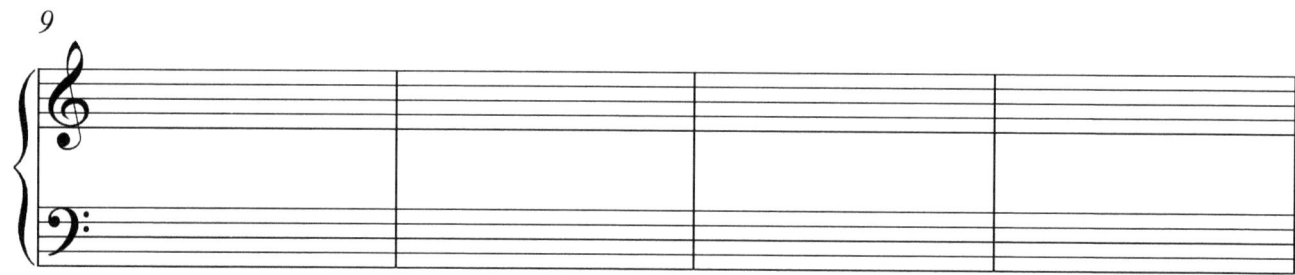

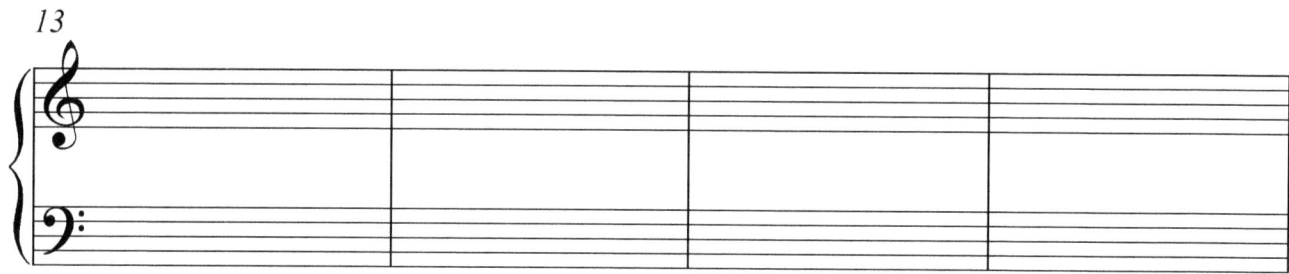

Dance type: _____

key:

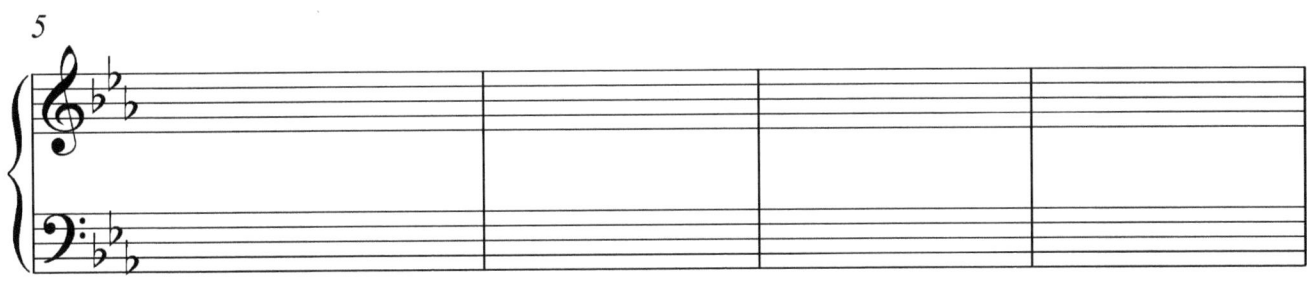

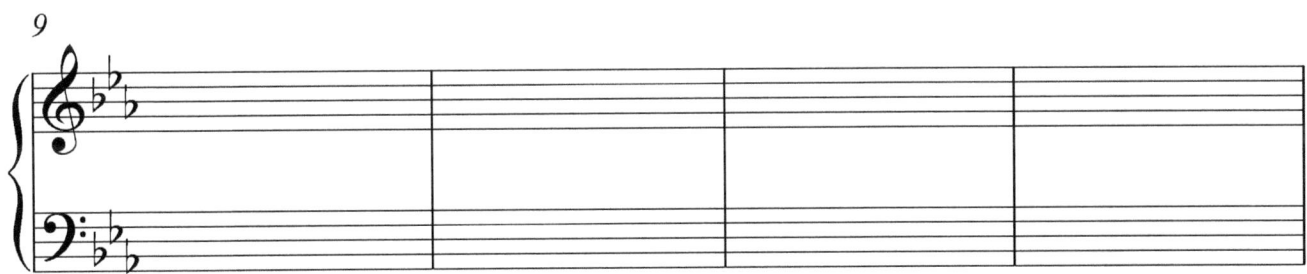

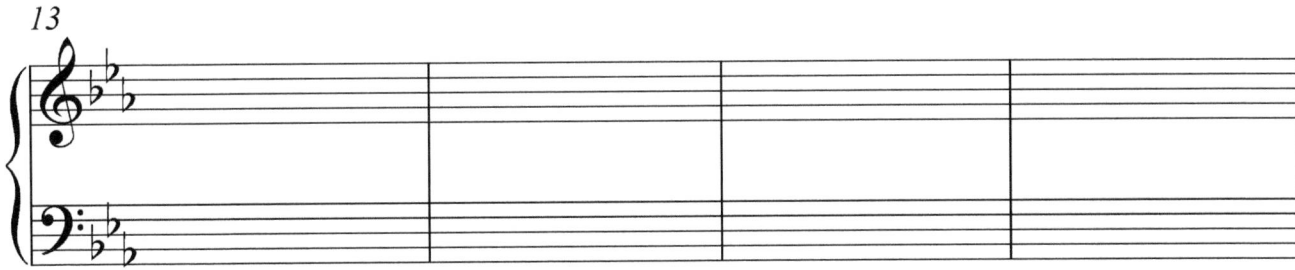

Chapter 22: Melody Writing

Dance type: _____

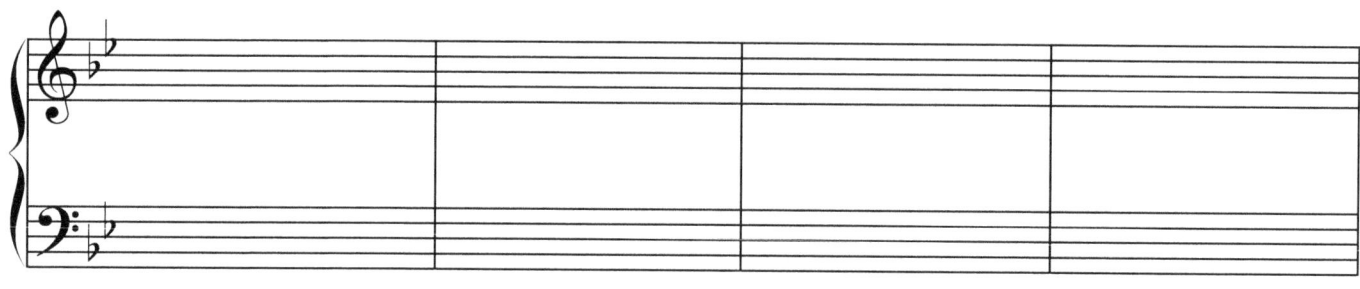

key:

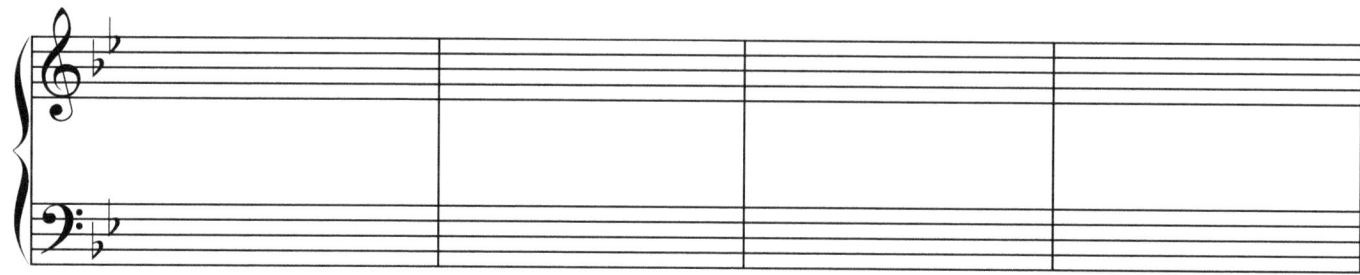

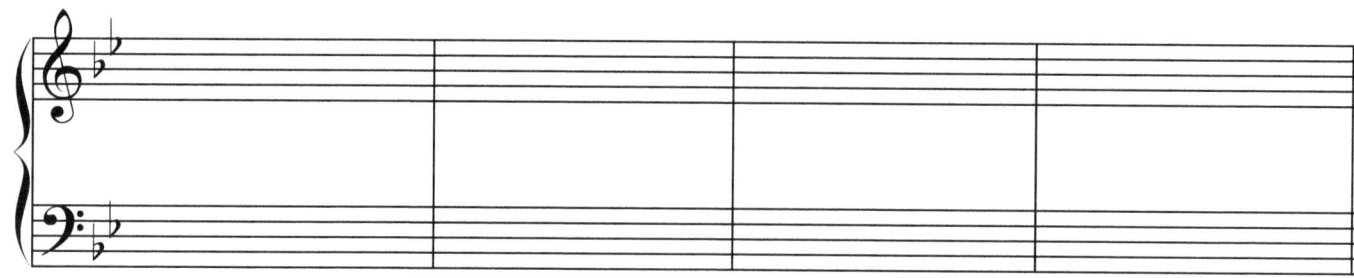

23
Counterpoint

The term counterpoint comes from the Latin expression *punctus contra punctum* which means point against point or note against note. Generally, counterpoint involves the writing of musical lines that sound different from each other but sound harmonious when played together. Counterpoint focuses on the interaction of melodies. Secondary to this interaction are the harmonies produced by the counterpoint. Still, you cannot separate the harmony from the counterpoint. It is impossible to write two lines of music without creating harmony, and impossible to create harmony without linear activity.

Counterpoint was used extensively in the Renaissance period, especially in the music of Giovanni Palestrina (1525 - 1594), but it reached its culmination with the composers of the Baroque period. It is often referred to as *polyphony* and the two terms are almost interchangeable. Historically, music created in the Baroque period is described as *contrapuntal*, while music composed before the Baroque period is described as *polyphonic*.

The Baroque was a very active period for contrapuntal writing. Prominent composers from this period that were in Germany are Johann Sebastian Bach (1685-1750), Dietrich Buxtehude (1637-1707), Johann Pachelbel (1635-1706) and Georg Phillipp Telemann (1681-1767). In Italy and Spain composers of this genre were Arcangelo Corelli (1653-1713), Antonio Vivaldi (1678-1741) and Domenico Scarlatti (1685-1757). In France composers included François Couperin (1668-1733) and Jean-Phillipe Rameau (1683-1764); and in England George Frideric Handel (1685-1759).

Figure 23.1 is an example of two voice counterpoint from the 18th century.

George Frideric Handel
Passepied

Figure 23.1

Writing Two Part Counterpoint

This chapter focuses on writing two part counterpoint in 18th century style. An important aspect of this writing can be seen in the intervals that occur between the two voices. Figure 23.2 shows the intervals that occur between the two voices of the Handel Passepied.

Figure 23.2

George Frideric Handel
Passepied

Two part contrapuntal writing in 18th century style involves three basic types of motion between the voices.

Similar Motion
Similar motion is when two voices move in the same direction either by step or by leap. The numbers in Figure 23.3 indicate the intervallic distance between the voices. If the voices move in the same direction by the same interval (as in this example in parallel 3rds) it is considered parallel motion. Note that we are expressing compound intervals in their simple form. (e.g. 10 = 3, 12 = 5, etc.)

Figure 23.3

Contrary Motion
Contrary motion is when two voices move in the opposite direction. Figure 23.4

Figure 23.4

Oblique Motion
Oblique motion is when one voice moves and the other voice remains stationary. Figure 23.5

Figure 23.5

Intervals Between Voices

The following intervals are considered consonant and are used frequently between voices in two part counterpoint.

major 3rd, minor 3rd, major 6th, minor 6th, perfect octave, perfect 5th, perfect unison

Two dissonant intervals that are used fairly frequently since they imply dominant 7th harmony are the:

augmented 4th, diminished 5th

Other dissonant intervals that may be used are:

minor 7th, perfect 4th, major 2nd

Two dissonant intervals that are **not used** are:

minor 2nd and **major 7th**

Most Commonly Used Intervals ———▶ **Least Commonly Used Intervals**

major and minor 3rds	perfect octaves	perfect 5ths	augmented 4ths
major and minor 6ths		perfect unisons	diminished 5ths
		minor 7ths	
		major 2nds	
		perfect 4ths	

We can study these vertical intervals and their uses beginning with the most commonly used.

Thirds

Vertical major and minor 3rds are used frequently. The 3rd often implies a triad in root position. You can use up to four vertical 3rds in a row. Using more than four in a row can make the counterpoint sound boring or uninteresting.

Figure 23.6

C: I   ii   I⁶   V   I

Chapter 23: Counterpoint

Sixths

Vertical major and minor 6ths are used frequently. The 6th often implies a triad in first inversion. You can use up to four vertical 6ths in a row.

Figure 23.7

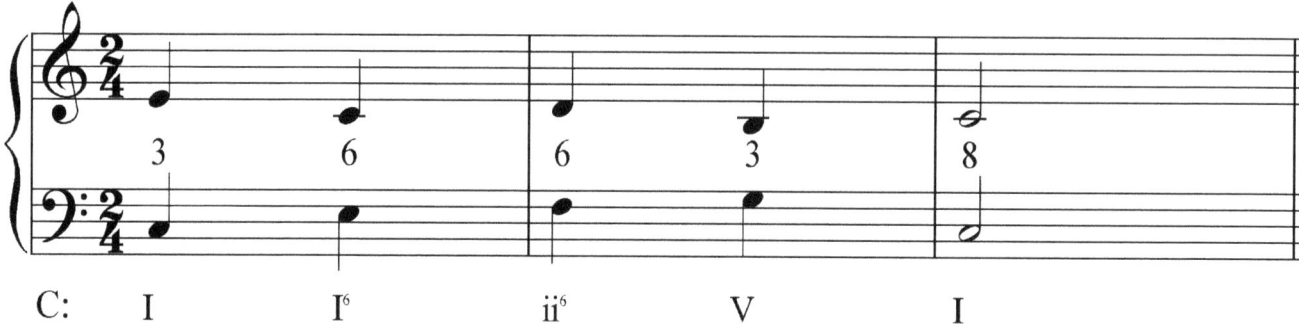

Perfect Octaves

Perfect octaves occur most commonly at the beginning and ends of phrases. They may be used elsewhere in a phrase but are usually found on a weak beat. Perfect octaves are found most frequently on the tonic and dominant notes of the key, but may occur on any note of the scale except the leading tone.
The approach to the octave is important. It is most often approached by contrary motion as in m.2 of Figure 23.8. It is correct to approach the octave in similar motion as long as the melody moves by step (mm.3-4). This is a common progression that occurs at the ends of phrases with an authentic cadence.

Figure 23.8

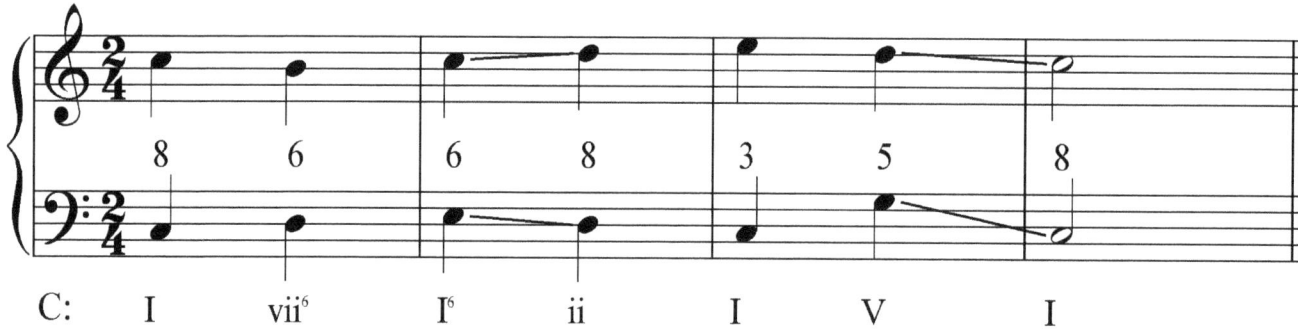

Do not use more than one octave in a row. This is the error of parallel octaves, and is considered wrong Figure 23.9. (a) The passing tone in (b) does not hide the faulty parallel octaves. When octaves are approached by a leap in similar motion, the error of hidden or direct octaves occur Figure 23.9 (c). Do not leap to an octave with similar motion.

Figure 23.9

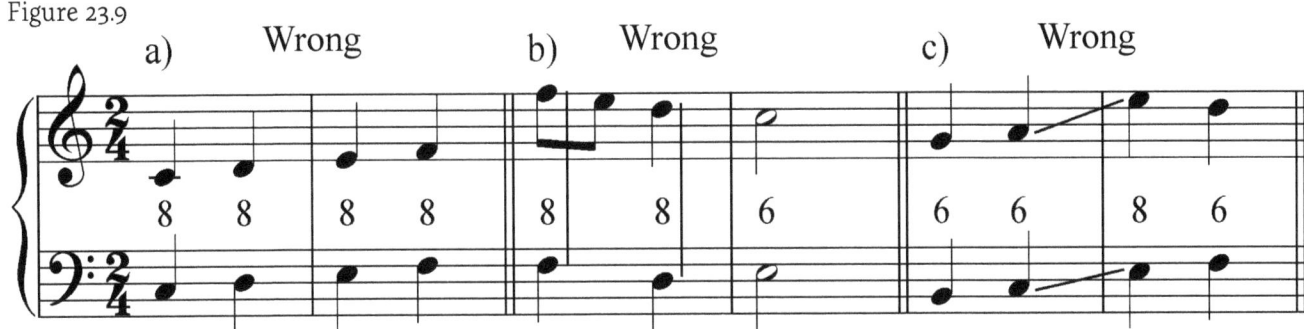

Perfect Fifths

The perfect 5th is most commonly used at the beginning and ends of phrases. It has a hollow sound and if it is used within the phrase it is usually found on a weak beat. The perfect 5th is usually approached by contrary motion Figure 23.10 (m. 2). An approach by similar motion is possible if the melody moves by step (mm.3-4).

Figure 23.10

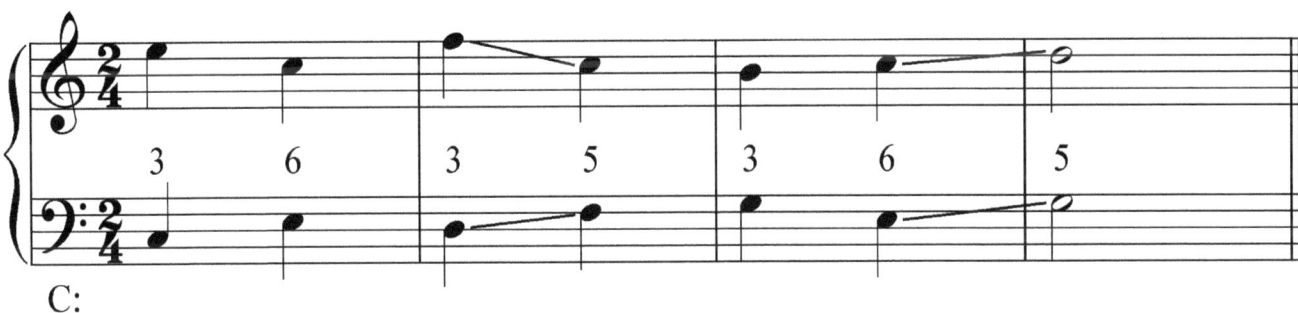

Do not use more than one 5th in a row. This is the error of parallel 5ths and is wrong Figure 23.11 (a). The passing tone creates faulty parallel fifths in (b). When 5ths are approached by a leap in similar motion an error called hidden or direct 5ths occurs Figure 23.11 (c). Do not leap to a 5th with similar motion.

Figure 23.11

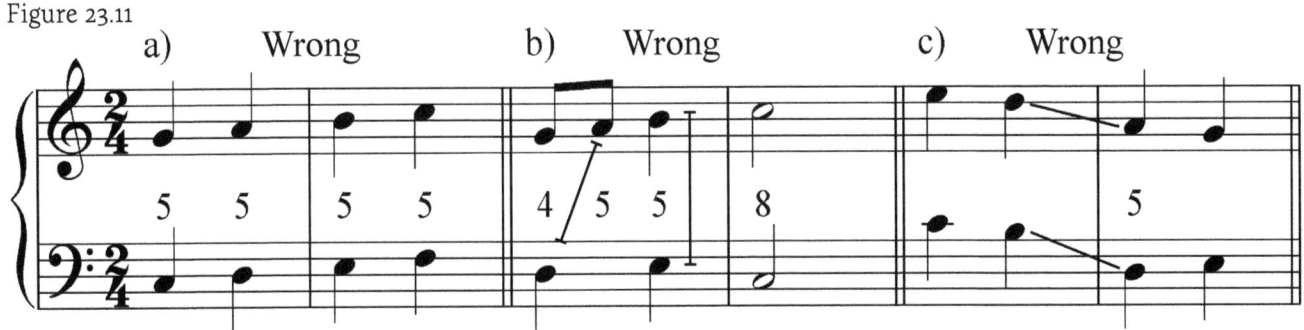

Sevenths

Major 7ths are almost never used because they are very dissonant. We do however use the minor 7th to imply V^7 or ii^7. The root of V^7 rises a 4th or falls a 5th to the root of I and the 7th falls a step to the 3rd of I Figure 23.12(a). In the progression V^7—vi, the root of V^7 rises a step to the root of vi and the 7th falls a step to the 5th of vi Figure 23.12(b).

Since ii^7 resolves to V certain rules of resolution are required. The 7th of ii^7 is prepared with common tone motion and falls a step to the 3rd of chord V. The root of ii^7 move to the root of chord V Figure 23.12(c). **Note that the leading tone must always rise to the tonic in two part writing and the implied 7ths must always resolve downward by step.**

Figure 23.12

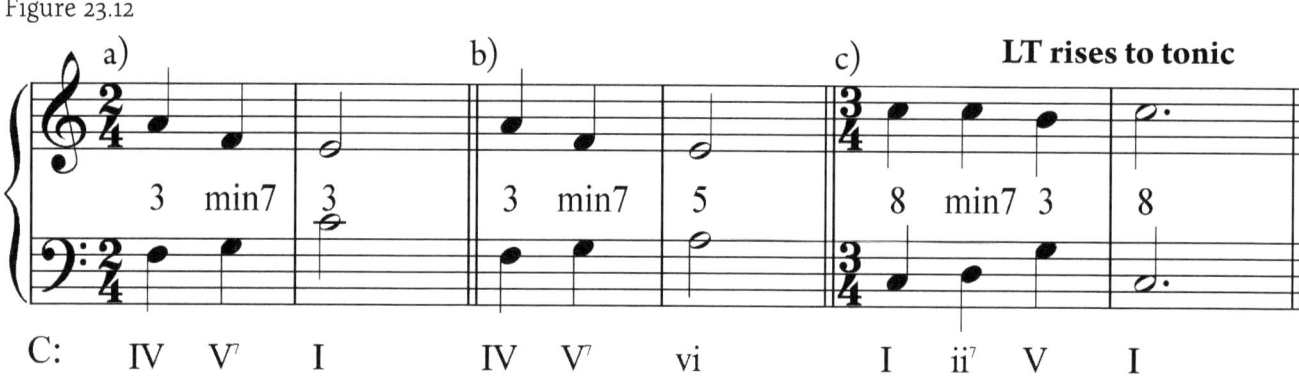

In Figure 23.13 the 7th of V^7 falls a step in its resolution to I and the 7th of ii^7 falls a step in its resolution to V.

Figure 23.13

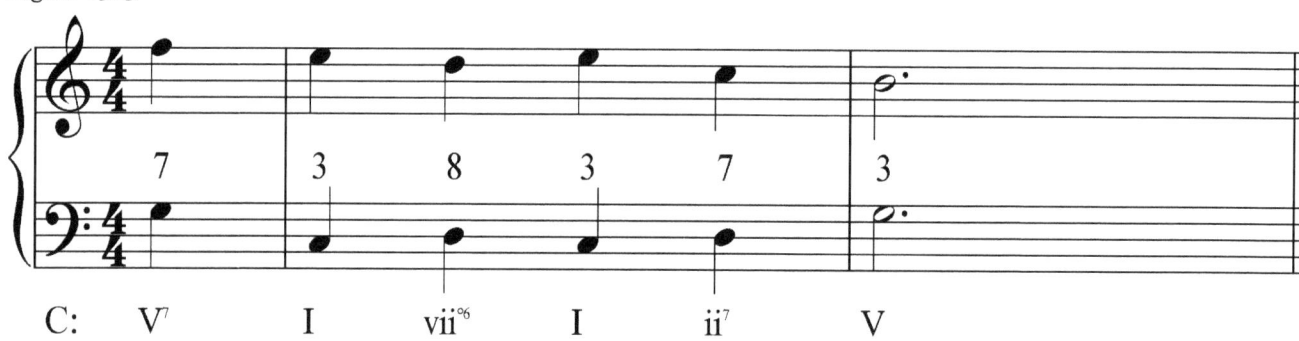

Chapter 23: Counterpoint

1. Complete the following progressions in two part counterpoint according to the following chord symbols. Be sure to resolve the 7ths in each 7th chord correctly.

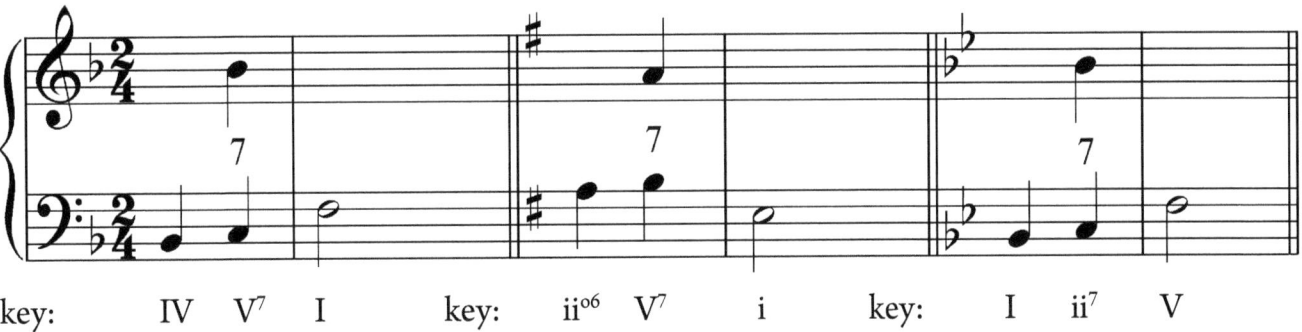

key: IV   V⁷   I   key: ii°⁶   V⁷   i   key: I   ii⁷   V

2. Complete the following progressions in two part counterpoint according to the following chord symbols.

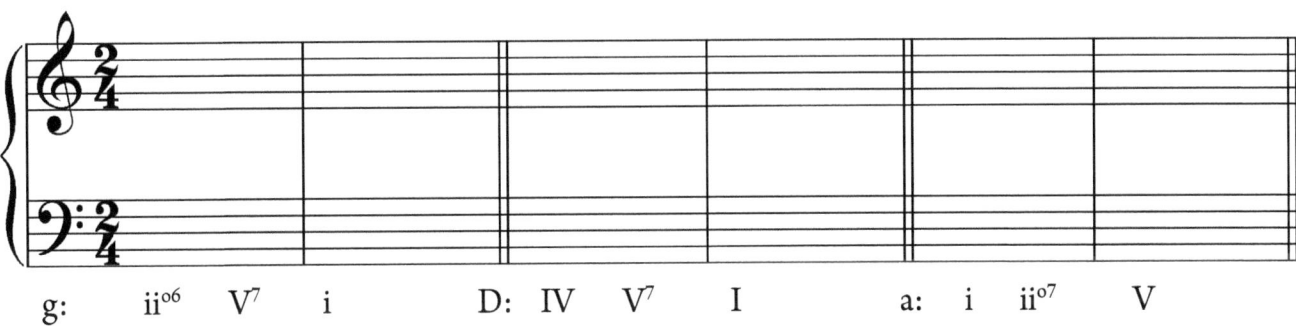

g: ii°⁶   V⁷   i   D: IV   V⁷   I   a: i   ii°⁷   V

The Perfect Unison

The perfect unison is used at the beginning and ends of phrases. It is not often used in the middle of a phrase because a unison can cause the counterpoint to sound like one voice has dropped out. It is best to approach a unison by contrary motion. Do not use more than one perfect unison in a row. Parallel perfect unisons are wrong.

Figure 23.14

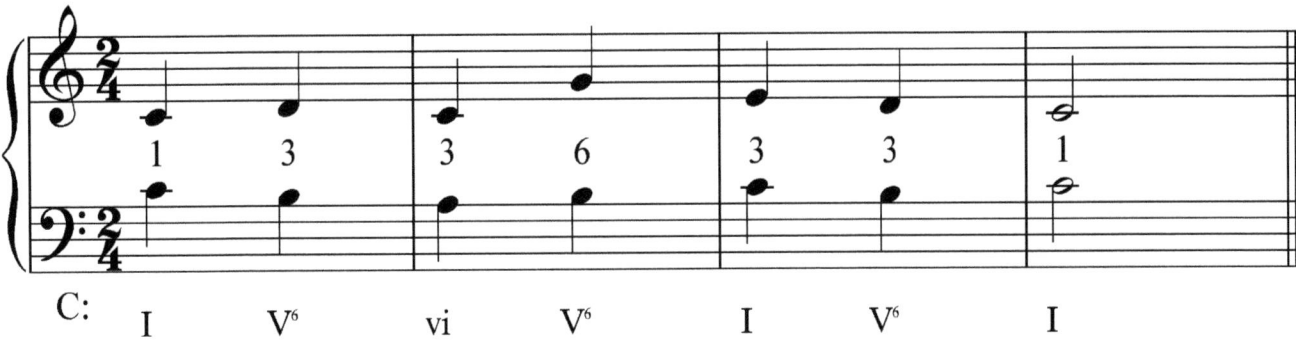

C: I   V⁶   vi   V⁶   I   V⁶   I

The Augmented Fourth and Diminished Fifth

The augmented 4th and diminished 5th are vertical intervals that require resolution. These two intervals imply inversions of the dominant 7th chord. The diminished 5th occurs between the leading tone in the bass and the subdominant in the treble. This implies the V^6_5 chord or less frequently an inversion of a diminished 7th chord.

The subdominant is the 7th of V^6_5 and must resolve down by step to the 3rd of chord I. The dim 5th resolves inwardly to the interval of a 3rd. Dim 5ths should be approached by contrary or oblique motion.

Figure 23.15

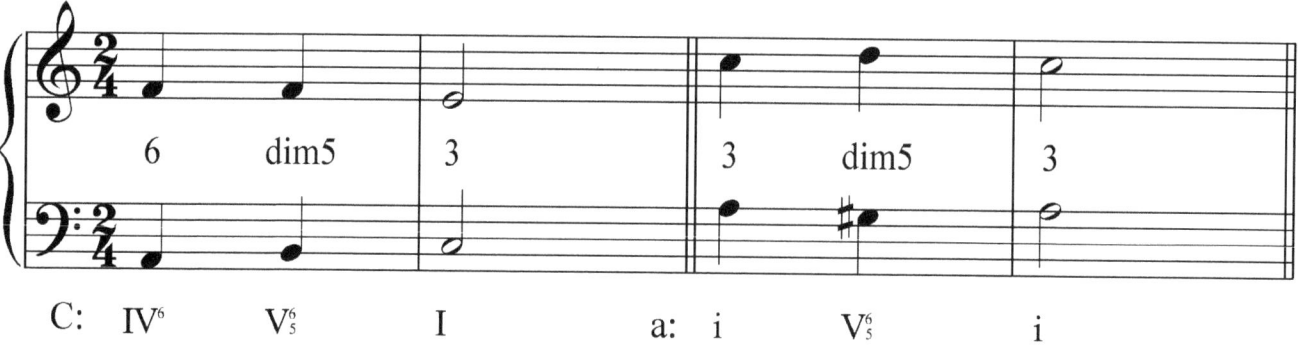

The augmented 4th implies V^4_2, or less frequently, an inversion of a diminished 7th chord. The aug 4th occurs between the subdominant in the bass and the leading tone in the treble. This interval resolves outwardly to the interval of a 6th. Augmented 4ths should be approached by contrary or oblique motion.

Figure 23.16

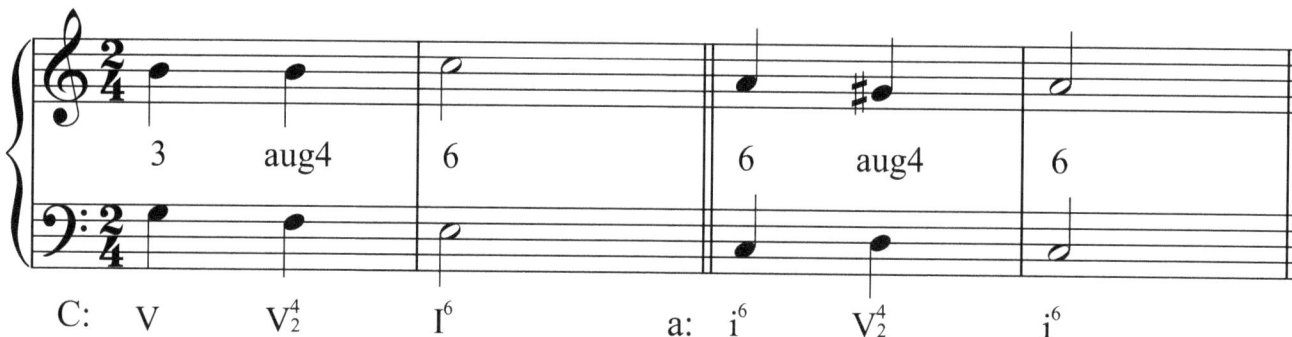

3. Complete the following progressions in two part counterpoint according to the following chord symbols.

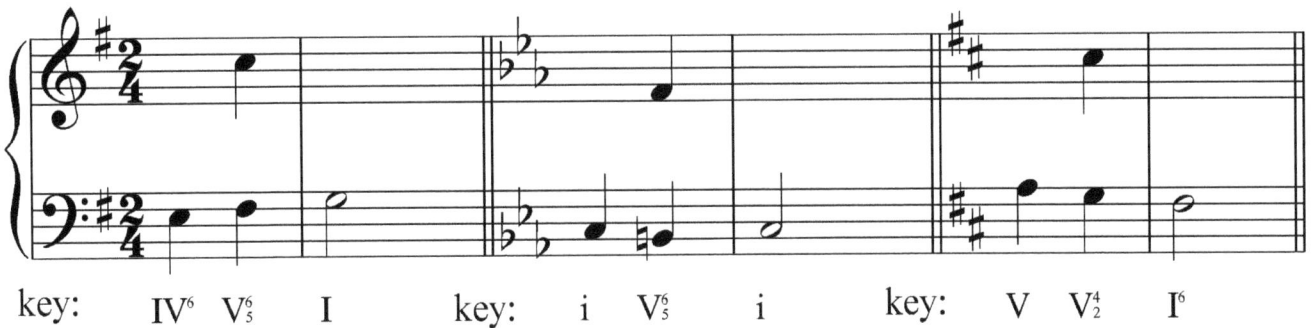

key: IV⁶   V⁶₅   I   key: i   V⁶₅   i   key: V   V⁴₂   I⁶

4. Complete the following progressions in two part counterpoint according to the following chord symbols.

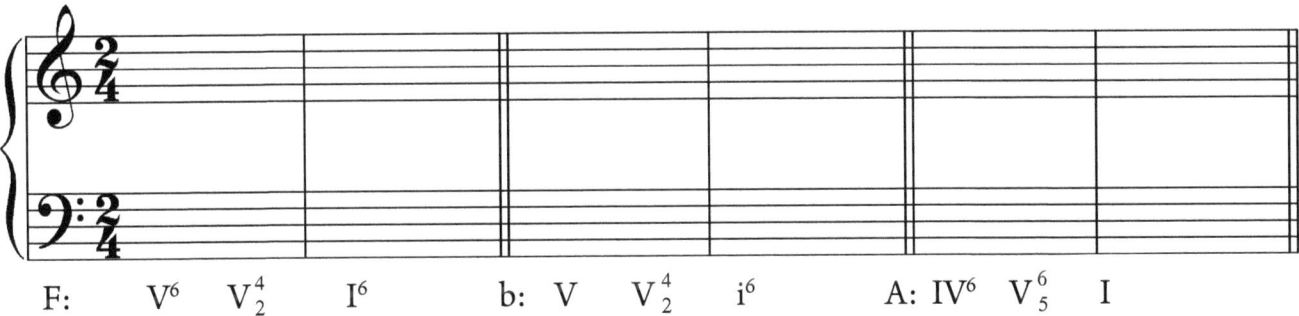

F: V⁶   V⁴₂   I⁶   b: V   V⁴₂   i⁶   A: IV⁶   V⁶₅   I

The Major Second

The major 2nd can be used as an interval between voices. The minor 2nd however is not. This interval is used occasionally to imply V⁴₂ or ii⁴₂ . Here, the bass note is the 7th and must resolve downward by step to a first inversion chord. The upper note may repeat as a common tone as in Figure 23.17 (a), or leap up a 4th as in Figure 23.17 (b).

Figure 23.17

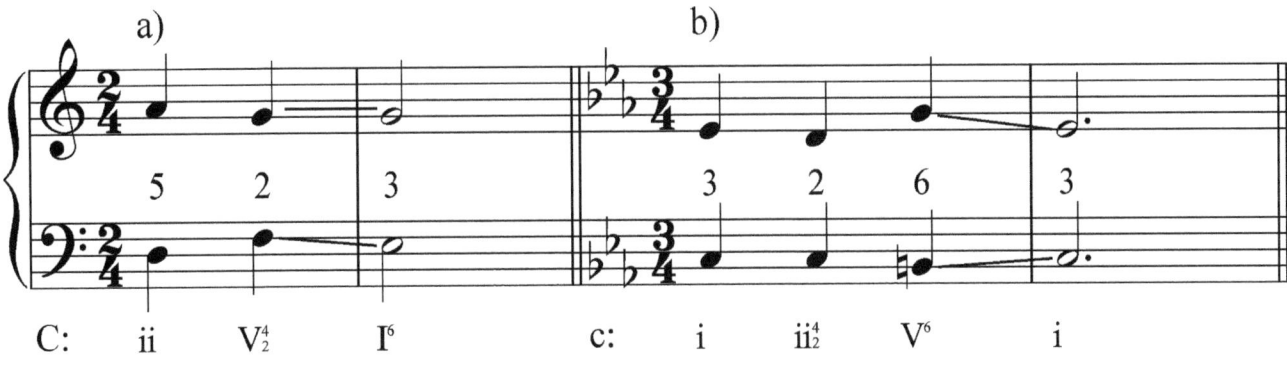

C: ii   V⁴₂   I⁶   c: i   ii⁴₂   V⁶   i

The Perfect Fourth

The perfect 4th used between two voices is usually found at the end of a phrase and implies a cadential six-four. Because the 4th is considered dissonant it requires resolution.

Study the following examples using the perfect 4th. In Figure 23.18 (a) the 6 resolves to 5 maintaining the dominant in the bass. Here, the bass drops an octave, but it could also repeat.
In Figure 23.18 (b) the 4 resolves to 3 over the dominant in the bass. Care should be taken when approaching the 4th. It is usually approached by common tone or by stepwise motion from above.

Figure 23.18

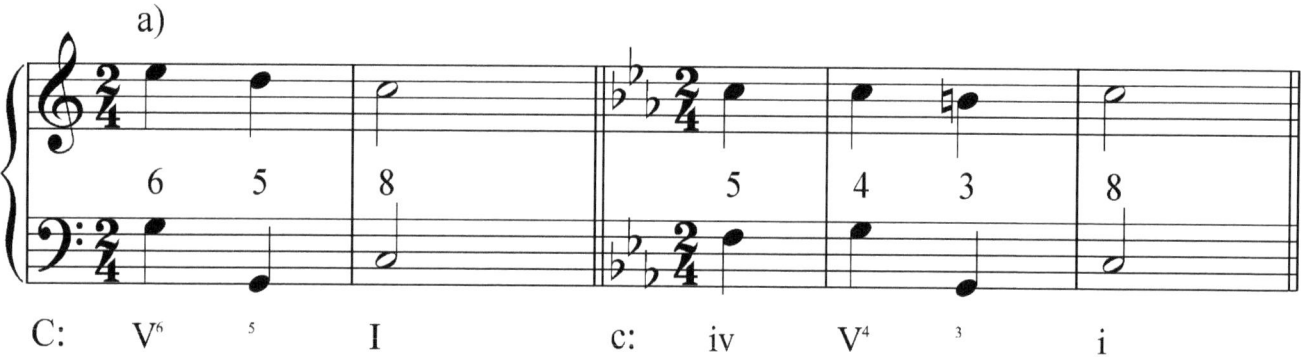

5. Complete the following progressions in two part counterpoint according to the following chord symbols.

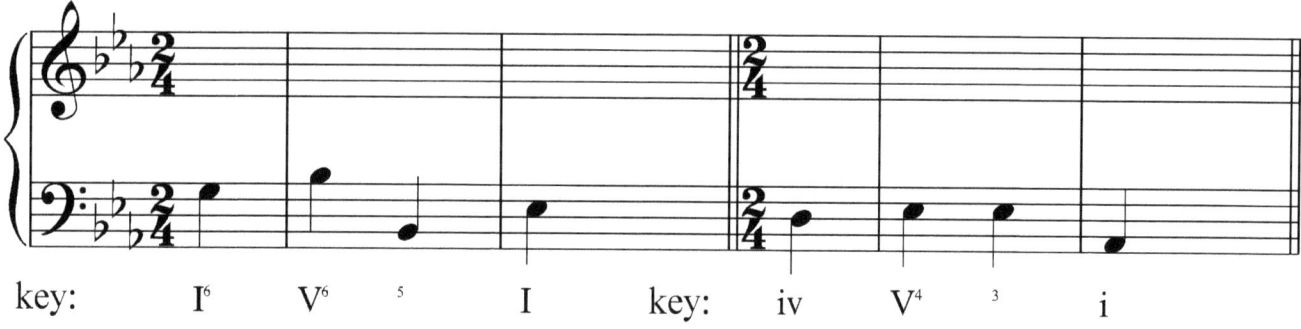

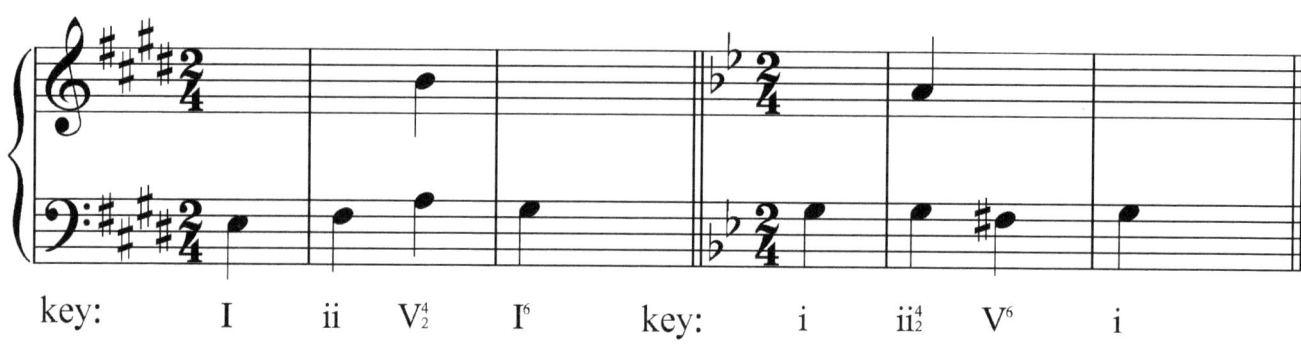

Implied Harmony

In 18th century counterpoint not only are the interval combinations considered, but also the harmonic progressions implied by the interval combinations. The music must be logical and have a sense of direction both as independent melodic lines and as a harmonic progression.

It is best to keep the progressions simple. Following the plan of: beginning tonic – predominant– dominant- ending tonic is effective most of the time. Staying within this harmonic framework in your two part writing will help to make your work harmonically sound and give it musical sense.

Figure 23.19 shows two different harmonies for the same bass line. Both examples function in the same way. Measures 1 and 2 are a prolongation of the beginning tonic. Measure 3 contains the predominant and dominant harmony followed by the ending tonic in measure 4.

Figure 23.19

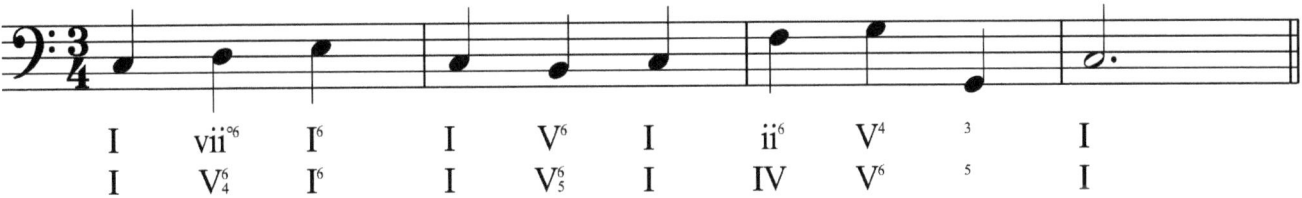

6. Study the following progression. Using Roman numerals indicate the implied harmony under the score.

key:

Strict note against note counterpoint is not used very often for an entire composition in 18th century style since it provides very little rhythmic interest when both voices use the same note values. We often see the addition of non chord tones or chordal skips to provide rhythmic interest and movement.

Study the example of strict note against note counterpoint in Figure 23.20.

Figure 23.20

Figure 23.21 is the same example with the addition of passing motion in m.2. These notes give interest and movement to the melody. However, care must be taken when adding non chord tones. Always check your work to see if the addition of non chord tones has created faulty parallel motion.

Figure 23.21

Chapter 23: Counterpoint

Tips for Writing Counterpoint Above A Bass Line

Study the following steps for writing counterpoint above a given bass.

1. Study the given example and name the key.

2. Decide on a harmonic plan. Here it may be best to start at the end of the phrase, deciding on a cadence and a good pre-cadential chord. Sketch in the predominant and cadence.

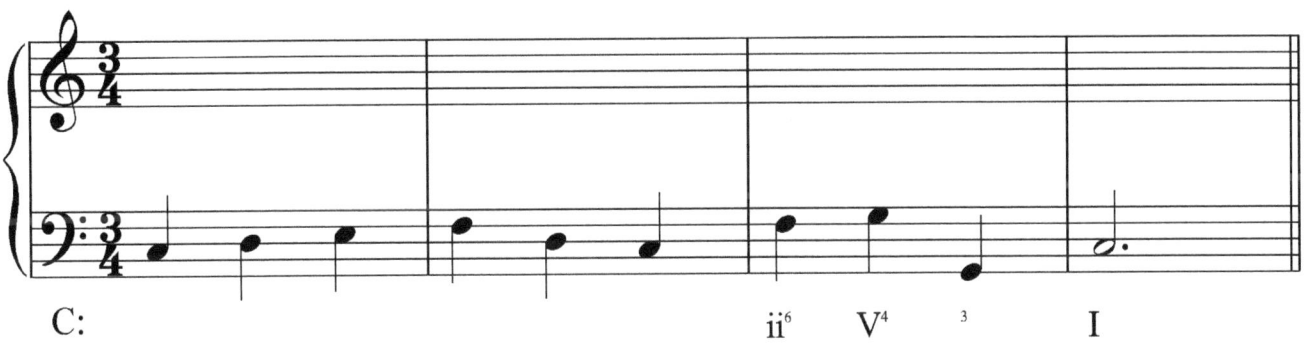

3. Start at the beginning and complete the harmonic plan for the exercise. Try to follow the basic harmonic plan of: beginning tonic—pre-dominant—dominant—ending tonic if you can. Look for common and idiomatic progressions like I-vii°6 –I6 shown below. Sketch in a basic chord progression bearing in mind that you may have to make changes when you actually add the upper voice.

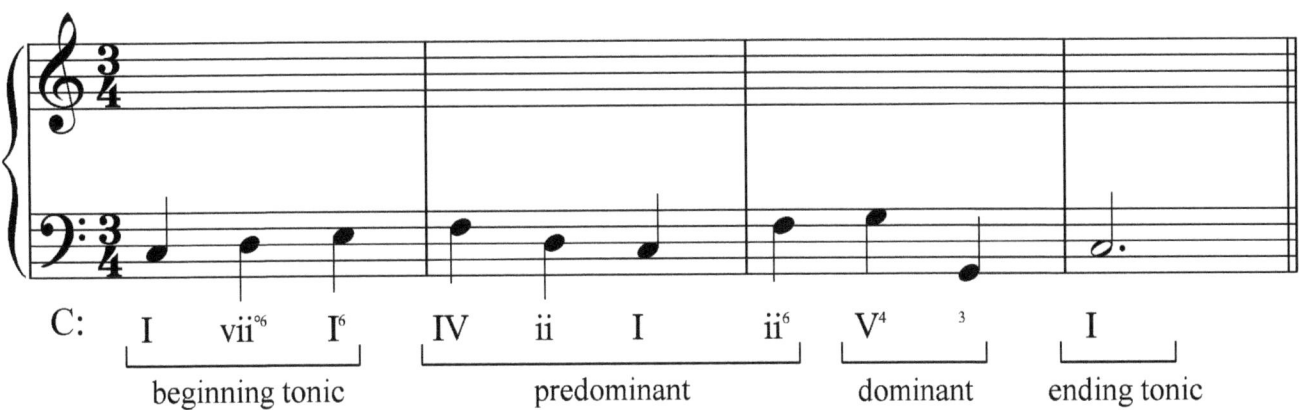

4. Write the counterpoint according to your harmonic plan. Write out the vertical intervals occurring between the voices. Check your work for the following:

- Are there any incorrect parallel perfect unisons, 5ths or octaves?
- Are there any melodic intervals that are not allowed like the aug4th and major 7th?
- Are there more than four vertical 3rds or 6ths in a row?
- Are all perfect unisons, 5ths and octaves approached correctly?
- Are 7th chords and six-four chords resolved correctly?
- Are large leaps treated correctly and left with stepwise motion in the opposite direction or an interval within the leap?
- Are there too many leaps in one direction outlining a dissonance?
- Does the phrase contain a climax?

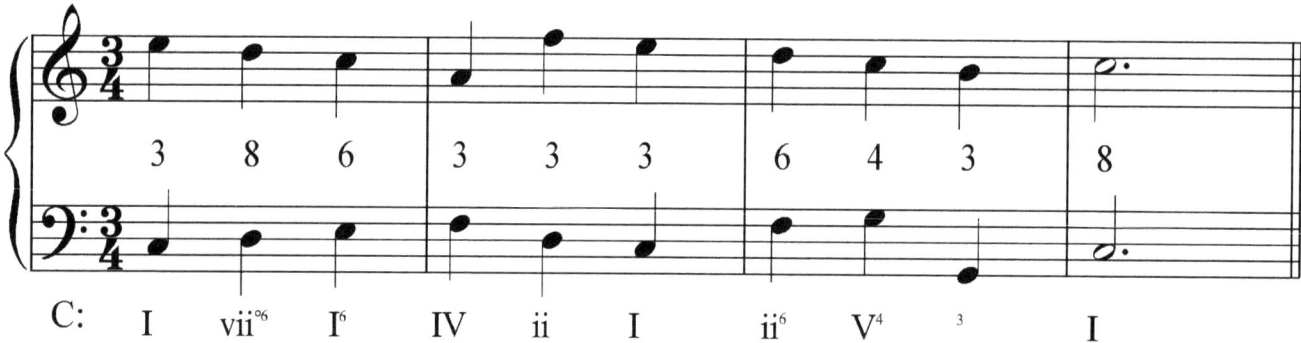

5. Think about adding a few non chord tones or chordal skips to give the example rhythmic momentum and interest, but be careful to avoid faulty parallels. Here a paassing tone is added to m.1, a chordal skip to m.2, and an suspension to m.3. The chordal skip works here because it outlines the notes of the IV chord. When writing these skips be careful avoid a dissonant interval. The suspension is an extension of cadential six-four. 4 is held off for a half beat longer before it resolves to 3.

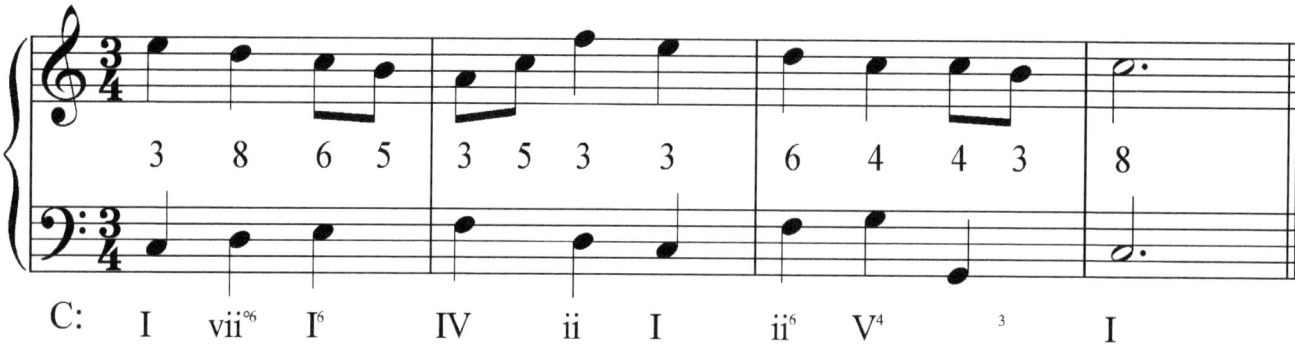

Chapter 23: Counterpoint

7. Name the key, provide chord symbols, and write a melody to accompany the following bass lines in two part counterpoint.

Chapter 23: Counterpoint

Johann Sebastian Bach's Two-Part Inventions

Bach's Two-Part Inventions were composed as teaching pieces for his eldest son Wilhelm Friedemann Bach. They were written between 1720 and 1723, when Bach was chapel master in Köthen.

According to the opening statement from the edition published in 1723, his intention was to provide examples of two-part pieces to be played on the keyboard to create independence of the hands. As well, they were designed to show how to compose using simple musical ideas in different ways.

Invention is a word derived from Latin that means "to find by investigating." The two-part inventions are short two-part contrapuntal works composed for the keyboard. Each one consists of two musical lines that weave and work together to create a complete composition.

All of Bach's Two-Part Inventions start with a small musical idea called the *subject.* These subjects may differ in character but are always the basis for the entire composition. Figure 23.22 contains the subject from the first Invention in C major BWV 772. Bach builds the entire Invention on this short idea.

Figure 23.22

Figure 23.23 shows how Bach introduces and treats this subject in the opening measures. It first appears in the upper voice in the treble clef in the tonic, C major (a). It then appears as imitation one octave lower in the bass clef (b). In the second measure, the subject occurs up a 5th, first in the upper voice (c) and then in the lower voice (d). This opening section where the subject is first introduced in each voice is called the *exposition*.

Figure 23.23

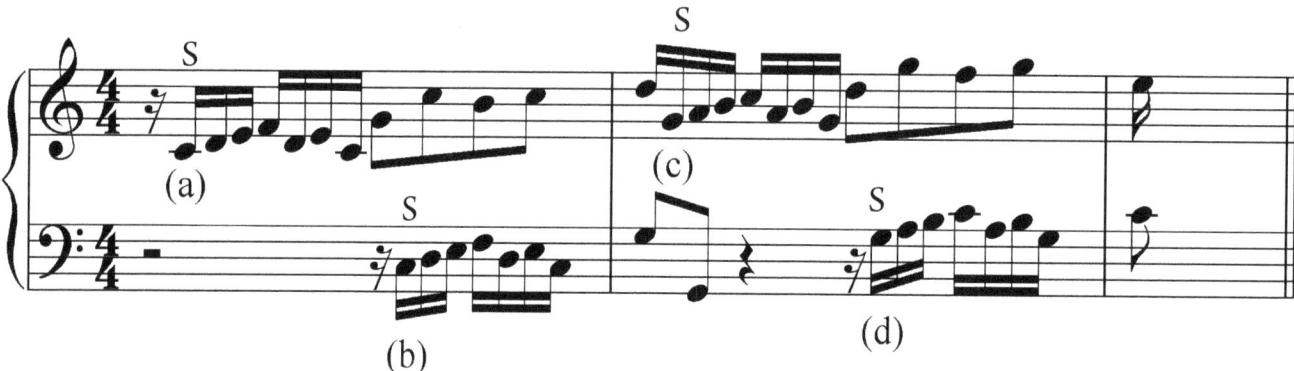

Using the material from the subject Bach employs a number of techniques that are common in most of the Inventions. Figure 23.25 shows his use of a sequence. Here the opening subject is seen in *inversion* in the treble clef and it descends. When a melody is inverted it becomes a mirror image of itself. The ascending intervals are changed to descending ones, and vice versa (Figure 23.26).

In the lower voice he uses a technique called **augmentation**. Here the rhythmic values of the first four notes taken from the subject are doubled. The sixteenth notes are augmented becoming eighth notes, and they are used in the sequence in the bass.

Figure 23.24

Figure 23.25

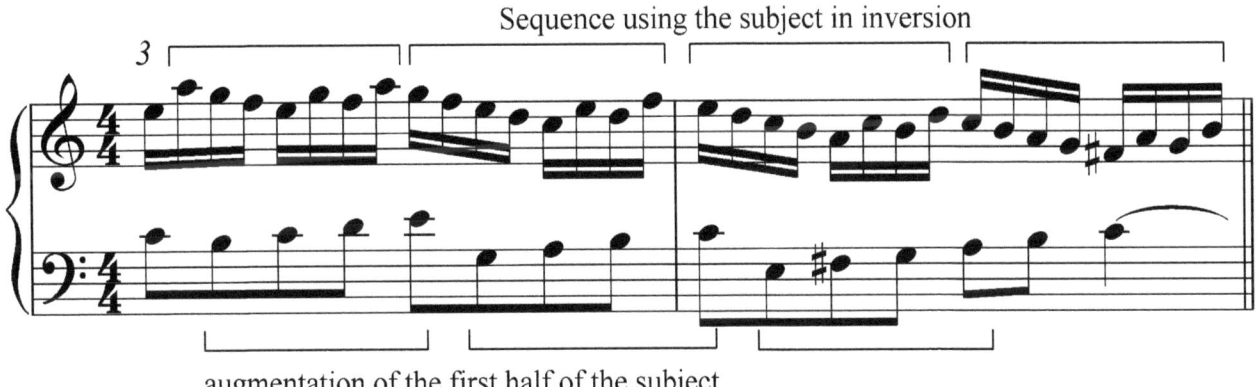

augmentation of the first half of the subject

Figure 23.26

Invertible counterpoint at the octave is used in mm. 7-8. This means what was played in the upper voice in mm.1-2 is played in the lower voice in mm. 7-8 and vice versa. Basically, the voices exchange position. This passage (mm.7-8), is in the dominant, G major.

Figure 23.27

Some, but not all of the Two-Part Inventions contain an element called a **countersubject**. A countersubject acts like an accompaniment to the subject. It is a melody that accompanies the subject and usually occurs in the other voice each time the subject is heard. Figure 23.28 is an example of a countersubject.

Figure 23.28

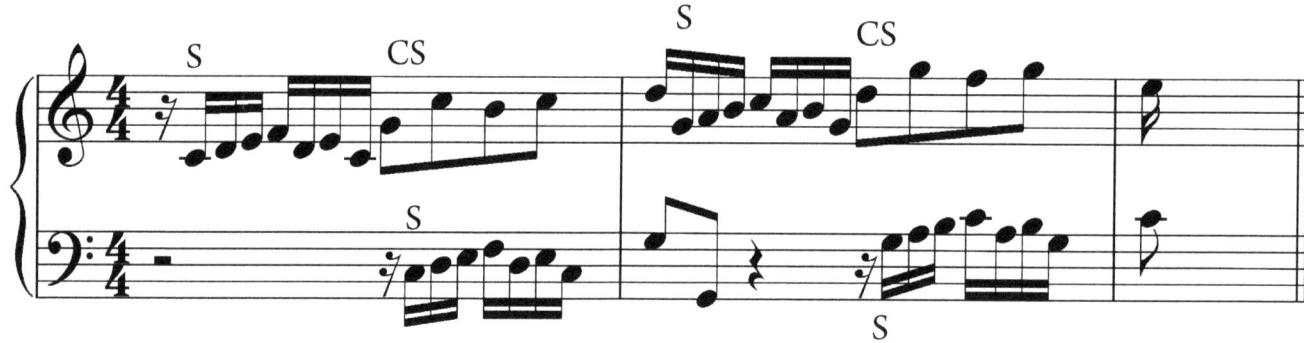

Chapter 23: Counterpoint

Another element in many of the Bach Inventions is *imitation*. Imitation is the repetition of a subject or a melody in a different voice. In Figure 23.29 the subject is imitated one octave lower in the bass clef. This example also contains the element of *transposition*. Here, the subject is transposed up a 5th in m.2.

Figure 23.29

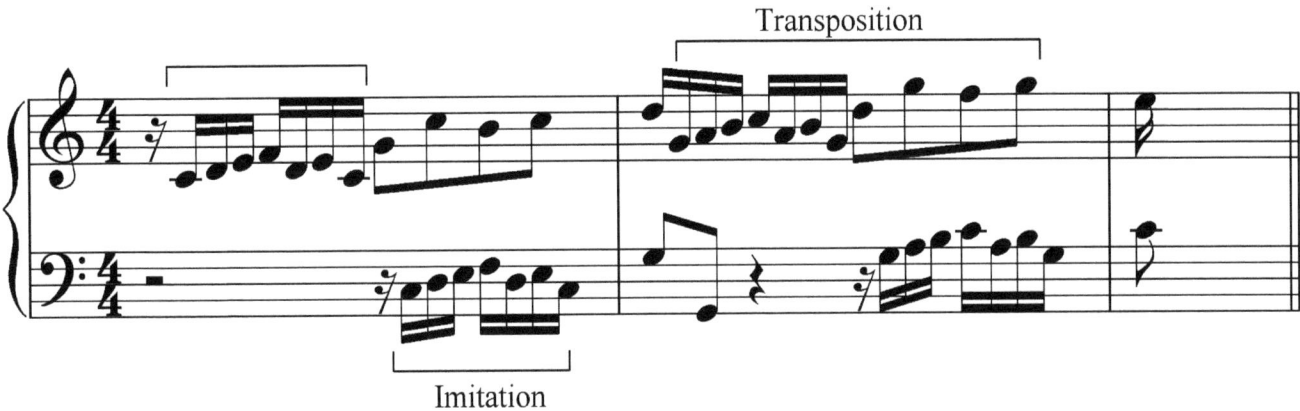

The element of *fragmentation* occurs when a portion of the subject is repeated, often using sequential movement. Figure 23.30 contains fragmentation. Here, the second part of the subject is inverted and than repeated in an ascending pattern. Essentially, fragments of the subject are repeated during fragmentation.

Figure 23.30

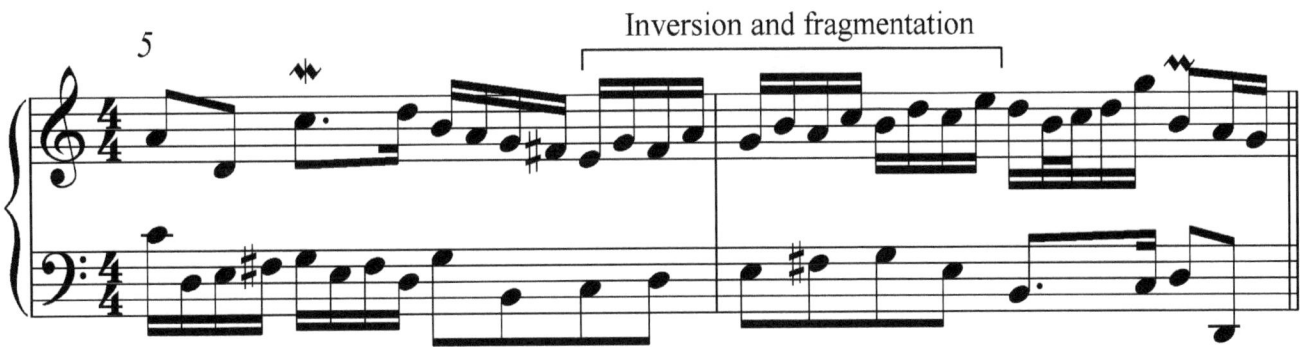

Sometimes the first entry of the subject is accompanied by the countersubject as seen in Figure 23.31 and 23.32. Also note that the subject in Figure 23.31 can be divided into two motives. Here, motive b is an inversion of motive a.

Figure 23.31

Figure 23.32

Figure 23.33 is an example of *canon*. In a canon we hear an initial melody, which is then imitated by one or more other parts. This imitation might be an exact replica of the original melody, or it might be altered in some way. In this example, the bass imitates the soprano at the octave up to the first beat of measure 7.

Figure 23.33

Chapter 23: Counterpoint

Inventions usually consist of three main sections:

Section A: An invention begins with an *exposition* section that introduces the main subject in the tonic key. The first voice plays the subject while the other accompanies in free counterpoint. The voices then switch, with the second voice playing the subject and the first providing counterpoint. Inventions may also have countersubjects that accompany the subject.

Section B: This is the longest section of an invention, the main subject usually moves through a number of closely related keys in short sections called *episodes*. These modulatory episodes may be based on the subject, but are not complete statements of it. This is where we see imitation, fragmentation, transposition, inversion, sequence and other techniques.

Section C: In this section the Invention returns to the tonic. Many times there will be a return of the subject. However, this return may be brief and is not seen in every Invention.

8. The following is an excerpt from the Two-Part Invention BWV 775 by J. S. Bach.

   a. Name the key.
   b. The subject and countersubject are identified. Using the letters S and CS find and label another statement of each.
   c. Explain the relationship between mm. 3-4 and mm. 5-6.

   _____

   d. There is no statement of the subject from m. 7 to m. 12. Give a term for this type of passage.

   _____

   e. Name the key and the type of cadence at mm. 17-18. Add functional symbols at this cadence point.

Chapter 23: Counterpoint

9. The following excerpt is the subject and counter subject from J.S. Bach's Two-Part Invention in F major BWV 779. Study it and answer the questions relating to the example on the next page.

a. Identify two statements of the subject and two statements of the countersubject and label them S and CS on the score.

b. State the key of these entries. _____

c. How is this key related to the tonic key, F major.
_____

d. Is it a closely related key?_____

e. The voice in the bass clef in mm. 21-22 is derived from the subject. How is it different?_____

f. Identify the implied chords in the boxes in mm. 21 and 22. Label them with root/quality chord symbols.

10. The following is an excerpt from the Two-Part Invention BWV 784 by J. S. Bach.

   a. Name the key.

   b. The subject is identified. Using the letter S find and label any other statements of the subject.

   c. State the implied harmony using functional chord symbols from m. 3 to m. 6.

   d. Name the sequence in mm. 3 and 4.

   e. Name the cadence in m. 6.

www.ingramcontent.com/pod-product-compliance
Ingram Content Group UK Ltd.
Pitfield, Milton Keynes, MK11 3LW, UK
UKHW051302180426
11947UKWH00020B/1854